Geosi Interviews
Fifty Writers World Wide

Geosi Interviews
Fifty Writers World Wide

Geosi Gyasi

LITERARY PRESS
LAMAR UNIVERSITY

ISBN: 978-1-942956-27-3
Library of Congress Control Number: 2016951465

Book Design: Theresa L. Ener

Lamar University Literary Press
Beaumont, Texas

To all writers who connected me to other writers

Recent Nonfiction from Lamar University Literary Press

Jean Andrews, *High Tides, Low Tides*
Robert Murray Davis, *Levels of Incompetence: An Academic Life*
Ted L. Estess, *Fishing Spirit Lake*
William Guest, *Places You Want to Go*
Dominique Inge, *A Garden on the Brazos*
Terry C. Maxwell, *Tales of a Journeyman Naturalist*
Jim McJunkin, *Deep Sleep*
Jeanetta Calhoun Mish, *Oklahomeland*
Jim Sanderson, *Sanderson's Fiction Writing Manual*
Steven Schroeder, *What's Love Got To Do With It? a city out of thin air*

For more information on these and other books go to
www.lamar.edu/literarypress

Preface

Aesop said that we are known by the company we keep, and the old sage's advice still seems sound. The fifty writers interviewed by Geosi Gyasi in this collection are in good company indeed. They are practicing writers, aspiring writers, whose commitment to the craft is in strong supply.

The private nature of creation, however, often makes writers solitary souls who practice their solipsism by turning inward upon their weaknesses. The great Russians said that we were defined by our illnesses, and Dostoevsky's Underground Man asserts that to be acutely conscious is a disease, a real, honest-to-goodness disease. Isolated and alienated within themselves, writers anguish to find hope in their mortality, working without community and frequently alienated as much by a lack of capital success as by creative seclusion. They put themselves in their stories and poems, their paintings, their sculpture and musical chords. Some see themselves as frauds—uncertain about their true natures—and help widen the divide between artists and the general public. But they often fail to recognize that their alienation itself makes them a part of a larger group.

America's Oscar Wilde, Oliver Herford, said that a man is known by the silence he keeps. Writers have a tough time keeping silent—excepting, of course, the neglect of the reading public—but Herford knew that a person must love a thing very much to practice it without hope of fame or money with little expectation of doing it well.

All artists, all creative people feel disarmed and alienated. So much the better. And the lessons we take from them help us to perceive and understand the world and perhaps even to find a place where we ourselves may take a stand. But there are more than lessons in Gyasi's interviews. Even after we learn their lessons, we have a hard time putting away these writers' books.

So if man is perishable, let us, as Miguel de Unamuno insists, perish resisting. The indomitable spirit of these writers defies non-existence. Good company indeed.

Jerry Bradley

CONTENTS

Roald Hoffmann was born in 1937 in Zloczow, Poland. Having survived the war, he came to the U. S. in 1949, and studied chemistry at Columbia and Harvard Universities (Ph.D. 1962). Since 1965 he is at Cornell University, now as the Frank H. T. Rhodes Professor of Humane Letters Emeritus. He has received many of the honors of his profession, including the 1981 Nobel Prize in Chemistry (shared with Kenichi Fukui).

"Applied theoretical chemistry" is the way Hoffmann likes to characterize the particular blend of computations stimulated by experiment and the construction of generalized models, of frameworks for understanding, that is his contribution to chemistry. The pedagogical perspective is very strong in his work.

Notable at the same time is his reaching out to the general public; he participated, for example, in the production of a television course in introductory chemistry titled "The World of Chemistry," shown widely since 1990. And, as a writer, Hoffmann has carved out a land between science, poetry, and philosophy, through many essays and three books, *Chemistry Imagined* with artist Vivian Torrence, *The Same and Not the Same and Old Wine* (translated into six languages), and *New Flasks: Reflections on Science and Jewish Tradition*, with Shira Leibowitz Schmidt.

Hoffmann is also an accomplished poet and playwright. He began writing poetry in the mid-1970s, eventually publishing the first of a number of collections, *The Metamict State*, in 1987, followed three years later by *Gaps and Verges*, then *Memory Effects* (1999), and *Soliton* (2002). A bilingual selection of his poems has appeared in Spanish. He has also co-written a play with fellow chemist Carl Djerassi, entitled *Oxygen*, which has been performed worldwide, translated into ten languages. A second play by Hoffmann, *Should've*, has had several workshop productions since 2006; a new play, *We Have Something That Belongs to You*, had its first workshop production in 2009.

Unadvertised, a monthly cabaret Roald runs at the Cornelia Street Café in Greenwich Village, "Entertaining Science," has become the hot cheap ticket in NYC.

> Gyasi: Can we start the interview this way? You were born Roald Safran. How did you come to be known as Hoffmann?

Hoffmann: First, my mother remarried right after the war, to my stepfather, who lost his wife in the war. So I became Roald Margulies. A year later, on the way out of Poland, we thought we would get into the US easier if we were German and not Polish. The Poles were making life uncomfortable for the ethnic Germans left in Silesia, and a German village priest found a way to support his flock, which did not hurt anyone—selling birth certificates of Germans killed in the war. So overnight Naftali Margulies, my stepfather, became Paul Hoffmann. My uncle forged a wedding certificate with my mother; my birth certificate was lost. And so I became Roald Hoffmann. Americans have trouble with these stories, as you can imagine.

> Gyasi: You were born in Złoczów, Poland, to a Jewish family. My

question is, do you have any memories about the place where you were born?

Hoffmann: Nothing from before the war, just a colorful wooden automobile I played in, and a tropical house plant that I tried to eat, a mistake. We came back there in summer 1944, on being freed by the red Army. Now I remember a little more, our house, bombed out other houses.

Gyasi: I wish I could ignore this question, but do you harbor any painful memories about the circumstances in which your family perished in the Holocaust?

Hoffmann: My father, three of four grandparents, and two aunts were killed, and so on. And a good Ukrainian family, the Dyuks in the village of Univ, hid us for 15 months at the end of the war. Ukrainian-Jewish relations are complicated, strained. I have written an autobiographical play, *Something That Belongs to You*, about those times, how people made choices for good and evil in terrible times.

Gyasi: You're a well-renowned chemist and won the 1981 Nobel Prize in Chemistry. How did you get into the literary world?

Hoffmann: Well, it all goes back to a general education at Columbia, wonderful introductions to art history and literature, a course with a great poet of the time, Mark Van Doren. I remember him reading Wallace Stevens's "Sunday Morning" to us. I began to write poetry in midlife, at age poetry. And plays later.

Gyasi: Is there any relationship between Science and Arts?

Hoffmann: Of course. Both are man or woman made, artifactual. Sculptures do not grow on trees, neither do new molecules, even as the trees are made of molecules. In both, craftsmanship is valued, and an economy of statement and intensity. Both reach out to others, communicate. Both have an aesthetic and try to understand the world within and outside of us. But there are differences, too.

Gyasi: Does your study and work in chemistry have any influence on your writing?

Hoffmann: I try from time to time to write poems with chemical themes. They usually don't work. But if I relax, and look for metaphor in science, it goes better.

Gyasi: Do you think winning the Nobel Prize put unnecessary burden on your public life?

Hoffmann: Fortunately, in America one is let alone. I survived, did not make a fool of myself. And I did not become an administrator. I just went on to do good science, and had fun in the process.

Gyasi: Under what category would you classify your book *Chemistry Imagined*—poetry, essay, fiction, or non-fiction?

Hoffmann: It is modeled on the Emblem Books of the Renaissance—an image by Vivian Torrence, my collaborator, which then evoked a short essay by me, sometimes a poem. It is mixed genre, not really classifiable.

Gyasi: The idea behind your play *Oxygen* often baffles me. In your view, do you think there will ever come a time when the Nobel Foundation will inaugurate a "retro-Nobel" award?

Hoffmann: Now that was a good idea, the retro-Nobel. No, they are unlikely to do it. But if they did, and that's what the play is about, they would run into the same questions of priority, history, and personalities that are a part of any kind of discovery. Then or now.

Gyasi: What would you like to be remembered for?

Hoffmann: For having done good science, and for trying, just trying, at all times to be a decent human being.

Greg Kosmicki is a poet and social worker living in Omaha, Nebraska. He founded The Backwaters Press in 1997 and is currently in the process of passing the operation of the press along to others.

Kosmicki's own poetry has been published in numerous magazines since 1975, both print and online, including *Briarcliff Review*, *Chiron Review*, *Cimarron Review*, *Connecticut Review*, *Cortland Review*, *New Letters*, *Nimrod*, *Paddlefish*, *Paris Review*, *Poetry East*, *Rattle*, *Sojourners*, and *Solstice*. He received artist's fellowships for his poetry from the Nebraska Arts Council in 2000 and 2006. He is the author of three books and 9 chapbooks of poems. Two of the poems from his book from Word Press, *Some Hero of the Past,* and one poem from his newest chapbook from Pudding House Publications in 2011, *New Route in the Dream,* have been selected by Garrison Keillor and read by him on *The Writer's Almanac*. His newest collection, *Sheep can Recognize Individual Human Faces,* was published by Stephen F. Austin University Press in 2014.

He and his wife, Debbie, who is also in the social work field, are the parents of three children and grandparents of one.

Gyasi: Do you mind telling me anything about Omaha, Nebraska?

Kosmicki: Omaha is a great place. It's a city of a little over 600,000 people, right on the Missouri River, with great restaurants, great art scene, great poetry scene, lots of parks, beautiful old and new buildings, and lots of jobs. It's one of the few places in the United States that didn't get hit by the recession. You all should move to Omaha, and bring your wonderful cultures with you.

Gyasi: How do you combine your work as a poet and a social worker?

Kosmicki: I write about the things that happen to me in my life, but I don't write about the people with whom I come into contact in my job because that would be a violation of their trust. When I retire, I will be able to loosely base stories on my work that I do now, but to write about it now would not be possible. As far as the time that it takes to write versus having a full-time job, I work my job in the day, and in the evenings after work, after supper and the dishes, and errands, and taking care of stuff for the press, I spend some time writing at the tail end of the day if I have any energy left. As I get older, I can't do that as much because I need more rest.

Gyasi: Could you tell me what you do as a social worker?

Kosmicki: I work for a part of the State Health and Human Services agency, and my job is to go out and visit with adults over age 18 who can't take care of themselves very well, and about whom we received reports from the public, to see if they are being abused or neglected, and if so, to try to take measures to alleviate their situations.

Gyasi: Being an editor and publisher of The Backwaters Press, where does your writing fit in?

Kosmicki: As noted above, it fits in less and less, since I am getting less energetic in my 60s. In light of that, I approached the board that oversees the press and asked that we find a new editor to take over my duties so that I can retire from the press and devote my free time to writing. We are in the process of slowly turning that over to the new editor, James Cihlar, and it is working out very well. He is phenomenally gifted.

Gyasi: What do you think of young poets coming out of America?

Kosmicki: It's really not possible to say—you would need a huge anthology—and there are lots of different kinds of poetry going on now. Contrary to the rumor that poetry and poets are dying breeds, there is an explosion of it all over the US, and in the world. I was in awe when I looked at your blog-site and saw all the brilliant poets coming from your continent. So if I were to say one statement about young poets in America, I guess that it would be that there are very many young poets and that they are very good poets.

Gyasi: Tell me about The Backwaters Press.

Kosmicki: My friend and mentor, Greg Kuzma, from whom I took poetry writing classes at the University of Nebraska in Lincoln, Nebraska, back in the early 70s, used to run a little press for which he hand-set the type and hand-printed on a monstrous old platen press he had in his basement. His wife, Barb, suggested the name Best Cellar Press for it, since the press was in the cellar. Seeing him do that got me excited about making books, and I carried the idea with me for years. He also had a little literary magazine called *Pebble* that he printed the same way. It was very demanding work. Eventually, late in the 90s, I decided to try it myself, and started The Backwaters Press. I wanted a press that would make books that were more utilitarian though, rather than hand-made, so I have printed only perfect-bound paperback books. Since beginning, the press has published about 100 titles. Many of the books that we published in the last few years were selected by Rich (David) Wyatt, the co-editor, when we had an open submissions policy. He is a very astute reader. The press has an annual contest for a collection of poems by a single author. Our website is www.thebackwaterspress.org.

Gyasi: Is it more difficult to edit than to write?

Kosmicki: Do you mean edit other people's work or my own?

Gyasi: Yes, your own work.

Kosmicki: I don't edit mine a lot—I'm pretty much one of those "First thought best thought" types. As far as editing other's work goes, I don't spend a lot of time going over people's manuscripts, telling the poets what to cut, etc., because I think that if someone has gotten to the point that they have put their poems into book form, they think that the poems are finished. I will read the manuscript and if I don't like the poems, then I don't publish it. That doesn't mean that the poems aren't any good, it just means that I don't like them for some reason and I don't want to publish them. The only time that I will do line-by-line edits is when a poet I know asks me to do so, but they've got to know me pretty well, because that's asking a lot. That's difficult work! If someone I don't know insists that I read something and edit, I charge for it, but I don't like to do that. Too much other stuff to do in my life, and it's time-consuming.

Gyasi: How long did it take you to complete *How Things Happen*?

Kosmicki: I'm not really sure. The poems in that collection were part of a longer manuscript that I had submitted to Harry Duncan, who used to run Abbatoir Press, a fine letter press at the University of Nebraska in Omaha. He said that he would like to publish it, but that he had so many projects to do he was afraid that he wouldn't get them all completed—by that time he was in his 70s. So he passed the manuscript on to a former book-making student of his, Denise Brady, who runs Bradypress in Omaha, another fine letter press. She selected about 15 poems out of the longer manuscript that she really liked and published those as *How Things Happen*. I'm surprised you know about it—it was a very limited, handmade edition of about 150 copies. But the poems weren't written as a book, but rather, like all of my books, the poems from many years were collected together into a loosely arranged book manuscript. The poems in *How Things Happen*, which was published in 1999, I think, were written in the time period from about 1977 through about 1987 or so. Another book, which contains many of the poems that are in *How Things Happen*, but that is about 120 pages long, titled *nobody lives here who saw this sky,* came out less than a year later from Missing Spoke Press in Seattle. Those books are very rare, too, because the press only published about 250 copies and then went out of business about 2 years later.

Gyasi: Tell me about *How Things Happen*.

Kosmicki: The book itself is a work of the book-makers art, being printed on fine papers, and with covers made of handmade paper that has cornstalks and coffee grounds in it. Denise Brady is a meticulous craftsperson and the book is beautiful, with each book hand-sewn by Denise, as well as all the typesetting and printing done by her by hand on a Van de Graf proof press. It's gorgeous! The poems are all based on the poet-as-storyteller, talking about what's happening in his life. I have always thought that, because we are all human beings, we will relate to each other's lives if the writers talk about what is going on in them, and that will form a bond somehow between you and me when you read my poems, and with that bond comes understanding of each other, and when we understand each other, then we are less likely to follow the idiots who run countries and go out and kill other people, because we understand each other. That's always been my justification for all the time that I spend with writing.

Gyasi: Where and when did you write *We Have Always Been Coming to This Morning*?

Kosmicki: The poems in this book were written over many years. The first section reprints some poems, up through "History," from a little chapbook I self-published in 1988 called *When There Wasn't Any War*. Those poems were all written from the time when I was a student at the University of Nebraska circa 1974 ("Eating

5

Supper, Watching the News") to some that were written when we lived in Alliance, Nebraska, and I was working for United Parcel Service, from 1981 through 1988. The remainder of that section are poems that were written between 1988 and 1991 when my wife and I were living in and working in a group home in Omaha, with six developmentally delayed young men. Section two is comprised of poems written after we moved out of the group home and into a tough part of town, while I worked for an agency as a case manager that provided services for homeless mentally ill people, and my wife was in administration at the company where we both worked before. That neighborhood is reflected especially in the poems "4-17-94," "7-8-94," and "Packing." We moved to a quieter neighborhood in 1995 when I got my job with the state, and the poems in section three are from that time period, from about 1995 through about 1998 or so, though some of them are reminiscences, rather than being based on events of the current day that the poem was written. Several of the poems from the third section about our youngest daughter Briana were collected together with other poems about her and published as a chapbook by Black Star Press in Lincoln, Nebraska, under the title *Marigolds*.

Gyasi: You are a 2000 and 2006 recipient of the Nebraska Arts Council's Merit Award. Why do you think you were given this award?

Kosmicki: The award is given to people who live in Nebraska who submit poems to the Nebraska Arts Council to be judged by an independent panel of judges. The Arts Council awards are cyclical: one year is for plastic arts, one year for performing arts, and one year for writing arts, in rotation. The Arts Council sends the submissions to the judges, who are recognized poets from another state, and they judge the writing without knowing the identity of the poet who submitted it. Each poet can submit up to 5 poems, and the Arts Council has the latitude to give out the awards however they deem fit, based upon the statements of the judges. For instance, if the judges think that all the award money should go to only two poets, then they will each get a fairly large sum, around $7,000 apiece. Usually though, they choose several poets to get smaller awards, such as $1,000 to $2,000, and one poet to receive the highest recognition with a $5,000 award. The money comes from state tax funds, so the Arts Council is extremely scrupulous about ensuring the integrity of the process.

Gyasi: Do we have a defined way of life for writers?

Kosmicki: Starting in the late 50s in the US, poets and fiction writers began to get hired by English departments at major universities to teach "creative writing" as a sort-of "side salad" to a serious English Literature degree. Then a few universities realized the potential for these programs and started offering creative writing degrees. The first in the US was the Iowa Writer's Workshop, I think, followed closely by Stanford University's program. The concept grew slowly, but steadily, until today there are creative writing majors and minors at practically every college and university in the country, and now it appears that we have a glut of "certified" poets and writers in the country—so I'm guessing that many of them, most, probably, can't find full-time employment teaching writing in creative writing

6

programs, and are forced back into the workaday world doing other jobs, while writing furiously away on their novels and poems before and after work. There has also developed a huge system of prize-giving and awards and grants, so that if you're lucky to have entered one contest or another and won it, you can win a fair amount of money and recognition through those. I'm not in that field—teaching—only because I couldn't find work in it back in 1978 and gave up on it since I had to feed my family, so I really can't say that I know it for a fact, but if you do the math, you come up with a lot more Master of Fine Arts graduates than there are teaching positions in the country. So I suspect that I was just ahead of the curve at least in that respect. (Not finding work with my English degree with a creative thesis.)

Gyasi: Your poem "April 2, 2013" sounds like one written out of an event. Was it written from a personal experience?

Kosmicki: Yes, it was. Most of my poems are based on my personal experience in one way or another.

Gyasi: Do you do many drafts?

Kosmicki: I don't really do much re-writing at all. I got in the habit when I was younger of writing at breakneck speed, trying to hang on to get where the poem was taking me. Some nights 40 years ago I would stay up for hours and write numerous poems—sometimes as many as ten. Most of them didn't turn out well, so I'd write some more the next time. Once in a while, years ago, I would spend a lot of time reading and re-reading a poem to try to get it to say what I thought I wanted it to say, especially when I first started writing. But later, I got in the habit of not going back much—now maybe I re-read, change a word here or there, and abandon it, because I figured out (after 20 years or so) that I should let the poem figure out what it wanted to do, not me with my big dumb ideas. Months later I will find them in my notebooks and see that some of them turned out okay if I just clip off, say, the last stanza or two, or the last line or two. Usually I try to let the poem take over so that I'm not in charge of it, and when I get back in charge, then it usually goes sour, so I stop there. Those are the lines/stanzas that get clipped off. Then, it might not be finished, but I rarely go back and work on something, because if I don't finish it in the first sitting, I've lost the thread and I usually can't get it back, so I don't try. I just write another poem. I do go back through poems sometimes and cut out words that aren't necessary to the poem, to tighten them up a bit—I look for "the," "and," "and then," "that," "then," and other words like those that don't contribute much and make the poem flabbier. Sometimes you need them, but often not. I try to keep those words off the ends of lines, unless they are pivoting the poem in a pretty important way somehow at the end of a line.

Gyasi: What's the most difficult part of writing?

Kosmicki: Waiting. Getting started. Writing when you think "I don't have anything to say." Writing when you don't feel "inspired." Just writing at all—it's a discipline, and there are about sixty-eight million trillion distractions out there, waiting to jump all over you and keep you away from the page where you belong if you are a writer. Nowadays, with cell phones, iPads, music everywhere, TVs everywhere, computers everywhere, the distractions are as ubiquitous as mushrooms on the forest floor after a month of rain. Those distractions will kill you as a writer if you don't abandon them because they are sucking away the two elements you need to write: time, and quiet time in your mind.

Gyasi: When you write, do you care about style?

Kosmicki: I wanted to be a smart-ass and reply, "Do you mean that it's not obvious from reading my poems that I don't care about style?" but I guess that I do care enough about it that I write in the manner that I do—that's my style, I guess—rather than in some other manner. I don't sit around and think about it though, I just write and try to get from the first line that appeared on the page that night to the one that feels like the last one, based upon what the first one was. I guess that my style is to more or less meander around on the page until the place where I've meandered to feels like the place that I was going to when I started out not knowing where it was I was going to. I guess that if I have a style, it could be called "conversational."

Gyasi: Does writing come easy for you?

Kosmicki: Yes, it does in some respects. At least, I feel like it does once I get something finished, but when I was a young writer, I was furious, I was mad to write, I had to write, and I wrote all the time. Now I don't agonize over it, but I don't feel good generally when I don't write. I don't feel good because if I'm not writing, I'm not connecting with the world. The most difficult part for me is having the discipline to sit down and do it, and the longer I go without writing, the harder it is to get back into it, and the easier to let distractions take over. When I do write, I just spew and whatever comes out builds a little step-stool for me to climb onto to see where I'm going next. Then I go there and see where I can go to next. It's not something that I think about consciously. If I think about it a lot, I get self-conscious and then my brain intrudes and tells me what I'm writing is dumb and I should stop. So I try to ignore that and keep going. Sometimes when I go back and read the poems a few weeks later, it appears that my brain was right sometimes, but sometimes not. Sometimes the words have a spark that seems right. But I have a hard time telling with my own poems because I'm too close to them, which is why I like going to the writing group I go to—The Poetry Warriors—they can tell me where it looks like a poem went off track, or if it stayed on.

Gyasi: What's the most interesting aspect of writing?

Kosmicki: I think that it's the little surprise that comes at the end of a poem sometimes (all the time in successful poems), that lots of times I don't even recognize, I just feel like I'm giving up on this poem, I quit, it's not going anywhere, and then later when I come back to it, I see that the poem ends right here or right there, and its done something that I didn't realize it was doing. Then I feel really smart for a minute! But I know that it's the poem, it's not me, I'm just taking it down and it's writing itself out, and I'm the lucky one who gets the credit for it.

Gyasi: What's your plan for your readers in the foreseeable future?

Kosmicki: Right now I'm collecting together all the poems that seemed to have worked out as okay poems about my relationship with my older brother and me. He was killed in a car accident when I was about 16 years old and I became pretty self-destructive for a few years after that, and I think that his death is probably why I ended up writing poems. I guess that was my introduction, or one of my introductions, to what life is all about. When I was in college, I wrote a couple poems about it, and one that I wrote, "Letter to a Dead Man," was one that I thought was pretty much the definitive poem about his death and my relationship to it, and that I was all over his death, but then I have been revisited by poems about him for the next 40 years. It seems that the dead never die as long as someone is alive who knew them. So I want to get those together. If I can get them all together, I'll try to find a publisher. It will be called *The Sun Has Stayed Where It Is* which is also the title of my Master's Thesis. And I'm continuing to write in the nights, and I've about got a collection-sized group together that I think I will call *It's as Good Here as It Gets Anywhere,* from a line in one of the poems.

Philip St. Clair is the author of four books of poetry: *Acid Creek* (Bottom Dog, 1997), *Little-Dog-of-Iron* (Ahsahta, 1985), *At the Tent of Heaven* (Ahsahta, 1984), and *In the Thirty-Nine Steps* (Shelley's, 1980). His two chapbooks are *Divided House* (Finishing Line, 2005) and number 176 in Pudding Press's *Greatest Hits* series (2003). Awards include grants and prizes from the National Endowment for the Arts, the Kentucky Arts Council, and the Bullis Prize from *Poetry Northwest*; he was a finalist in the National Poetry Series in 2001 and 2013. His poems have been published in *Beloit Poetry Journal, Black Warrior Review, Gettysburg Review, Harper's, Main Street Rag, Oyez Review, Paper Street, Prairie Schooner, Ploughshares, Poetry Review, Rattle, Shenandoah,* and elsewhere. His work has appeared in anthologies from the University of Akron Press, Bottom Dog Press, and Southern Illinois University Press, and in 2009 he was included in the University Press of Kentucky's *What Comes Down to Us: 25 Contemporary Kentucky Poets.* After his honorable discharge from the United States Air Force in 1965, he attended Kent State University from 1966 to 1974, receiving B.A., M.A., and M.L.S. degrees; in 1985 he earned an M.F.A. from Bowling Green State University. In addition to work as a librarian, a bartender, and a writer/indexer/editor (both in-house and freelance), he has taught at Kent State University, Bowling Green State University, and Southern Illinois University. In 1991 he came to Appalachian Kentucky to teach at Ashland Community College (now Ashland Community and Technical College), where he directed the Jesse Stuart Writers' Conference and chaired the Humanities Division. He retired from ACTC in 2010 and resides with his wife, Christina, in Ashland, Kentucky.

Gyasi: I understand that after your graduation from high school in 1961 you enlisted in the United States Air Force and were assigned to the Military Air Transport Service. Tell me about that experience.

St. Clair: I came from a working-class background, so college wasn't an option. In addition, I was a disaffected, overweight rebel in high school and my grades wouldn't merit a scholarship. My choices were either working in one of the local steel mills or joining the military, so I decided to enlist in the Air Force. In those days there was a draft, so every able-bodied male knew that he would have to somehow fulfill a six-year obligation. After basic training I was assigned to Dover AFB in Delaware, where they moved a great deal of cargo around the States and to and from Europe. I worked on the flight line, loading and off-loading Korean-War-era transport planes as well as more recent aircraft such as the C-130 Hercules. As a consequence, I have great affection for cargo planes, especially the C-124 Globemaster (affectionately dubbed "Old Shakey") and the classic DC-3 (C-47 in military terms). During the Cuban Missile Crisis, I was twice sent to Tyndall AFB, a SAC base on the Florida panhandle, as part of the support for the invasion of Cuba, which of course never happened. In June of 1963, I was transferred to Prestwick Air Base, a tiny outfit appended to the large international airport near Glasgow, Scotland. Our main task there was to support the passenger flights of military aircraft to and from the States; we also moved cargo to and from the U.S. Navy's atomic submarine base at Holy Loch. In September of 1965, I was sent back to the States for discharge from active duty and spent two additional years in the inactive reserves, a don't-call-us-we'll-call-you situation. In 1966, Prestwick AB was deactivated, and the Military Air Transport Service was renamed Military Air Command. And in that year it was very apparent that our role in Viet Nam was beginning its tragic escalation.

Joining the Air Force was the best single decision I ever made: it got me out of my hometown and put me in the (vastly) larger world. The experience gave me much-needed discipline, carved away excess flesh, and introduced me to G.I.s from all races and nationalities and all walks of life. I was also eligible for the extended G.I. Bill, which helped finance my undergraduate degree at Kent State.

Gyasi: Do you often write from the experiences you had with the Military Air Transport Service?

St. Clair: No, not that much. At present I'm between projects, and I just might begin writing about some Air Force experiences.

Gyasi: What does it take to be enlisted in the United States Air Force?

St. Clair: That question I can't answer—it's been over fifty years since I joined up. Back then, the Air Force and the Navy were regarded as "more intelligent" than the others—they weren't in the business of creating combat soldiers. I'm sure Air Force basic training, while difficult, was much easier than basic training in the Marine Corps. There was also a draft at that time, which drove many young men into the Navy and Air Force who wanted to avoid being drafted into the Army. (I probably would have joined up anyway.) Today I think the "no-draft" military is smaller, leaner, and more selective.

Gyasi: So how did you settle down to writing?

St. Clair: I began writing poetry during my senior year in high school. I began reading the Beat poets and found kindred spirits there—it was a short step from admiration to emulation. I also became interested in my high school literature classes: Chaucer, Pope, Addison and Steele, and Dr. Johnson were my favorite Brits; among the Americans I liked Edgar Lee Masters (*Spoon River Anthology*) and Carl Sandburg. Outside school my favorite poets were Don Marquis (Archy and Mehitabel) and the Beats—especially Ginsberg's "Howl" and Ferlinghetti's *A Coney Island of the Mind*. That was the beginning.

> Gyasi: You earned an MFA (Poetry) from Bowling Green State University. What influenced your choice to study at Bowling Green State University?

St. Clair: After Ahsahta Press published *At the Tent of Heaven*, I began to consider MFA programs that might possibly lead to a teaching gig in higher education. The Iowa workshop came to mind, of course, but I had a somewhat opinionated poetry workshop instructor who was rapidly against what he called the "Iowa School"; that stuck with me. In addition, I had the idea that I wanted to be an "Ohio Poet," and never applied to Iowa; BGSU in Ohio was one of the older MFA programs, so I applied there.

> Gyasi: In your opinion, what makes a good writer?

St. Clair: The best single work I've ever read about the artistic process is Ben Shahn's *The Shape of Content*. He believed there were three things necessary to form an artist: Education (a "formal" education that exposes the acolyte to those artists who have gone before—their work, their importance, their traditions), Culture (immersion in the total world spectrum of creative endeavor—literature, music, painting, sculpture), and Integration (a healthy, interactive relationship with the everyday world). To these I would add the virtue of persistence and the importance of a spirituality not born of dogma and ideology.

> Gyasi: Tell me a little bit about *Acid Creek*.

St. Clair: *Acid Creek* is a collection of poems based on family history and personal experience—a shift from the two earlier books, *At the Tent of Heaven* and *Little-Dog-of-Iron*, which were based on the Native American experience. The title is taken from a stream of industrial waste that ran behind the house in Warren, Ohio, where I grew up. There was a steel mill close by; it rolled red-hot ingots of steel into thinner sheets and coils, and the liquid waste used to treat the product during its manufacture was diluted with water and then pumped into a ditch that eventually fed into the Mahoning River. During the 1950s it was enclosed in concrete pipes, and some of it was dumped into large pits on the mill's property called "waste lagoons." I remember that the liquid was a dull orange in color and marbled with blue swirls of oil.

> Gyasi: Was it difficult finishing *Little-Dog-of-Iron*?

St. Clair: No. And when I had written the final poem, I had the definite sense that the spirit of Coyote had left the building.

> Gyasi: The title of your book *At the Tent of Heaven* seems fascinating. Could you explain the title?

St. Clair: *At the Tent of Heaven* is a series of poems based on the experiences of Native Americans who lived in the 1830s—just as the white power structure was preparing a concerted effort to take their land and to drive them across the

Mississippi. I needed a title, and came across a passage in the fortieth chapter of the book of Isaiah: "Have ye not known? Have ye not heard? Hath it not been told you from the beginning? Have ye not understood from the foundations of the earth? It is he that sitteth upon the circle of the earth, and the inhabitants thereof are as grasshoppers: that stretcheth out the heavens as a curtain, and spreadeth them out as a tent to dwell in: That bringeth the princes to nothing; he maketh the judges of the earth as vanity."

Gyasi: What inspired *In the Thirty-Nine Steps*?

St. Clair: I had no real plan or theme in mind—the book was just a collection of unrelated poems. I used the title simply because there were 39 poems in the book; no ties to the Hitchcock movie.

Gyasi: Do you gain anything at all from writing?

St. Clair: Yes, the virtues of engaging in a sometimes-difficult process; a sense of completion when it's done. And always a bit of a thrill if and when the poem is published. Some sort of spirituality at work here ...

Gyasi: What time of the day do you like to write?

St. Clair: Late mornings and early afternoons.

Gyasi: Is it true that without passion you can't write?

St. Clair: No. A great deal of terrible work has been done in the heat of passion, but without passion the task of writing becomes a chore and a burden—and often an embarrassment.

Gyasi: Do you have any writers you look up to?

St. Clair: Some months ago I decided to closely read and study six male writers who are more or less my contemporaries: Gerald Stern, Philip Levine, William Matthews, Jack Gilbert, Seamus Heaney, Ted Hughes. The list could just as well include Sharon Olds, Carol Ann Duffy, Deborah Digges, Mary Oliver. Also Charles Simic.

Gyasi: Do you get time to read?

St. Clair: Yes, these days I make time to read; I seem to be between projects.

Gyasi: Have you ever been rejected for a piece of writing?

St. Clair: No, but I've been ridiculed for being a poet ...

Gyasi: What do you find as the most difficult part of writing?

St. Clair: That first draft—going from Point A to Point B the first time. I know that the revision process is much longer, and in some ways more frustrating, but the first stab at a poem is, for me, the most difficult part.
I also have problems sometimes with closure—the "getting out" of a poem.

Gyasi: Do you consider style when you write?

St. Clair: Style, for me, is good sound. Whether one calls it "musicality" or "a good ear," it's something that very much concerns me.

Gyasi: When not writing, what are you likely to be caught doing?

St. Clair: Watching PBS, streaming movies and television shows, going for walks in the park or the neighborhood, baking bread, reading.

Gyasi: Who reads your works?

St. Clair: I really don't know. Five years ago some of my poems were published in the University Press of Kentucky's *25 Contemporary Kentucky Poets*, and the anthology was picked up by some of the Commonwealth's public schools.

Gyasi: What's the most important mail or letter you've ever received from a fan of your books?

St. Clair: I don't get much feedback on my work, but what's been given has been positive. For that I am humbled and thankful.

R.G. Evans's debut collection *Overtipping the Ferryman* won the 2013 Aldrich Poetry Prize. His poems, stories, and reviews have appeared in *Rattle, Paterson Literary Review, Tenebres* (France), and *Weird Tales*, among other places. His original music, including the song "The Crows of Paterson," was featured in the 2012 documentary *All That Lies Between Us*. Evans teaches high school and college English and Creative Writing in southern New Jersey.

Gyasi: Let's begin the interview this way. You're a poet and songwriter/singer. Which of them came first into your life?

Evans: I have to say I got involved in both around the same time, when I was a teenager. I began to write songs and poems in high school, but I had been playing guitar and singing for several years before I wrote my first poem, so if I think of it as a race, I suppose my singing/songwriting beat my poetry writing by a couple of lengths.

Gyasi: How does the art of writing poems differ from that of writing songs?

Evans: It's most similar, obviously, when writing a song with lyrics than an instrumental piece. In songwriting, though, you can create mood or atmosphere through your choices of chords, minor or major keys, etc., whereas with poetry your primary tools are the words and verbal images—which isn't limited at all. If anything, I find poetry writing more liberating than songwriting.

Gyasi: Do you feel your poems sing?

Evans: I have been told they do. I defer to those who have said so to answer this question.

Gyasi: How does it feel to perform your songs before an audience?

Evans: It's very immediately gratifying to sing a song and see and hear the reaction of an audience: facial expressions, applause. Sometimes, though, I get fairly profound stage fright when singing songs I've written, whereas I seldom get nervous when singing someone else's songs or reading my own poems. I've tried to reason why this might be, but so far it's a mystery to me.

Gyasi: Do you do poetry readings? How does it feel to perform poetry before an audience?

Evans: Yes, I do readings, quite a few since the publication of my first book, *Overtipping the Ferryman,* last January. In fact, I'm very excited to have been invited to read for the first time at the 2015 Geraldine R. Dodge Poetry Festival to be held in October in Newark, NJ, the largest poetry festival in North America. The human voice reading poems can be a very powerful instrument, as I learned when studying with W.D. Snodgrass as an undergraduate at the University of Delaware. After singing a song, one expects to hear applause. Not so after reading a poem. What I listen for during poetry readings are those little grunts of recognition or emotion—what I've called in a poem "The Sound We Make after Poetry." Those visceral grunts can be as heady as the most thunderous round of applause.

Gyasi: How does an idea for a song occur to you?

Evans: I usually look for an unusual turn of phrase, maybe something ironic or comic. The poet Stephen Dunn has said that if a line in a poem sounds like it could be part of a country western song, get rid of it. I sometimes think of songs as a haven for all of those lines that have been orphaned or abandoned in poems.

Gyasi: How does an idea for poems come to you?

Evans: Sometimes I think it's not so beneficial to think of it as "an idea for poems," because what drives a poem may not be an idea, but a mood or a musical collision of words instead. I tend to find inspiration in personal experiences, things I've heard people say, events that happen during the course of the day. This can be rather limiting, though, considering the mundane ways most days unfold. My most recent poems have been inspired by phrases or passages from the book *The Unquiet Grave* published in 1944 by Cyril Connelly. Creating poems in dialogue with another writer's published works relies much less on happenstance and more on the discipline to sit down and interact with that writer on a daily basis.

Gyasi: I'm not sure why I should be asking this question, but do you get writer's block when writing songs?

Evans: I think that's a perfectly fair question. My poetry output far outpaces my song output, primarily I think because I'm fairly limited as a musician. I get far less concerned about being blocked writing songs than I do when writing poems, because I feel like I have more tools to use to jump start my poetry than I do when writing songs.

Gyasi: Your first collection, *Overtipping the Ferryman*, received the 2013 Aldrich Press Poetry Prize. And it was your debut?

Evans: I was delighted to receive that honor. The publication of that book has been a lifelong dream, and it has opened up many doors that had been previously shut.

Gyasi: You teach high school and college English and Creative Writing. How do you manage your time teaching and writing poems and writing songs and singing?

Evans: Many writers I know take teaching jobs to support themselves while they write, writers who teach, in other words. I've always seen myself as a teacher who writes. The teaching comes first—that's what I'm paid to do. I make time for my writing whenever I can, usually during holidays or summer recess—although I have been known to procrastinate grading a set of student papers if the writing comes begging for my attention.

Gyasi: Your song "The Crows of Paterson" was featured in the documentary *All That Lies Between Us*. Could you tell me what this documentary was all about?

Evans: *All That Lies Between Us* is a film about the life and work of the Italian

American poet Maria Mazziotti Gillan. The directors are friends of mine, and they asked me if I could write some songs and instrumental music for them to use in the film, something I had never done before. Gillan tells writers that we all have a crow that sits on our shoulder and speaks to us in the voices of all our critics who tell us we're not smart or attractive or worthwhile enough. She says you have to ignore the crow and go deep down inside yourself to a place she calls "the cave," where our deepest stories and talents lie. My song "The Crows of Paterson" is a tribute to Maria's allegory of the crow and the cave and also her hometown of Paterson, New Jersey. (You can see a clip of my performance of this song from the premiere of the film here: https://www.youtube.com/watch?v=TtNIcWeKYhw)

Gyasi: Who inspires you as a singer/songwriter?

Evans: The list is endless, although my first and greatest influences were Warren Zevon and Bruce Springsteen.

Gyasi: Who inspires you as a poet?

Evans: William Shakespeare, Walt Whitman, Emily Dickinson from the Pantheon. Among contemporary writers, Stephen Dunn, Charles Simic, Martin Espada, Thomas Lux, Mary Oliver. It's another endless list, really.

Gyasi: Marly Youmans, the 2013 Aldrich Prize Judge, said of your book *Overtipping the Ferryman*: "While reading for the Aldrich Poetry Award, I tripped and fell into the world of a skeptic obsessed with what he doubts—who takes the symbols and stories of creation and wrests them to his own uses, though God and the skeletons under our skin are never far away, and lend power and support to his poems." Now, what do you think about this statement?

Evans: I am forever grateful to Ms. Youmans for selecting my book for publication. I found it doubly gratifying to read her commentary on my book because it showed me that she understood and appreciated all the elements of my work that I would hope an ideal reader would.

Gyasi: Do you have any formal background in songwriting?

Evans: None. As I said previously, my skills in that area are rather limited.

Gyasi: Singing and writing poems—which of the two do you make enough money from?

Evans: Enough for what—to live? Neither! Remember, I'm a teacher who writes.

Gyasi: How do you reconcile fatherhood with writing and singing and teaching?

Evans: You might think it a juggling act, but not really. Although it would be painful, I could stop writing, singing, and teaching in an instant if I had to. I will always be my daughter's father.

Diane Seuss was raised in rural Michigan. She is the author of three collections of poetry: *It Blows You Hollow* (New Issues Poetry Press, 1998), *Wolf Lake, White Gown Blown Open* (Juniper Prize, University of Massachusetts Press, 2010), and *Four-Legged Girl* (Graywolf Press, 2015). She has published widely in literary magazines. A poem that originally appeared in *Blackbird* received a 2013 Pushcart Prize. Her poem "Free Beer" is included in *The Best American Poetry 2014*. Seuss was the MacLean Distinguished Professor in the Department of English at Colorado College in 2012. She is Writer in Residence at Kalamazoo College in Michigan.

Gyasi: Perhaps, let's begin from your poem "Song in my heart." What inspired the poem?

Seuss: The personal dimension of "Song in my heart" is that it arose out of all of the feelings and realities that followed the difficult ending of my marriage. Once I got through the period of grief, I started to realize that there was great freedom in living alone and steering my own vessel, so to speak. When that realization came, it was sort of a "Song in my heart"; I came alive again. But of course it wouldn't be much of a poem if it had been written and experienced without texture. Once one begins writing, the speaker, of course, is no longer the writer, but a sort of performance of self. This performed self has a kind of swagger, and kind of silliness. The reader may feel that the speaker is in fact deluding herself, especially as she audaciously compares herself to God toward the poem's end. "Song in my heart" was really one of those poems that wrote itself and surprised me in its completion.

Gyasi: Are you a fan of shorter poems?

Seuss: Yes, I am, and I'm not very good at writing them. When they have come, my shorter poems have been very satisfying. The sonnet is just fourteen lines for a reason. There's something very satisfying in poems that can get a lot of work done in a relatively small space. Even without the rhyme and meter, a poem that is approximately the length of a sonnet feels like it holds an ideal balance between the spoken and the pressure of the unspoken outside the poem's margins.

Gyasi: Are you so much into prose poetry?

Seuss: Yes. I write and publish brief prose "pieces" which sort of exist in the hazy space between brief nonfiction and prose poetry, sometimes teetering more in the direction of one or the other. There is an elegance to that prose "box" that I find very appealing. Robbing oneself of line breaks by writing in the prose line may allow for a certain density of language or an extension of voice that works for some subjects. I could happily write a whole book of prose poems!

Gyasi: You feature "God" in most parts of the poem "Song in my heart." Are you a Christian? Do you believe in God?

Seuss: Good question. I was not raised in a particular church. When I was very young we lived in a small village, and it was a time in which children could wander without parents being too worried about them. I wandered on Sundays from church to church—all Christian, as there were no alternatives to Christianity in this small town. From a young age I sought out the spiritual, then. My father was ill for most of my early childhood and died when I was seven. His illness, his suffering, made my upbringing very complicating and confusing and scary. We reach for the Mystery, perhaps, when faced with pressures beyond our capacity to understand. I cannot say I now follow a particular religion, but I do believe in the Mystery, and

I do attempt to live a compassionate life. Of course, the God I reference in "Song in my heart" is not really God, or my notion of the spiritual. It's the performed speaker's view of God, which I play for a kind of sad comedy.

Gyasi: Where did you get the idea to write *Wolf Lake, White Gown Blown Open*?

Seuss: If you mean the entire book, that's a very big question! The title poem is probably one of the more complex poems I've written thus far. Wolf Lake itself is a real place. It's a beautiful little inland lake near the place where I currently live. There are no houses built around it. It's deep and spring-fed. I spent a summer going there nearly every evening, fishing with my young son and my then-husband, trying to save the marriage. The lake, the situation, the hour of dusk, the glowworms around the shore, all worked their way into my imagination and became representative, I guess, of the edgy, in-between spaces of grief and the erotic, the self and the other, poetry and everything else. The book as a whole arose out of a time in my life in which I was rediscovering desire and embodiment, and also working hard to survive and understand many difficult losses.

Gyasi: Tell me about winning the 2009 Juniper Prize for Poetry.

Seuss: Winning that prize was hugely supportive for me. It made my work more available to a wider readership, but more importantly, it confirmed to me that my work was on the right track. As you know, writing is an act of solitude. It's difficult to know if one's poems hit the mark, if they offer anything important to the reader. I was very heartened to know that the book "landed" for the judges of the prize, at least. Of course, prizes aren't why we write, and once the book is published there is still an endless stack of blank sheets of paper to fill with whatever comes next.

Gyasi: What do you do as a writer-in-residence at Kalamazoo College?

Seuss: I teach in the Department of English, primarily creative writing courses but also a seminar for first-year students and a literature course, Contemporary Poetry. I also bring important writers to campus, am faculty advisor for the student literary magazine, and attempt to serve as a bridge between the campus and the larger Kalamazoo community. It's been an incredible privilege to teach students at a place that encourages a global perspective and supports the students in finding their voices, in whatever field they choose.

Gyasi: What are your interests as a writer?

Seuss: Wow. Big question. I could go on and on, and my interests change as my work evolves. I will only say that I seem to always be interested in exploring beauty, desire and desirelessness, how I learned what it is to be a woman, people who live in rural spaces, and loss. Loss has been my subject since I was a very young child, and there is no solving it, no resolving it. On the level of language, my interests vacillate between an eye and an ear for lushness and an attraction to spareness. I seem to journey between those two poles.

Gyasi: How do you manage life as a single parent and writer?

Seuss: Very great question, with no perfect answer! It's been very difficult to balance the needs of my son with the needs of my students and the requirements of my profession—which I needed in order to make a living for myself and my son—and to still have a rich and informed life of the imagination. I'm lucky in that I think I have a natural tendency toward multi-tasking. What has been especially challenging is that my son went through a long period of struggling with addiction. But these are the issues that so many parents face. Like other parents, I have done my best, and often my best wasn't good enough. Writers, just like brick-layers and seismologists, carry the weight of the gap between what they wish they could have done and what they were able to do. I guess that all becomes part of the writing, of what I have to express.

Gyasi: Do you write mostly from your experiences?

Seuss: I'm not sure we can ever fully escape our own experiences; they're certainly often a starting-off point for me. But just as the speaker is a performed version of myself, at best, the content of the poem isn't fact-based journalism but an intersection between the real and the imagined. Poems are such an act of imagination that even content that seems related to my own lived experience is more the product of dream than reality. Lately, I've been writing about and from visual art. We're always moving between the binaries of "out there"—the world—and "in here"—the self, the inner life, like a bead on a string.

Gyasi: Do you mind sharing the inspiration behind the poem "Glosa"?

Seuss: "Glosa" is obviously a formal poem. The form is so compelling; it arises out of 14th- and 15th-century Spain and was constructed as a way to pay tribute or expand upon four lines from another poet's work. I've written a few glosas. This, I believe, was my first. Rather than choosing another writer's poetry to expand upon and structure the poem, I choose prose, from a story by Chekhov, who happens to be my son's favorite writer. You'll notice that the glosa uses each of the four borrowed lines as the last line of one of the four ten-line stanzas. As happens when we work from restrictive forms, I surprised myself. I found myself telling part of my son's story, of his struggle with depression and addiction, but weaving in Chekhov's story as well. I know it's a pretty dark poem, and I'm glad you found meaning in it.

Gyasi: Is *It Blows You Hollow* indeed your first book?

Seuss: Yes. *It Blows You Hollow* was published many years ago by New Issues Press, thanks to the editor of the series, poet Herbert Scott. I had always written poems, but hadn't been very proactive about publishing. He sort of grabbed up the manuscript and worked with me tirelessly to get it right and to get it published. I'm eternally grateful to him. When I look back at that book, I witness a much younger self, but she's still a part of me, and in some of the poems I'm proud of what she was able to express.

Gyasi: What do you like about poetry?

Seuss: I love so much about poetry. I love its capacity to create empathic connections between people. I love its music. I love how, when writing, one's imagination can be given free rein and can lead the writer places she didn't intend to go. I love how the artfulness of the poem, and moving through stages of revision, allow the writer to hold even the harshest experiences away from themselves in order to get the art "right," even when life itself cannot be so easily brought into balance. I love that I can read a poem written hundreds of years ago and feel the humanness of that poet as if their flesh and blood was nestled next to me. I love that writing poems demands that I look at things closely, that I name my feelings and experience, and that I abandon easy judgments for difficult complexities. I love being astounded by another writer's approach to language and how that opens up space for my own experimentation. I love falling asleep with a book of poems in my hands!

Gyasi: Do you read lots of poetry?

Seuss: Yes, I read a great deal, partly because I teach and have to stay current in order to keep my students interested, and partly because for me, poetry is my food and my spiritual text.

Gyasi: You were honored in 2003 with the College's esteemed Florence J. Lucasse Award for Excellence in Teaching. My question is, are you a great teacher?

Seuss: Oh boy, I'd never claim to be great at anything! (Although I do make pretty great pie ...) I love teaching, and I care about my students a great deal. I try to be the kind of teacher I needed when I was their age. I work very hard at teaching, and I try to keep it new, making sure I change things up and don't get stale. My spiritual philosophy of teaching is to find a way to hold each student in positive regard, and to work hard to help them respect their own imagination and their own power. I also try to make the atmosphere of the classroom fun and edgy, so that students feel they can bring their whole selves to the party. And I don't believe in suffocating students with work. Much can be learned from teaching with a light touch.

Gyasi: Do you keep a strict writing schedule?

Seuss: No, I wish I could, but that doesn't work given the nature of my life. During the teaching year I write when I can, which often means on holiday breaks. I get a great deal of writing done in the summer. I am actually in the process of applying to residencies for next summer, as getting away from my needy house and my needy dog and my everyday landscape allows me to really immerse myself in poems. If I suddenly became a millionaire, I probably would keep teaching, though I would give myself a lighter schedule, because I think giving back, via the classroom, is crucial to my own writing. When left to my own devices, I would write daily—or probably stay up most of the night and write.

Gyasi: Do you know when you've come to the end of a poem?

Seuss: Hmm, good question. I usually do know, as I feel a sort of emotional and even physical release when I've reached the poem's ending. Now and then I write past the ending and need to hack off the false ending. At other times, I realize I haven't really found the poem's true ending, and the current ending is a cop-out. Usually, however, I write until I find the place the poem wants to lead me, and it's usually a place of discovery and surprise.

Gyasi: Do you think about critics when you write?

Seuss: No, I don't. Partly, I'm freed from that concern because not too many critics have written about my work! But also, I think the critic plays an important function in understanding and evaluating the work after the fact, but isn't a very helpful presence while the work is being created. I've certainly been hugely helped by writing colleagues who offer up their critical point-of-view on my work. I am not offended by criticism unless it's delivered with meanness or ill-intent. I think that most criticism, even if it stings, contains a core of truth, and I sit with it until I can accept and act upon that truth. So no, the critic does not haunt my writing process, but certainly helps the process of revision.

Gyasi: What do you do when not writing or teaching?

Seuss: I'm going to assume that "grade papers" falls under the category of teaching, so I won't mention that long process! I love to cook, hang out in my little back yard with my dog, read, take road trips, see my mom and sister and son and friends, and be with the natural world. I love and live for experiences of solitude, silence and peace.

Gyasi: Do you mind ending the interview with anything in mind?

Seuss: I deeply appreciate your questions. I always learn something from being called to answer for myself and my work. Life is difficult; we all lose so much. I see poetry as the holy language that can now and then serve as a bridge between the land of the living and the land of the dead. The poem represents a larger spiritual process, and for me is the antidote to death. I am eternally grateful for what poetry teaches me. Thank you.

Dan Albergotti is the author of *The Boatloads* (BOA Editions, 2008) and *Millennial Teeth* (Southern Illinois University Press, 2014), as well as a limited-edition chapbook, *The Use of the World* (Unicorn Press, 2013). His poems have appeared in *The Cincinnati Review, Five Points, The Southern Review, The Virginia Quarterly Review,* and *Pushcart Prize XXXIII,* as well as other journals and anthologies. A graduate of the MFA program at UNC Greensboro and former poetry editor of *The Greensboro Review,* Albergotti is a professor of English at Coastal Carolina University in Conway, South Carolina.

Gyasi: You were about 35 years old when you decided to pursue an MFA at UNC-Greensboro. Now, what motivated your decision?

Albergotti: I had completed a PhD in literature when I was 31 and spent the next several years teaching at the University of Alabama and then at Auburn University. I loved the classroom, but found myself less and less interested in scholarship. Instead of working on turning chapters of my dissertation into publishable articles, I would spend time writing poems. One day I just admitted it to myself: I'm a writer, not a scholar. So I made the very unorthodox decision to enter an MFA program *after* having completed a PhD—quite a midlife path change. Like Dante, at 35 ("midway through life's journey") I'd found myself in a dark wood, and needed to find my way out.

Gyasi: Did you benefit from the MFA program at UNC-Greensboro?

Albergotti: Absolutely! It's a wonderful program, one that emphasizes community, individual attention, and the time to write. I couldn't be happier with my choice of MFA programs.

Gyasi: Were you writing before you started your MFA program?

Albergotti: Yes, I'd been writing poems since I was in high school, and I'd taken it very seriously even in college. But I had never taken a creative writing course until my final semester of coursework in the PhD program at the University of South Carolina. That semester, I took a poetry writing workshop from James Dickey. I really think my new trajectory began there.

Gyasi: Are you the routine type of writer? Do you keep a strict schedule?

Albergotti: No, I've never been able to do that. I've always suspected that strict routines are more important to prose writers than to poets. But having said that, I do wish I could "clock in" at the desk more regularly. In another interview, I once compared my method to making soup. Instead of working through many drafts on the page, I gather lines and ideas for poems and work them pretty obsessively in my mind over weeks or even months before completing even a first draft. The obsessive thought is the heat of the stove in my metaphor, and every three months or so, soup is ready—I will produce fairly advanced drafts of 6-8 poems in a very condensed period. Then my imagination is back to cutting vegetables.

Gyasi: Do you have literary influences?

Albergotti: There are some writers that I deeply admire and try to emulate: John Keats, Elizabeth Bishop, Thomas Hardy, Philip Larkin, Brigit Pegeen Kelly, Larry Levis, Jack Gilbert. I'm sure there are more whose influence on my work is equally strong and I just can't recognize it. One of my favorite definitions of a writer is by Saul Bellow: "A writer is a reader moved to emulation."

Gyasi: You were the former poetry editor of *The Greensboro Review*. Tell us about the work you did there.

Albergotti: I was the poetry editor of *The Greensboro Review* for one academic year, fall 2001 to spring 2002. That role was my assistantship in my second year of the UNC Greensboro MFA program. It was a wonderful apprenticeship to editing under the tutelage of the magazine's long-time editor, Jim Clark. I learned from the best there. It was also an experience that gave me a very healthy appreciation for the difficulty of publication. For the first issue I worked on, we read approximately 2800 submitted poems ... and published 13.

Gyasi: You also edit the online journal *Waccamaw* at Coastal Carolina University in Conway, SC. What interests me is the name of the journal. How did it come about? Is the work you do there any different from what you did at *The Greensboro Review*?

Albergotti: I founded *Waccamaw* in 2008. The journal is named after the Waccamaw River, which runs through the town of Conway. The river itself takes its name from a regional Native American tribe. The work I did on *Waccamaw* was a little more extensive than my work on *The Greensboro Review* because I was the founding editor, and putting together issues for the digital format also demanded that I be more involved in production. I'm very proud of *Waccamaw*, but I retired from editing in the spring, passing on the editorship of the journal to my colleague

Cara Blue Adams.

Gyasi: You teach creative writing and literature courses at Coastal Carolina University. Are there any major differences between the terms "Creative Writing" and "Literature"?

Albergotti: That's a good question. Ideally, there should be virtually no difference. You should be able to call the classes "Literary Study" and "Literary Production." But of course the literature that we study is far more sophisticated than the literature that most students can produce at that stage in their lives. Still, I always tell my creative writing classes that the goal is not to write passable poems that will garner them the praise of their friends and family, but rather to begin a long, arduous journey that will result in their inclusion in the *Norton Anthology of American Literature*. Donald Hall has said in an essay that he sees no point in dedicating yourself to the writing of poems unless your goal is to write *great* poems. I agree.

Gyasi: I am wondering how students are taught how to write. Is it possible?

Albergotti: This is a question that's often aimed at creative writing programs. Certainly you can't mechanically teach anyone how to produce poems like those of John Keats or Emily Dickinson. But I do believe you can cultivate the *discovery* of writing in the creative writing classroom. It's not a one-size-fits-all approach; it's giving people the tools of discovery. I once heard a rather cynical old literature professor say dismissively of creative writing programs, "You know, Shakespeare didn't need an MFA." Under my breath, I responded, "Yeah, well Flannery O'Connor earned one."

Gyasi: Let's talk about your full-length collection of poems *The Boatloads*.

Albergotti: *The Boatloads* is my first full-length collection. It won the A. Poulin, Jr. Poetry Prize from BOA Editions and was published in 2008. The manuscript grew out of my MFA thesis that was finished in 2002.

Gyasi: What are you currently working on?

Albergotti: My second full-length collection, *Millennial Teeth*, was just published by Southern Illinois University Press in September. Unlike *The Boatloads,* which consists entirely of free verse poems, *Millennial Teeth* is made up of both free and formal verse. Though it is a bit different in terms of form, the new book does continue to explore my thematic obsessions with mystery, doubt, ephemerality, and silence.

Eric Paul Shaffer is author of five books of poetry, including *Lāhaina Noon*; *Living at the Monastery, Working in the Kitchen*; and *Portable Planet*. More than 400 of his poems have appeared in more than 250 local and national reviews as well as reviews in Australia, Canada, England, Ireland, Japan, New Zealand, Scotland, and Wales. Shaffer received the 2002 Elliot Cades Award, a 2006 Ka Palapala Poʻokela Book Award for *Lāhaina Noon*, and the 2009 James M. Vaughan Award for Poetry. He teaches composition, literature, and creative writing at Honolulu Community College. Shaffer joined the poetry faculty at the Jackson Hole Writers Conference in Wyoming in June 2015.

Gyasi: From Wikipedia, you've been described as a Hawaiian novelist and poet. Could you spend some time talking about Hawaiʻi?

Shaffer: Hawaiʻi is a vibrant and exciting place for me, the end of a long journey moving mostly west. I was born in Massachusetts and as a child and young man lived in Maryland, Michigan, Indiana, New Mexico, and California. Then I moved to Okinawa, Japan, for my first job as a university teacher, where I lived for eight years. Only then did I start east again, but I traveled only halfway back across the Pacific, settling in Hawaiʻi, a place that includes the best of the East and the West. I'm not actually a Hawaiian novelist and poet; I'm a writer of poems and novels who lives in Hawaiʻi. In other words, a great deal of my work addresses living in Hawaiʻi, but I also write about events everywhere on the planet and publish my work all over the world from Hawaiʻi, to the mainland (which is what we in Hawaiʻi call the forty-eight contiguous states of America), to other countries, like Australia, Canada, England, Ireland, Japan, New Zealand, Scotland, and Wales.

When I lived in New Mexico, I wrote of New Mexico: see *Kindling* and *RattleSnake Rider*. When I lived in California, I wrote of California: see *RattleSnake Rider* and the first book of *Portable Planet*. When I lived on Okinawa, I wrote of Okinawa: see the other two books of *Portable Planet* and *Living at the Monastery, Working in the Kitchen*.

Lāhaina Noon was written only on and about Maui and the islands after I arrived on Maui in 1998, and since I've lived on Maui and Oʻahu, much of my work concerns life in the islands. A writer must address the events and issues of the place where he lives, and I find that the islands are constantly part of my new work. I have been making Hawaiʻi my home since I arrived, by studying the culture, the literature, the islands, and the language. Knowing a place well is the best way to inhabit it respectfully, and for me, that learning always leads to writing.

Gyasi: What does it mean to be a novelist and poet?

Shaffer: For me, writing poetry and fiction means that the formal, familiar distinctions between the two genres become blurred. I've been told that my poems are "narrative" and "novelistic" and that my fiction is "poetic." I think what those readers are sensing is that my poems and my novels are built at the sentence level, and there, I use all literary skills, strategies, and techniques equally, no matter what they are, so when readers come to my novels, they encounter language that is vivid and compressed, which is not a familiar feature of fiction. When readers come to my poetry, they discover dialogue and plot and dramatic scenes, which are too often not common characteristics in poetry.

I love sentences. In fact, when I was writing my first novel, I used to tell my wife that I was going to the office "to make sentences." I make poetry the same way. I often unravel my lines when I'm revising poems and make a paragraph or sequence of sentences so that I can study each individually and review their progress through the work. No matter what, I want sentences to be clear.

One kind critic even placed me in the "Clear Pool School of Poetry," indicating that my language was clear and deceptively deeper than the words might at first appear. I am still pleased with her assessment. Poetry is the attempt to say something significant and beautiful to our fellow humans, and the most important feature of our statement is clarity. Readers cannot appreciate what they cannot understand, and the writer's first and essential task is to communicate, to make a poem clear. Poems are not riddles, and every poem should immediately provide a worthwhile reward. Readers should be glad they read a poem the first time and be intrigued enough to return and read the lines again, and when they do read again, they should find more and more excellence and significance in the lines every time.

I come to poetry and fiction with the same attitude, and those readers who observe the genre distinctions more carefully than I do are sometimes surprised.

Gyasi: Do you find the time involved in writing novels boring?

Shaffer: That is a great question, one I've never heard before. When I am writing, I am immersed in the making of sentences, so, no, I am not bored when I'm writing novels. Completing a novel takes more time, but again, all of the time that goes into composition, revision, and finishing a novel is absorbing and rewarding. Making sentences, whether in poetry or fiction, is a pleasure. Fooling with words is fun.

The worst part about writing novels or poems is the effort to get them published. The effort is time-consuming and often frustrating, and the effort takes time away from writing. On the other hand, there is no way around making that effort unless one wants to write only for him- or herself, and I am a writer because I want to communicate with an audience. Therefore, I must at least attempt to publish.

Gyasi: Is it true that writing poems does not involve lots of research?

Shaffer: Well, that's not true for me. For me, all writing requires research, some formal and most informal. One of my guiding lights as a writer is accuracy: I want to be sure that all the details I include in my work are factual and verifiable because when readers don't trust our observations, they don't trust our work. In other words, when I write that the Southern Cross is visible on an early summer evening over the breakwater in Waikīkī, I not only saw that myself, I also verified the fact with my star charts. Getting the words right starts with our experience, but requires verification.

As for how much research is needed, once I was asked how long it took me to write a particular poem, and I responded jokingly, "All my life." Later, I realized that answer was the truest one I could have given. In the most essential way, everything in our experience is our research for writing poems or novels or plays or essays. All of what we know comes into play when we write, so writing anything involves research as well as our experience. As for formal research concerning poems, I find that I must look up, read, or research all kinds of information just as often as I do when I am writing novels.

A better way to answer might be to say that for every 1,000 words of finished writing, I end up doing some big or small amount of formal research, whether the writing is poetry or fiction.

Gyasi: When did you become a novelist?

Shaffer: Hmm. Well, I started writing fiction in high school, and I continued to write stories infrequently for many years. I began writing what became my first novel in 1985 after reading Richard Brautigan's *The Tokyo-Montana Express*, which I found inspiring and liberating. Brautigan, Kurt Vonnegut, and Tom Robbins became my guides as I wrote. I finished the first draft of *Burn & Learn*, my first novel, in 1991. I revised the novel for many years until the book was finally published by Leaping Dog Press in 2009.

So when exactly did I become a novelist? Was it when I began writing? Was it when I finished the first draft of my first novel? Was it when the novel was published? Good questions. I'll say I became a novelist when I actually started writing one in 1985, and I became an author when the novel was published in 2009.

On the other hand, most of my short stories and novels are still unpublished, so I am better known, if I am known at all, for my poems.

Gyasi: When did you become a poet?

Shaffer: Uh-oh, that's a tricky question. Okay, well, I've been writing poems since the second grade when I wrote a rhyming piece about Halloween, in which I rhymed "witch" with an unfortunate choice. The uproar was surprising, exciting, and gratifying, and I continued to write poems.

Luckily, I began to read poems when I was young, and I began to get an idea of what poetry is, was, and does. I've become a much more frequent reader of poetry than I am a writer of poetry, which seems to surprise people since I write and publish so many poems. I really do read more poetry than I write. When I find a great poem or a great poet, I am as excited as I am by writing a poem of my own. As for becoming a poet myself, I will only say that I write poems. I think it is up to my readers to decide whether I'm a poet or not. A poet has a lot of responsibilities and duties, and I try to meet as many of them as I can, so I aspire to be a poet. Yet "poet" is not really a title one can assign to him- or herself; it's a cultural recognition, one awarded by our fellow humans in recognition of good work. I'm glad when people who have read my work call me a poet, but I don't call myself that.

Gyasi: You're a professor of English at Honolulu Community College. Could you tell us some of your interests as a teacher?

Shaffer: I am interested in guiding students to become better readers and better writers. For expository writing, I focus on the basics: sentence construction and clarity, organization and presentation of points, discovery of good examples and complete explanations of evidence, and development of editing and proof-reading skills.

For creative writing courses and literature courses, I focus on the techniques of fiction, non-fiction, and poetry, recognizing and employing effective literary strategies, using figurative language appropriately and well, and appreciating fine works of literature, both classic and contemporary.

What expository and creative writing have in common is the requirement to communicate. I teach my students that the most important person in the world is the reader because without the reader, the writing means nothing.

> Gyasi: You also taught American literature at Maui Community College and the University of the Ryukyus on Okinawa. Could you say a thing or two about American literature?

Shaffer: Yes, American literature is my specialty, especially twentieth-century American literature, with an emphasis on poetry after 1950 and contemporary poetry. As an American, I find much to love in our literature, the range, the depth, the incredible number of perspectives, and I find that the literature awakens me to all kinds of insights that I might otherwise have missed.

It's also great to see how American literature is influenced and influences literature all over the world. Writers respond to writers they admire, and writers also incorporate ideas and images from everywhere, so whether I am reading Murakami, Borges, Calvino, Achebe, McEwan, Rushdie, Franzen, or somebody else, I see a pleasant mix of world history, mythology, and literature in every work. I am glad that there are many good writers everywhere, each reading and writing for each other and all of us, but we probably should have expected that. There are more humans alive now than any other time in the planet's history, which means that there are more great writers alive now than at any other time. Like you, Geosi, I love to read, and this is an age where readers will have their choice of anything they desire.

> Gyasi: What do you think of the young generation of American writers?

Shaffer: If you mean the American writers that are younger than I am, and there are more every year, many are talented and skilled, and I enjoy reading them. And, as my elders recommended to me, I would recommend to all of them—and to everyone else who writes—to read more and participate in the current literary conversation fully and with their whole hearts. Literature changes the world, one mind at a time. And that is the permanent pace for change that will endure.

> Gyasi: You received the Elliot Cades Award for Literature, Hawaii's highest literary honor, in 2002. Why do you think you were chosen for this award?

Shaffer: The ways of literary awards committees are often difficult to discern, and I didn't meet anyone on the committee until the awards ceremony, so I am hoping that I received the award because they read my books and the letters of those who nominated me and decided that I was worthy of the prize. I hope they saw solid and illuminating literary work, but I didn't ask, and they didn't say.

One interesting outcome of winning the Elliot Cades Award for Literature was a conversation I had with a few writers attending the ceremony. They asked whether I had written much about Hawai'i. I had, but not much had been published at that time, so I decided right there to make my next book exclusively focused on Hawai'i. Three years later, Leaping Dog Press published *Lāhaina Noon*, which, as

I mentioned earlier, was only of and about the islands.

Gyasi: What inspired "Portable Planet"?

Shaffer: "Portable Planet" is a poem I wrote because I was living in Okinawa, and I was corresponding with one of my poetry pals who lived in Florida. We realized that we were on nearly opposite sides of the planet, and as a joke, she sent me an inflatable globe to remind me of both how large and how little the world is these days. Once I had received the globe and inflated it, I found all sorts of unusual uses for the globe, and I wanted to explore and describe them and their implications in a poem.

One of the most important qualities for a writer is to be observant, so I realized as I wrote that there were personal and cultural implications in my uses of the inflatable globe, and I tried to incorporate them in a thoughtful but funny poem. One of the best benefits of writing poems is what we discover and learn about ourselves and the world in the process of saying what we mean. It's always great to surprise ourselves.

Gyasi: What do you think now if you look at your first book?

Shaffer: My first book was actually half of a book of poetry called *Kindling: Poems from Two Poets* (1988); the other half was poems written by my good poetry buddy James Taylor III.

When I look at my poems in that book, there are still eight of the twenty-one that I am proud of and that I read in public on the proper occasions. Some are still among my favorites of all my work: "Recognition," "Grandmother's Frame," "Clearing the Library Shelves," and "Goat Rock Beach, North California Coast." Considering that I was in my early thirties then, that's a pretty good percentage. My first book on my own was *RattleSnake Rider* (1990). That book also contained many of the poems that defined my direction and voice for years to come, and many remain my own favorites: "Instant Mythology," "An Irregular Ode to the Idea of My Pierced Ear," "For Veronica, Instead," "Hawk in October," and my long poem, "RattleSnake Rider."

All in all, I am still pleased when I read my early work, but not as pleased as I am when I read or write my current work. The best poem is always the one I am working on.

Gyasi: You are the author of five collections of poetry and one novel. What accounts for the high number of poetry books?

Shaffer: I've always written poetry first. What I mean is that daily when I sit down to write, nearly always what comes out is a poem. Another reason that I have more poetry books is that I'm more involved in poetry. I read poetry all the time. I make a point of reading at least ten new poems a day, and I often go far beyond that. I subscribe to poetry magazines and read the ones that come to the library. I order books by people who've written poems I like, and I am always pleased whenever one of my poems and one of their poems appear in the same literary magazine. I also have more books of poetry published because I write fiction very slowly, and I write creative non-fiction even more slowly. Finally, I am very pleased with my work in fiction and non-fiction, but I believe my best writing is in poems.

Gyasi: Where do you get inspiration to write?

Shaffer: I get inspiration to write from my Lux Minute Minder kitchen timer, which, when I sit down early in the morning, I set for one hour, and then I write madly for those sixty minutes. On good days, when I don't need to go anywhere early, I set the timer two or three times before I move on to other daily necessities. Once the timer is ticking away, I am free to focus on words. The timer becomes a shield against interruptions and distractions and a watchman who reminds me where the morning is going. Once an hour, I can look up and get my bearings so that I can decide if I will continue writing or I must move on to something else. I am dead-set against waiting for inspiration. I've watched many of my fellow writers do that, and often, they never write again. My publisher coined a term for those who once wrote and write no more, "wroters." I don't want to be a "wroter," so I write every day, with or without inspiration.

Gyasi: Do you care about bad reviews?

Shaffer: Sure, I do, but I care more about not being noticed at all, which is a fate likely to many of us in this age of the internet information avalanche. Even a review ambivalent about my poetry would be a review posted or printed, and somebody may notice. Also, none of my books have ever really gotten a bad review. The reviews of my poetry are generally very positive, and that is satisfying. At this point, along with the five books and three chapbooks of poetry, I have published more than 400 individual poems in more than 250 local, national, and international reviews, so I feel confident that I must be doing something right enough for most readers.

Gyasi: Do you think so much about imagery when writing?

Shaffer: Hmm, I don't "think" about imagery when I write, but I always begin with an image. I visualize the scene, situation, and action of the writing, and I describe the whole thing in a way that creates the poem in the reader's mind's eye. We often say, "I see what you mean" when we understand, and that is what I want my readers to say when they read my work. Often, the scene is in my mind before I even start, and I start pitching out the details. Other times, I have a line in mind, or I overhear somebody speaking brilliance, or I wake up with a voice speaking in my ear, and when I write that down, the whole poem springs to mind, and I have to race to get it all down.

Gyasi: Tell us about your poem "The Word-Swallower."

Shaffer: "The Word-Swallower" is a great example of what I said in answer to your last question. I was reading over the list of circus performers in some magazine or online, but when I saw the words "the sword-swallower," I read, "the word-swallower."

Immediately, the image of the circus tent, small, green, mildewed, and out-of-the-way, occurred to me. I entered and saw the word-swallower sitting on a cheap, rickety, old folding chair. I realized that, of course, if the attraction was watching someone swallow words, not many people would care, so the poem became one of close description and an ironic interplay between the narrator who spoke at length about the word-swallower and the word-swallower who says nothing ever. I was in a tough spot until I realized that someone must also speak *for* the word-swallower *in* the poem. The dog-faced boy leaped into that void and fit the poem perfectly.

I have often found in my fellow writers a curious and simultaneous love and contempt for language, and this poem allowed me to play a little bit with those contrasting impulses in these lines as well. In this poem about a man who refuses to use words for any purpose, I used more "fancy" words than I ever usually use—among others, "verbiage," "riposte," and "grandiloquence" (a perfect word that I tripped over as I closed the poem)—to further widen the contrast between the silent central figure and the narrator and to underscore the magnitude of the word-swallower's commitment to silence.

May I ask myself a question to end the interview?

Gyasi: Sure!

Shaffer: Okay, here goes: What are you working on now?

I am working on three projects: one each of poetry, fiction, and non-fiction. I have put together *Even Further West*, my sixth book of poems, and I am circulating it to various publishers. The manuscript contains about 45 poems, including "The Word-Swallower," all of which have been published in literary reviews around the planet. I think the book includes some of my best poems to date.

As for fiction, I am working extremely slowly on a novel about a fifteen-year-old who works on a Christmas tree farm in Michigan. He wants to help his mother and family make ends meet after the father abandons them. Fiction is fun to write, but I don't find time for this project very often.

In non-fiction, I'm working on a book I call *A Mockingbird on Maui*, which addresses what it's like to live upcountry in Kula and how exploring and studying a place makes one feel at home. At 1900 feet, far from the beaches, Kula is a rural part of Maui, and in the book, I write about examining the flora and fauna of the fields around the house and the sky at night.

I enjoy having so many different writing projects in progress since whenever I sit down and wind the Lux Minute Minder, I can turn to whatever book I wish and write.

Maria Mazziotti Gillan is winner of the 2014 George Garrett Award for Outstanding Community Service in Literature from AWP, the 2011 Barnes & Noble Writers for Writers Award from Poets & Writers, and the 2008 American Book Award for her book, *All That Lies Between Us*. She is the Founder/Executive Director of the Poetry Center at Passaic County Community College, editor of the *Paterson Literary Review,* and director of the creative writing program/professor of English at Binghamton University-SUNY. She has published 20 books, including: *The Silence in an Empty House* (NYQ Books, 2013); *Ancestors' Song* (Bordighera Press, 2013); and *Girls in the Chartreuse Jackets* (Cat in the Sun Books, 2014).

Visit her website at http://www.mariagillan.com.

Gyasi: Are you comfortable with the label American poet?

Gillan: Yes. I am an American poet and proud to be part of the multi-cultural fabric that is America. My parents were immigrants from Italy, and I was born in Paterson, NJ. I did not speak English until I went to school.

Gyasi: How long have you been writing?

Gillan: I've been writing since I was eight years old.

Gyasi: Do you remember your first piece of work?

Gillan: Yes. It was a poem about a dog that was published in *St. Anthony's Messenger*. It was a dreadful poem, and by the time it actually appeared in the magazine, I recognized how bad it was.

Gyasi: Do you find poetry easy to write?

Gillan: I love poetry, and it is so much a part of me that I don't think I could ever stop writing it. Writing it is easy; revising it is hard.

Gyasi: What factors inspired you to enroll in a Ph.D. program at Drew University? In other words, why Drew?

Gillan: I thought that I wanted to learn more and I thought I needed the Ph.D. to get a full-time teaching job in a university. My children were still young and I needed a school close to home.

Gyasi: How do you get the idea to start a poem?

Gillan: Usually it comes to me when I've been reading poetry. Also, I always write when my students write.

Gyasi: At what time of the day do you write best?

Gillan: I used to get up in the middle of the night to write when my children were young. Now, I can write anytime.

Gyasi: You are the founder of the Poetry Center at Passaic County Community College in Paterson, NJ. Do you remember the beginnings of this poetry center and how is it doing?

Gillan: I started the Poetry Center in 1980, the year that I obtained the first small grant from the New jersey State Council on the Arts, and we're now in our 35th year. It's grown enormously since 1980, and I'm very proud of what I've done and of its reputation for excellence.

Gyasi: As the editor of the *Paterson Literary Review*, do you edit your own work?

Gillan: I am the sole editor of *PLR*. I choose all of the work.

Gyasi: Could you tell us how you came to write *Ancestors' Song*?

Gillan: *Ancestors' Song* is a collection of poems about my family and my Italian roots. It is a celebration of my mother and of San Mauro, Italy, the small Italian village where she came from.

Gyasi: Can you talk about your poetry collection *The Place I Call Home*?

Gillan: Much of my work deals with family and *The Place I Call Home* is rooted in family, place, and love.

Gyasi: Do you know who reads your books?

Gillan: People from all over the world. For example, in the last week, I got a series of emails about my work from a young woman in England, and I also received emails from a woman who teaches at the American Embassy School in India. People write to me very often about my work, and it is very gratifying.

Gyasi: What actually inspires you to write?

Gillan: My ordinary life inspires me. I've written a great deal about growing up in poverty as the child of immigrants, but I've also written about a long marriage, loss, grief. I am writing more and more about my fear for all we've done to destroy the environment.

Gyasi: Have you gained anything from writing?

Gillan: Writing has given me a voice. When I was young, I was very shy and poetry has always been my way of telling my story and reaching out to the world.

Gyasi: You've published 18 books to date. I'm not sure if that is accurate. But do you see yourself publishing more books in the future?

Gillan: Actually, I've written 20. I continue to write and to publish in journals, and I'm working on a new manuscript.

Gyasi: What sort of theme(s) do you often write on?

Gillan: Family, marriage, love, loss, grief, environment, social justice.

Gyasi: Is there any way you could compare Italian literature to American literature?

Gillan: For a long time, because we spoke Italian at home, I thought I was Italian, but then, when I went to Italy, I realized that there is a difference between being Italian-American and being Italian. The Italian poetry I have read has been much more philosophical than American poetry. I think that my type of poetry is much more narrative than Italian poetry.

Gyasi: Do you still live in Hawthorne, New Jersey? If so, my question is, how is the literary scene?

Gillan: Yes, I still live in Hawthorne, NJ, and that is a blue-collar suburb of Paterson, NJ. For me the literary scene is in Paterson at the Poetry Center, and it exists for me everywhere I sponsor readings or I go to read myself. I love readings and I revel in sharing my work with audiences.

Gyasi: In 2008 you received the American Book Award for your book *All That Lies Between Us.* Do you know why you won this award?

Gillan: I am not sure why they chose that particular book, but I was thrilled to receive it. It was national recognition that justified all the work I had done in my life and through my writing.

Gyasi: What is the most boring part of writing?

Gillan: Nothing. I love writing, and it's never boring for me. It is my passion.

Gyasi: Do you have a favorite among all the books you've written?

Gillan: They're like my children. I love them all and can't choose one above the others.

Gyasi: What legacy do you want to leave behind as a poet?

Gillan: I want to leave poems that touch people, that move them to laughter or tears. I want what every writer wants—to be remembered.

Dominika Wrozynski is Assistant Professor of English at Manhattan College in New York City. Her latest poems have appeared in *Crab Orchard Review*, *Slipstream*, *Kritya: A Journal of Poetry*, *The Spoon River Poetry Review*, *Saw Palm*, *Rattle*, *Proud to Be: Writing By American Warriors (Vol.3)*, and are forthcoming in an anthology entitled *200 New Mexico Poems*.

Gyasi: First, what is your relationship with Poland?

Wrozynski: I was born in Poland in 1979. I am the daughter of artists and teachers. My mother was a drama teacher and a community arts organizer. My father was an actor and director of stage productions. Poland was a communist country when I was born and my parents were active in underground arts movements that opposed the communist government. One day, a government agent stopped my mother on the street. He said if she and her husband did not cease their activism, they would be arrested and I would be taken to an orphanage. We would never see each other again. My mother and father began the process of getting us out of Poland that very day. We eventually took a Christmas cruise to Germany (when I was 6 years old). We got off the ship in Hamburg, went to a homeless shelter, and applied for political refugee status. My father found work and we lived in Germany for 2.5 years, waiting for sponsorship to Australia or the United States. We were sponsored by a church group in Washington State and came to America when I was 9 years old. I grew up in Seattle.

My mother and father are the only biological family I have in America. Everyone else stayed in Poland. So, though I've grown up in America, I will always have ties to the country of my birth. I visit Poland occasionally, but usually many years lapse between visits. I speak Polish and translate Polish poets into English; there's a poetic and artistic connection for me there as well. Mostly, I just find it difficult to answer the "Where are you from?" question.

Gyasi: Do you think America has provided you with the right environment needed to write?

Wrozynski: Yes—absolutely. I never had to struggle with being able to express myself artistically (like my parents did). My future was the reason they left Poland. Though we never had a lot (materially), I had the freedom to write, to grow up in a country that fostered my intellectual development (instead of a place that was under Communism's thumb for so long).

Gyasi: When did it all begin—I mean your writing career?

Wrozynski: I wrote as a young person—as an undergraduate at college (when I was at Seattle University). But it wasn't until I went to graduate school for English and Creative Writing that I considered making a career out of writing and teaching. When I went to graduate school (first at New Mexico Highlands University and then at Florida State University), I learned technique from the some of the best writers working today (especially Barbara Hamby, David Kirby, and James

32

Kimbrell). I also received mentorship and figured out that I could write and teach and make a living—and that I wasn't half bad at writing and teaching.

Gyasi: Do you have a special purpose for why you write?

Wrozynski: I don't set out to write with a specific purpose or agenda. I want my audience to know what it means to be human—for me, in a certain time and place. I do want to learn about things, people, and places that interest me. Often my writing (for myself) is a way into that knowledge.

Gyasi: What do you ascertain as the best time to write?

Wrozynski: I do really well when I have deadlines (self-imposed or imposed by outside factors). I often need the pressure of a deadline to work effectively. I don't write nearly as much as I could when I have multiple free days just stretching ahead of me. To me, there's something wildly intimidating about all of that "free" time.

Gyasi: Who are your literary influences?

Wrozynski: That's a really difficult question. There are so many writers I admire. There are also writers I read when I'm stuck in my own work. There are writers who speak louder to me at various times in my life than at others. There are writers who are really good at writing *about* writing (not just actually creating poetry or prose).

I'll just list a few writers here from whom I draw inspirations (technical, spiritual, craft-oriented, etc.)—there are really too many to name: Wislawa Szymborska, Czeslaw Milosz, Frederico Garcia Lorca, Elizabeth Bishop, Richard Hugo, Denise Levertov, Jack Gilbert, Robert Bly, Carolyn Forché, Emily Dickinson, Walt Whitman, and on, and on, and on.

I also wrote with a writing group for years—and still keep in touch with these amazing writers and friends: Laura Newton, Christine Poreba, Deborah Hall, Jane Springer, Jen McClanaghan, Sarah Grieve. They have read and workshopped most of my poems and fledgling prose pieces. Their guidance and influence has been invaluable to me. Their poetry and prose (they're all published) will take your breath away—it's that good.

Gyasi: You were the poetry editor for *Apalachee Review* from 2006 to 2013. Could you tell us a bit about the *Apalachee Review*?

Wrozynski: *Apalachee Review* is a literary journal that has been operating in Tallahassee, Florida, for more than 40 years. It's currently headed by Mary Jane Ryals and Michael Trammell, who are terrific writers and editors. I became involved when I lived in Tallahassee and attended Florida State University and I eventually served as the Poetry Editor for a few years. This journal is a true community effort. The staff members are all volunteers (mostly from in and around Tallahassee, Florida). But the writing that comes in is from all over the United States and from all over the world, actually. Staff members read and select submissions for publication. The quality of the prose and poetry is high and literary agents have contacted some of the writers in *Apalachee Review* based on the writing samples they read in the magazine. I'd encourage everyone to visit the website to check out some great poetry and prose. If you like what you read, you can also subscribe and receive the issues by mail. Here's the website:

http://www.apalacheereview.org.

Gyasi: You've also been an associate Fiction Editor for *Carve* magazine between 2004 to 2005. Where do you draw the line between editing poetry and fiction?

Wrozynski: I don't edit fiction anymore, but I loved editing for *Carve*. In some ways, editing fiction and poetry is a similar process for me. I'm looking for originality, images, specificity. I can usually tell if I want to keep reading a piece of fiction after the first page. With a poem, I can usually tell after the first few lines if I'm going to keep reading. I love stories (many of my poems are narrative, after all), and I love good storytellers. I admire good fiction writers for their abilities to sustain a complex and rich story over the course of many pages.

Gyasi: What do you do to rest when you're not writing or teaching?

Wrozynski: Of course, I read—in a variety of forms. Novels, books of poetry, newspapers, magazines, online content. I also love doing active things (especially when I can get outside). I play with my dogs. I run a lot (I ran my first marathon on September 28, 2014). My husband, Todd, rides a motorcycle, and I love riding on the back. I love to travel, and also to attend theatrical productions or concerts—I just wish I had more resources (time and money) to do that.

Gyasi: Do you earn a living from writing?

Wrozynski: I don't earn a living from writing, per se. Even if I win a prize or get paid for a poem, it's never enough to support myself. But writing and teaching are closely linked for me—and it's teaching that allows me to support myself and to have a writing career.

Gyasi: Is it appropriate to say that poetry is easier to write than fiction?

Wrozynski: That's like saying, what was more difficult to create, modern art or classical art? Both come with their own sets of challenges, right? Poetry and fiction operate in the same way—each form has its own set of challenges, techniques, skill sets. I would never say one is easier than the other.

Gyasi: As a poetry editor, what makes a good poem?

Wrozynski: When I was the poetry editor for *The Southeast Review* (at Florida State), I wrote this "manifesto." I think it still applies to my aesthetic:

I don't look for one specific thing when I read poetry. I only wish it were that simple. A well-written lyric will move me as much as a well-written pastiche or narrative. But I do wish for one major thing: Submit a poem that makes me want to go into the editorial meeting and put up a fight to see the poem in print. Give me an arsenal of surprising images, unusual word choice, and a critical awareness of what it means to be human. If I'm going to take the effort to fight for a poem, I want it to win.

Gyasi: What inspired "Desert Love Poem"?

Wrozynski: "Desert Love Poem" is a pretty early poem (that was recently published by *Rattle*). I was surprised, in a way, that it had gotten picked up for publication because I wrote it so long ago. The sentiment behind the poem, however, is still accurate. Sometimes it's hard for us to love the people who are the closest to us, whether those people are spouses, parents, or children. In fact, sometimes we don't love them at all, and that feeling can last a while. It usually makes us feel guilty—how can we fall out of love with someone? What's wrong with us? The poem seeks to address that uncertainty. But it also ends on an image of love, of two people who know each other and love each other so well that they don't need to say anything to express their feelings for each other.

Gyasi: What do you think of the current poetry coming out of America?

Wrozynski: I don't want to generalize my response because poets are individuals and their books are individual books. I'm just excited that I get to read and hear so much good poetry and that so many small presses and literary journals defy the odds, year after year, and bring us some of the most innovative and exciting art to date. I am lucky that I get to add my voice to this mix every time I publish a poem or piece of prose.

Gyasi: Is it true that poetry is dying?

Wrozynski: I hope not—otherwise I won't have a job! No—but in all seriousness, there have been so many things written about poetry as a dying art. One of the most famous essays written about this very topic is Dana Gioia's "Can Poetry Matter?" Though this was written in 1991, many people still refer to it when describing poetry's relevance as an art form. In this essay Gioia makes some compelling arguments for the "death" of poetry, citing an insular graduate school culture, an unwillingness of poets to collaborate with other artists (visual and musical), and unwillingness for critics and reviewers to review poetry in non-academic forums (among many, many other things).

Though I understand Gioia's arguments, I view the state of poetry differently. I teach in NYC where I can go and hear poetry (in various forms—traditional, slam, spoken word, etc.) any day of the week. Often that poetry reading is presented in collaboration with visual or musical art. People might say, "Well, of course, you're in NYC. What about elsewhere?" I found the same to be true in Tallahassee, Florida, and in Las Vegas, New Mexico. You just have to work a little harder in smaller towns to find artistic venues and opportunities—and there will be fewer opportunities to engage with art. But those opportunities are there—or you can do something to create them.

There are organizations that employ poetry as a tool of social change. Split This Rock is one such organization that hosts a yearly poetry festival in Washington, D.C. Hundreds of poets and activists participate in the festival. We have poet laureates—both in individual states and in a national position. There is poetry on television, on the radio, and in public spaces (like NYC subways). Could there be more of all of this? Absolutely. Could we value arts more in America and allocate more resources towards arts and arts education? Yes. But to say that poetry is dying seems inaccurate. Maybe I'm an eternal optimist when it comes to this topic.

Gyasi: Is it necessary for all poets to engage in poetry readings?

Wrozynski: It's not necessary, per se, but if you're a professional poet you will probably read your work to a variety of audiences. Many times if you have a book accepted for publication, that prize committee or press will sponsor a reading.

Often colleges and universities operate reading series or festivals and will ask you to come and participate by giving a reading. Usually you receive some sort of honorarium for the reading.

Gyasi: Tell us something about *American Accent*.

Wrozynski: My book project, *American Accent*, is a poetry collection in which I explore what it means to be American—geographically, psychologically, and linguistically—for a Polish-American émigré writer. Thematically, the manuscript begins with life in communist Poland, my subsequent escape from the country of my birth, and assimilation into American culture. Poems such as "My Mother's Biography"—a bilingual Polish and English poem—also explore a linguistic hybridity, and reflect my interest in contemporary translation projects. *American Accent* also addresses various American geographies, such as the mesas of New Mexico; the landscape serves as a backdrop for yet another version of America—one where small-town locals duel with Patrick Swayze and other figures once iconic in popular culture.

Gyasi: Do you ever regret being a writer?

Wrozynski: No. If literature communicates what it means to be human (for a certain writer at a certain time), I feel privileged that I am able to share my voice with my readers. Being able to write and to have readers is a great gift. I would never regret that.

Gyasi: If you had any advice for budding writers, what would it be?

Wrozynski: Read as much as you can. That is a cliché and young writers hear this all of the time, but it's true. How else can you know what other talented writers are doing and how it is that they are doing it? How else can you learn about techniques and forms? You need models. You also need to have writers whom you turn to when you're stuck or when you're trying something new in your own work. There's no way to find those writers without reading. Also, find someone who is better than you and see if you can learn from him/her. For many writers that learning occurs in a class or workshop. It doesn't have to be there—but find someone who is better than you and someone who writes differently than you do. That's a great way to expand your technique.

Teresa Mei Chuc was born in Saigon, Vietnam, and immigrated to the U.S. under political asylum with her mother and brother shortly after the Vietnam War while her father remained in a Vietcong "reeducation" camp for nine years. Her poetry appears in journals such as *EarthSpeak Magazine*, *Hawai'i Pacific Review*, *Hypothetical Review*, *Kyoto Journal*, *The Prose-Poem Project*, *The National Poetry Review*, *Rattle*, *Verse Daily* and in anthologies such as *New Poets of the American West* (Many Voices Press, 2010), *With Our Eyes Wide Open: Poems of the New American Century* (West End Press, 2014), and *Mo' Joe* (Beatlick Press, 2014). Mei Chuc's poetry is forthcoming in the anthology *Inheriting the War: Poetry and Prose by Descendants of Vietnam*

Veterans and Refugees. *Red Thread* is her first full-length collection of poetry. Her second collection of poetry is *Keeper of the Winds* (FootHills Publishing, 2014).

> Gyasi: You were born in Saigon, Vietnam. Could you tell us why you immigrated to the United States?

Mei Chuc: I was born in Saigon, Vietnam, shortly after the fall of Saigon. I was about two years old when we immigrated to the United States under political asylum. After the fall of Saigon, during the time when my mother was still pregnant with me, my father, who served in the Army of the Republic of Vietnam (ARVN), had to report to "re-education." My mother told me that in the evening after my father reported to the Vietcong "re-education" camp, some soldiers came and checked if my father had gone. My mother said that if my father did not report when he was suppose to, he would have been taken out of the home, like some of the other villagers, and shot to death. My father was told to pack enough food and clothing for ten days, but he ended up being imprisoned for nine years. In a Vietcong prison, there was no sentence, the prisoners didn't know when they would be released or if they would ever be released.

Conditions were terrible for many South Vietnamese after the U.S. war in Vietnam. Vietnamese who were part of the ARVN or had family who were part of the ARVN, or those who worked in an American company or had some Chinese ancestry, were persecuted. My father had served in ARVN during the U.S. war in Vietnam, my family had worked for an American company selling music records in South Vietnam before the war, and we were ethnically part Chinese. On October 21, 1978, my mother took my brother and me and a bag of belongings, boarded a boat, and fled Vietnam before the Sino-Vietnamese War when the persecution of Vietnamese with Chinese ancestry was mounting. China invaded North Vietnam on February 17, 1979, and began the Sino-Vietnamese War, also known as the Third Indochina War, that lasted until March 16, 1979. My mother, brother, and I arrived in the United States on February 10, 1979.

> Gyasi: What do you remember about the Vietnam War?

Mei Chuc: I was very young then, two years old, when we fled Vietnam. What I remember are the physical, emotional, mental, and spiritual memories passed on from my family members and the stories that they would tell me about the war. I think my first remembrance of the Vietnam War came in the form of absence. I deeply felt my father's absence from my life since he was taken away when my mother was still pregnant with me. So this hollow space in my life and heart and spirit was so great that it consumed me as a child. My father was imprisoned for nine years in a Vietcong prison in Northern Vietnam. I first saw him when I was nine years old and he brought the weight of the war with him when he came. I felt my suffering, my family's suffering, and the suffering of those involved in the war. Over the years, I learned so much from my family about the war and from reading historical texts. Many poems from my first collection of poetry, *Red Thread*, are about my family's experiences through the U.S. war in Vietnam and about the war itself.

Gyasi: Do you write from personal experiences?

Mei Chuc: I think that I write from personal, universal, natural, and human experiences. I believe that our most intimate and personal spaces reflect the greater story of humanity, the earth, and the universe. So, the deeper I look inside myself, the further and wider I reach into the world.

Gyasi: What inspired you to become a writer?

Mei Chuc: I love words and languages and I think that I can best express myself in writing. Writing makes me feel human and allows me to share my heart and spirit. Writing also allows me to tell my story and my family's story through the Vietnam War. I believe that it's important to preserve many sides and voices in history, especially those of the oppressed because those are usually the voices that are silenced or overwhelmed into silence. It is almost a resistance against erasure.

Gyasi: You have a Masters of Fine Arts in Creative Writing from Goddard College in Plainfield. Why did you decide to pursue poetry?

Mei Chuc: Poetry is the form that I gravitate towards. I think that I fell in love with poetry early on when I was a child and learning English as a third language (my first and second languages are Vietnamese and Cantonese) because I finally felt that I had control of language when I was able to write poetry and express myself. I didn't have to follow any of the rules of English grammar or punctuation. I was able to recreate myself in a new world and country. Writing poetry was a way that I was able to reclaim a part of myself that had been exiled, dislocated, and torn apart through war and its consequences, into something that was wholly my own... something of compassion, love, and beauty.

Jane Hirshfield has a great quote that I think reveals my dedication to poetry. Hirshfield wrote, "... for giving oneself to the lion, or to poetry, is a vow—nothing more, nothing less than one's entire life will be asked."

Gyasi: You served for two years as a poetry editor for Goddard College's *Pitkin Review*. What do you consider as good poetry?

Mei Chuc: When I was in high school, my English teacher taught us that the difference between good poetry and great poetry is that great poetry transcends time and place and that there is a working that a poet must do between sound and sense ... a sort of balance or a sort of wisdom about the two, I think ... and that *sense* should never be sacrificed for *sound*. I think this is true of what I believe and also that poetry should move me deeply in some way either by its images or sounds or meaning and I should be both transported and transformed in some way after reading it.

Gyasi: Do you edit your own work?

Mei Chuc: Yes, I mostly work in my own poet cave and mostly edit my own work. I am very self-critical, so I am grateful to also belong to an email writing group called New Nada, consisting of a few friends. We email each other poems now and then and provide some feedback, and the group has been incredibly supportive over the years.

Gyasi: What inspired your poem "The Road"?

Mei Chuc: I went to an art exhibit at a local museum that was featuring paintings by Michelangelo Merisi da Caravaggio. The people in his paintings lit up. I

38

remember reading somewhere that Caravaggio painted in a darkroom and treated his canvas with a luminescent powder made from crushed fireflies.

The experience seeing Caravaggio's paintings in person and connections I made to my children, who are my biggest inspiration, became my poem "The Road."

Gyasi: Could you tell us about how you founded Shabda Press?

Mei Chuc: In the summer of 2011, I was sitting in my room and decided that I wanted to create something and support what I love—books and poetry. So, I decided to create a press to make poetry books and bring poetry into the world. I wanted to experience what it was like to go through the entire process from writing to publishing to distribution/sharing. I didn't really know how to go about doing this and began by learning along the way. The road was unpaved and dark before me, but I took my first step. Now, I am happy to have brought some wonderful poetry books into this world.

The first books that I used to make when I started to put my poems and writings together were made by hand; I would make photocopies of each page, cut, paste, and staple the pages together. I loved giving away the hand-made books to friends. I truly love the "do it yourself" process and making things.

Gyasi: I am wondering how it feels to translate your own poems into other languages.

Mei Chuc: I actually haven't translated my own poems into other languages, but I am very fortunate to have several of my poems translated into Vietnamese by some brilliant Vietnamese poets, Le Dinh Nhat Lang and Ngo Tu Lap.

Gyasi: Having studied the Russian language for about two decades, could you tell us anything about Russian literature and poetry?

Mei Chuc: Some of my favorite Russian writers are Fyodor Dostoevsky, Leo Tolstoy, Nikolai Gogol, Mikhail Bulgakov, and some of my favorite Russian poets are Marina Tsvetaeva, Anna Akhmatova, Nikolai Gumilyov, and Vladimir Mayakovsky. I really think that Russian literature and poetry speak for themselves in their brilliance of expression of humanity, society, and imagination. If you can read the literature and poetry in Russian, that is even better because the Russian language is so descriptive and versatile and musical.

Gyasi: Tell us about your first full-length poetry collection, *Red Thread*.

Mei Chuc: It took me about a decade to write *Red Thread*. Many of the poems are about my experience and my family's experiences in the Vietnam War and after the war. I also wrote about other aspects of the war such as Agent Orange, napalm, and the My Lai Massacre. Writing the book was important to me as I was documenting my experience as well as my family's experiences. Writing the book helped me to process the war in the most intimate and compassionate way possible.

Gyasi: Is *Keeper of the Winds* actually your second book? Do you mind sharing anything about the book?

Mei Chuc: *Keeper of the Winds* is my second full-length collection of poetry. The book came much sooner than I had expected. Since I write at odd times, I didn't even realize that I had enough new poems to make a second full-length collection.

I just started putting all the poems together and then realized that I really had been writing. This made me realize that if you write here and there and now and then, pretty soon all those poems add up. Some of the poems were earlier poems that I love but weren't included in the first collection. In *Keeper of the Winds*, I explore other aspects of the consequences of the U.S. war in Vietnam, such as the effects on the environment. In my poem "the decade the rainforest died," I explore the effects of Agent Orange used during the war on the rainforests in Vietnam. I have two poems in the book, "Jumping Jack: The M16 Mines" and "The Gambler," about the continuing effects of unexploded ordnance or landmines used during the war. "Con Son" is a poem about Tiger Cages used by the U.S. during the Vietnam War. My poem "Violin" is about my childhood experience with my father's Post Traumatic Stress Disorder. I also wrote about current wars in the book. My poem "Depleted Uranium" is about the consequences of the U.S.'s war in Afghanistan. "Pencil" is a poem about the use of drones in the middle east. "ocean in a conch shell" is a short poem about the use of F16s in the middle east. In the book, there are also poems about my name, about healing, about breathing, about being and not-being, about birds, about the nuclear plants in Fukushima ...

Gyasi: Do you care about critics of your books?

Mei Chuc: I try not to think about what critics say unless it's constructive and I can learn from the criticism. I think worrying too much about what critics say about one's work can be distracting from the real work of writing. I try to stick to what Rainer Maria Rilke taught me, to trust myself. Rilke wrote, "Everything is gestation and then birthing. To let each impression and each embryo of a feeling come to completion, entirely in itself, in the dark, in the unsayable, the unconscious, beyond the reach of one's own understanding, and with deep humility and patience to wait for the hour when a new clarity is born: this alone is what it means to live as an artist: in understanding as in creating...."

Gyasi: Where and when do you often write?

Mei Chuc: I work full time as a public school teacher and am also raising my kids, so I don't have much time. Many poems I write in the middle of things, in waiting rooms, waiting in line, stopping while in the middle of washing dishes and jotting down notes, late at night when everyone is asleep, or early in the morning when everyone is still asleep. Since there isn't a lot of free time, I write whenever I can. Many times, I record my poems using voice memo on my phone while driving to work and then type them later. Whenever I have some free time on the weekend or during spring break and summer break, I try to write as much as I can. Sometimes, on the weekends, I go out into the garden and sit on some bricks in the silence beneath the guava and orange trees and write.

Gyasi: Do you mind ending the interview in Russian?

Mei Chuc: Sure, here is a short poem by Marina Tsvetaeva that I translated. The translation was first published in an amazing journal, *Aldus Journal of Translation*, in Spring 2013, Issue 4. http://www.theartmovement.info/aldus/ My translation:

All the magnificence of
Trumpets—is the murmur of
Grass—before you.

All the magnificence of
Storms—is the chatter of
Birds—before you.

All the magnificence of
Wings—is the flutter of
Eyelids—before you.

by Marina Tsvetaeva
(translated from the Russian by Teresa Mei Chuc)

Original:

Все великолепье
Труб—лишь только лепет
Трав—перед Тобой.

Все великолепье
Бурь—лишь только щебет
Птиц—перед Тобой.

Все великолепье
Крыл—лишь только трепет
Век—перед Тобой.

—Мари́на Цвета́ева

Большое спасибо, Geosi Gyasi!

Vasiliki Katsarou was born and raised in Massachusetts, to Greek-born parents, and educated at Harvard College, the University of Paris I-Sorbonne, and Boston University. She's a Pushcart Prize-nominated poet whose first collection, *Memento Tsunami*, was published in 2011. Her poems have appeared in *Agave Magazine, Poetry Daily, Regime Journal* (Australia), *wicked alice, Wild River Review*, as well as in the anthologies *Rabbit Ears: TV Poems* (NYQ Books) and *Not Somewhere Else But Here: A Contemporary Anthology of Women and Place*. She has also worked in film and television production and directed an award-winning 35mm short film, *Fruitlands 1843*. In 2014,

Katsarou was one of seventy national and international poets to read work at the Dodge Poetry Festival, the largest poetry festival in the United States.

Her website is http://www.onegoldbead.com/

Gyasi: First, can we talk about your parents? You were born and raised in Massachusetts to Greek-born parents. Can you say something about your parents?

Katsarou: My parents both grew up in the same small town halfway between Athens and Thessaloniki, Greece. My father emigrated to the U.S. during the Greek Civil War in the late 1940s. He educated himself while working in shoe factories in Lowell, Massachusetts, where there was a large Greek immigrant population. When he turned 40 and was still unmarried, his father back in Greece created the circumstances for my father to meet and to marry my mother, who was 10 years younger than he and whose family lived across the street. It was an arranged marriage. My maternal grandfather had been a hunter and fisherman and subsistence farmer, as was common at that time in the small villages of Greece. My mother, who'd been a gifted young student, couldn't go to high school because there was no high school in the town—no father then was willing to send his daughter away to school. So my mother became a talented seamstress, running a small business from home with apprentices. She was so successful that she was the only one in her family to earn a cash income at that time. Her life changed radically when she married my father and came with him to a small town in western Massachusetts. That's where I was born. I don't think about it too often, but I'm actually the first woman on both sides of my Greek family to go to college.

Gyasi: You've worked in film and television production in France and Greece. When was this and how did you get involved with film and television?

Katsarou: I studied literature in college but also took a few film classes and became enamored with film as an art form. After college graduation and a job working at a museum in Boston, I picked up and moved to Paris, France. I found work at a documentary film company and also at a small production company where I was an assistant to the producer. I also pursued my (self) education in film by taking advantage of all that Paris has to offer in its independent, second-run, and repertory cinemas. I saw all the films of Bergman, Antonioni, Bresson, Tarkovsky, Mizoguchi. I was so moved and inspired that it made me want to try my hand at filmmaking.

Gyasi: You've also written and directed an award-winning 35mm short film, *Fruitlands 1843.* Could you tell us something about this film?

Katsarou: *Fruitlands 1843* is my MFA thesis film, made at Boston University while I was a graduate student there, after returning from France. I was living then in the beautiful hamlet of Still River, Massachusetts, where I became familiar with the true story of the short-lived utopian community that existed there in 1843, founded by Louisa May Alcott's father, Bronson Alcott. Bronson Alcott was a philosopher and pioneer in education reform, who was on the fringes of the

Concord circle of Emerson and Thoreau. My film is an imaginative retelling of the story of the commune. The film won several awards at film festivals in Boston and New York. I'm proud of it and when I look back now, I feel as if it's a poet's film—not narrative-driven but rather imbued with the atmosphere and associations I felt while immersed in the story and the landscape.

Gyasi: How did you start writing?

Katsarou: Well, I know I wrote little stories as a child and was encouraged by my English teachers. I wrote juvenile poems that were published in my high school newspaper, but it was only in my 20s that I started to get a sense of myself as a sort of metaphysical observer, if I can describe it as that.

Gyasi: Do you remember your first piece of literary work?

Katsarou: Depends on what you mean by literary! One of the first poems in my collection, *Memento Tsunami*, is an early poem of mine called "A Madame Malenfant" and describes the French Canadian lady who rented out a room to my father before he was married. As a child, my father used to take us to her house, which was in the country with lots of land and blueberries and wildflowers, and handmade doilies and dollhouses. It was a magical place for me and it got me to thinking about how I spent more time with this French-speaking woman than with my actual Grandma who lived in Greece and whom I saw very infrequently as a child.

Gyasi: Do you remember what inspired your poem "America"?

Katsarou: That poem is a somewhat surreal depiction of estrangement—the feeling of being torn between two families and two cultures, between an inside and an outside. I wrote it around the same time I was making my film *Fruitlands 1843*, and the dissonance between the ideals of the Transcendentalists and the realities of contemporary life fed the poem.

Gyasi: What sort of preparation goes into the writing of a single poem?

Katsarou: I take notes. Often it's a phrase that comes to me, or simply an incongruous sense of time passing that is very hard to put into words. I write and rewrite. I put the poem aside, and wait for something to remind me of it. Then I take it out again. Often the poem will sit for years as I search for a way to condense, to crochet, to strengthen the pattern and the purpose of the poem. Most of my longer poems go through seven substantial revisions, I've noticed.

Gyasi: What about "Portmanteau"? Do you often write short poems?

Katsarou: I don't set out to write short poems, but I do seem to have accumulated a series of haiku-length poems that have come to me as I write other, longer, poems.

Gyasi: Could you tell us about your college days at Harvard? What do you remember most when you were a student?

Katsarou: I remember the feeling of being at large in the city and reveling in all the art events, readings, film screenings, exhibitions that were available in Cambridge. It was a feeling of openness and independence from constraints. I also remember the day I discovered the poetry of Holderlin in a European Romanticism class. And the film theory classes I took with Vlada Petric at Harvard's Carpenter Center. I had work-study jobs all through college, and my favorite was working for the Office for the Arts with a supportive all-woman staff writing for the arts newsletter and promoting artists. I was always very, very busy at Harvard.

Gyasi: Your first collection, *Memento Tsunami*, was published in 2011. Could you tell us what inspired the book?

Katsarou: Well, I didn't set out to write that particular book. I accumulated a group of poems over close to twenty years. When I considered them—with the help of poet friends like Ellen Foos of Ragged Sky Press—and the US 1 Poets' Cooperative of Princeton where I first started to workshop my poems—I started to see the strands that tied certain poems together. The title poem refers to the tragic Indonesian tsunami of 2004, but also to the onslaught of materiality that permeates life. Some things (and some thoughts) become talismans and others become weights that tie us down.

Gyasi: How long did it take you to write *Memento Tsunami*?

Katsarou: At least a decade. As I mentioned, a handful of those poems date back to my early writing in France, twenty years before. From the moment I realized I had enough poems to make a book, it was probably four or five years. My new manuscript has come together much more quickly.

Gyasi: Do you enjoy reading your poems?

Katsarou: More and more. I've a bit of a split personality in that I'm naturally introverted but I've made a big effort to read my work in front of audiences over these many years, and it gets easier with practice. When I feel my work has resonated with others, I feel very gratified and grateful. Since I've been organizing many poetry readings over these last years, I've come to appreciate the importance of poets reading their work in public in a warm and thoughtful setting. Among other things, poetry is a gift of one's own breath.

Gyasi: You direct the Panoply Books Reading Series in Lambertville, NJ. Could you tell us how the reading series started?

Katsarou: The owner of the shop, Roland Boehm, was a friend of a friend. At the time of the very first reading, I was working with Ragged Sky Press of Princeton, and looking for a venue to launch a book by a poet I'd edited from San Francisco. When that reading went well, I decided to organize another, and Rollie was generous enough to agree. That was five years and some 40 poets ago.

Gyasi: Which writers have had the greatest impact on your writing?

Katsarou: I wrote my Harvard thesis on Maurice Blanchot, and his philosophical, self-reflexive writings seeped into my consciousness. I've also been influenced by prose stylists like Henry James and Proust, whose masterwork I read in French in its entirety twice, while I lived in France. I mentioned Holderlin already, and of course, the poetry in Greek of George Seferis and of Cavafy. Many Russian and German poets in translation were formative—poets like Rilke, Akhmatova, Tsvetayeva, Mandelstam, Celan, Milosz—so many great poets whose work has suffused my idea of what poetry is. I love the work in French of the Franco-Swiss poet Philippe Jaccottet. In English, I've been very influenced by the modernism of Eliot and Pound, Wallace Stevens, the poems of Gustaf Sobin, an expatriate American poet living in Provence whom I corresponded with and met on several occasions. William Bronk, early Anne Carson, Michael Longley ... I have eclectic tastes and many diverse influences.

Gyasi: Do you earn a living from writing?

Katsarou: Not yet. I would love to be able to combine my poetry advocacy, editing, and writing work into some sort of position that earns a salary and continues to benefit the larger artistic community here in New Jersey, but I have not yet worked this out.

Gyasi: Do you have a favorite among all the poems you've written?

Katsarou: Not really. That would be like choosing a favorite child—a cliche, but true nonetheless. But one of my favorite poems to read at readings is "Greek Family Myth" since the family dynamic I describe seems to resonate with many people, while being very specific at the same time.

Gyasi: Could you tell us about the time when you lived in France? Did you learn how to speak French?

Katsarou: Well, I lived in Paris from 1989 though 1994. I already spoke French when I arrived, having studied it since middle school and done a "Junior Year Abroad" program in Paris while at Harvard. However, I did learn other kinds of French—business French, colloquial *argot*, etc. I was very proud the day a police officer referred to me as a "Parisienne."

Gyasi: How do you compare French literature to American literature?

Katsarou: That's a big question. I feel that the conceptual, the surreal, the philosophical, the poetic, are all more accepted and mainstream in French literary culture.

Gyasi: You've said somewhere online that you're a literary poet. Could you break that down to our understanding?

Katsarou: I believe what I said is that I was a literary filmmaker and that I'm a visual poet. When it comes to filmmaking, I've been drawn to stories of poets and artists, to uncompromising characters, and to the invisible within the visible. And my poetry is often prompted by visual art, by landscapes, and atmospheres where physical details lend themselves to a series of associations. I'm fond of poet Mina Loy's statement: "Poetry is a music made of visual thoughts, the sound of an idea." I tend to go fine-grain in my observations, both in film and in poetry, and I imagine if I ever returned to filmmaking, it would be to the painterly and rather abstract filmmaking style that I admire.

Gyasi: What are your plans for the future?

Katsarou: I have a new full-length collection of poems that I'd like to see published. I hope to combine film and photography with poetry in some sort of project in the future. I also look forward to collaborations with other poets and artists.

Gyasi: Do you mind asking me just one question?

Katsarou: Geosi, who is your favorite poet of the past? Have you traveled to Europe and to America? Which is the most favorite place you've visited?

Gyasi: Pablo Neruda proves to be one of my all-time favorite poets of the past. My first travel out of Ghana was South Africa. While in South Africa, I traveled to almost every province while I worked on various odd jobs. My favorite place is Durban, where I spent most of my time writing at the beaches and parks and gardens.

Returning from his first day of kindergarten, **Marco Katz** broke down in tears because he had not yet learned to read. After remedying this situation, he became a voracious reader of novels, a habit he supported for decades by playing the trombone and composing music. Eventually, he followed daughter Nathalia Holt, author of *Cured* (Dutton, 2014), into academia, where he studied with Barbara Brinson Curiel, author of *Mexican Jenny and Other Poems* (Anhinga, 2014). Katz's essays and short stories in English and Spanish include "Correo Electrónico entre Eduardo Oso y Sancho Panza," which came out last year in *White Rabbit*. His book, *Noteworthy Protagonists* (Palgrave, 2014), brings together music, literature, and life in the Americas.

Gyasi: You tell me, how do you combine work as a writer and musician? Are the two jobs not demanding?

Katz: Combined, they are almost impossible! I played music professionally for decades and never even taught students during that time. It took all of my time and effort to play the trombone and later to copy, arrange, compose, and produce music. When I decided to study literature, I meant to give up music. A friend, guitarist Dan Andersen, convinced me to perform some gigs with him while I was going to school, and I have been endeavoring a balance ever since. For my undergraduate senior paper, I decided to write about the ways people write about music, coming up from behind the critics so to speak. I focused on new books about salsa, and found that each mentioned at least one of the bands I had played in professionally. This paper, "Salsa Criticism at the Turn of the Century," became my first academic publication. When I finally graduated with my BA in English, Dan and I celebrated by recording "In New Orleans," now available as an EP download.

Gyasi: But before I delve into your music proper, do you consider writing as a real job?

Katz: Yes, there are many writers who work at this and some manage to make a good living at it.

Gyasi: You were born in New York City in 1957, the same year my country, Ghana, gained independence from the British. Can you tell us about growing up as a child?

Katz: I do not remember my birth, but I have retained good memories of playing in Washington Square Park as a child. My parents, Kip and Ginny Gaylor, worked in theater, and Greenwich Village was a welcoming and affordable place for thespians in those days. At the age of six, I saw Robert Preston in *The Music Man* on Broadway and decided I that had to play one of those "Seventy-Six Trombones." Since the age of fourteen, I knew that I would have no other career.

Gyasi: Do you come from a family of musicians or writers?

Katz: Everyone in my father's family plays and sings music. Most sound better than I do, but few became professionals. My cousin Naomi is an exception. She sings so brilliantly that, even though we don't always get along, I had to have her record my difficult song cycle *Las piedras del cielo*. My parents both write stories, and my father has several fiction and non-fiction publications.

Gyasi: Do you agree with the reviewer Adam Gaines who said in a review of the *Bundee Brothers Bone Band* album that, "Katz's compositions are a real highlight of the disc ..."?

Katz: That's a wonderful line! I also liked, "His trombone writing is expertly idiomatic, and his music is harmonically interesting without being obtuse." Interesting music can make sense. His review made me very happy. Meanwhile, I try to remember the old Ann Landers line, "Compliments are like perfume; they should be inhaled but not swallowed."

Gyasi: At what age did you start playing the trombone?

Katz: Ten. My parents forced me to take piano lessons for a year, and finally gave up and let me go with the trombone. Like most elementary schools, mine had a process of weeding out untalented young people so I was not given an instrument. (Can you imagine if we stopped teaching reading and writing to kids who didn't pass aptitude tests with books?) My maternal grandfather managed to come up with a twenty-five dollar silver slide trombone and so the school music teacher was obliged, clearly against his will, to give me lessons. After the first half hour, when I couldn't even get a sound that any four-year-old can achieve in one minute, he seemed ready to strangle me. Things got better after that.

Gyasi: Could you tell us what a trombone looks like?

Katz: Trombones are simple instruments, basically a tube that goes back and forth on a slide with a mouthpiece at one end to create sound and a flared bell at the other to amplify it. Some instruments, saxophones and guitars, for example, can cost thousands of dollars; a decent trombone, in contrast, might run for as little as fifty. And because a player just needs to vibrate his or her lips and push a slide back and forth, this makes it an excellent choice for beginning musicians. I wish more people would take this up.

Gyasi: I am not sure if it is accurate to label you as a jazz and salsa trombonist.

Katz: Over the course of my life, I have acquired many labels. The ones you mention here are among my favorites. No title makes me happier than musician, and I enjoyed years of playing jazz and salsa.

Gyasi: In 1978, you were nominated "Trombonist of the Year" by *Latin NY* magazine for your recording work with the Alegre All-Stars director, Charlie Palmieri. Why do you think you were nominated?

Katz: Izzy Sanabria did a lot of great work for salsa musicians. His magazine, *Latin New York*, provided a place for us to get recognition and build our audience. The magazine also featured some of the greatest music photographs ever seen, taken by an Italian ex-priest named Dominique. (I wish I knew where to find him now.) Sanabria and his team based nominations for musicians on recordings released during the previous year. I had a featured solo, employing a plunger mute, on

"Tiene saber," a theme recorded by Palmieri on an album called *The Heavyweight*.

Gyasi: Could you educate us on the plunger mute?

Katz: Brass instrumentalists can purchase plunger mutes from music stores or suppliers of musical accessories. Or they can do what the big band brass players did when they came up with those wah-wah sounds: buy a toilet plunger and take off the stick. Years ago, hardware stores would take a nickel off the price if you didn't need the stick. I noticed, though, that they would never shake my hand afterwards.

Gyasi: Are you happy as a musician?

Katz: As a musician, yes, but as a working unit of the music business, no. North Americans despise musicians. Now lots of people tell me how much they love the arts, but few do anything substantial to demonstrate that affection. For the price of a couple of cups of fancy coffee, one can download most recordings, but people complain that they shouldn't have to make these so-called sacrifices. In my book, I suggest that patrons try going to the door of their favorite jazz venue and asking for a chance to play. In most cases, they will see an ugly change of facial expression and thus get a good idea of the disdain that we deal with regularly. Add to this that live music venues, like many music publishers, have given up on promoting music; in many cases we're expected to bring an audience, and if we fail, we're required to pay the owner for his or her losses. Major record company executives actually present panels at places like ASCAP to explain how we need to treat them properly in order to get a hearing for our music. And then they prove incapable of selling disks or downloads or in any way understanding their own business.

Gyasi: What took you to Spain between the years 2001 and 2002?

Katz: My wife, M. Elizabeth Boone, took many extended research trips in Spain while working on her first book for Yale University Press, *American Views of Art and Life in Spain, 1860–1914*, and I have been glad to tag along. During our first trips, I managed to pick up some gigs playing the trombone, and made quite a few friends along the way. From 2001-2002, she had a sabbatical and wrote a book in Spanish with a colleague in Toledo. At that time, I was able to get into the Universidad Complutense de Madrid, where I studied with Estefanía Villalba, Cándido Pérez Gállego, Isabel Colón, Álvaro Alonso, and other fine *filólogos*.

Gyasi: Could you give us some background to your book, *Music and Identity in Twentieth Century Literature from Our America: Noteworthy Protagonists*?

Katz: Friends who have known me for a long time tell me that they have been hearing these ideas for decades. It culminates important life work for me. The book focuses on connections between music and literature in American novels, providing new ways of reading and considering protagonists who play music but have not been recognized as musicians by literary critics. Understanding Florentino and Juvenal, the antagonists of *El amor en los tiempos de cólera*, as musicians makes it possible for readers to gain new understandings of that much discussed novel and to think about Gabriel García Márquez' works in new ways. Similarly, Zora Neale Hurston's often reviled final novel, *Seraph on the Suwanee*, becomes a different book when one pays attention, as so few critics have, to the musical abilities that Arvay passes on to her son Kenny. The American setting of these works also gains importance in my text as a means of comprehending García Márquez, Hurston, and the other authors under discussion. As I point out in the book, America is a continent—or a hemisphere, if you prefer—rather than a country. The Spanish language has a word for something or someone from the United States, *estadounidense*, and I have long been fascinated by the hegemony implicit in this adjective's omission from the French and English languages.

> Gyasi: What do you make of the reviewer in the *International Trumpet Guild Journal* who finds fault with your brass quintet arrangements of music by Juan Morel Campos?

Katz: Apparently, his ensemble had difficulty playing some of the works in the collection. I have heard from other brass quintet leaders who like them all, but I realize that some of my pieces require excellent players, and I encourage my publishers to rate their difficulty in promotional materials. This reviewer's biggest complaint was that I referred to the importance of the nineteenth-century composer Juan Morel Campos, even though his name did not appear in the *Grove Dictionary of Music*. In fact, no Puerto Rican composers formerly appeared in that August volume, an omission that Grove has since rectified, including a substantial section devoted to Morel Campos. I suppose that we may now consider him important.

> Gyasi: Do you have a godfather you look up to as a musician?

Katz: Multiple godfathers—and godmothers too! One of my publications, *Renaissance Music for Four Trombones* (International Music Co.), includes works by some of the many fine Baroque composers long ignored because they were identified as female: Maddalena Casulana, Vittoria Aleaotti, and Isabella Leonarda. As a young musician, I benefited from the advice of seasoned players and, if I had been intelligent, would have taken them all even more seriously than I did. These included salseros Charlie Palmieri and Mon Rivera, the Broadway show composers Stephen Schwartz and Stephen Sondheim, and Eph Resnick, the trombonists' trombonist. Another musician, although he does not refer to himself as one, that I admire is Timothy Brennan, who not only plays Dmitri Shostakovich on the piano but also explains many facets of music with extraordinary articulation in books and journal articles. All of these people have taken an interest in my work and have helped me greatly. Contemporary composers who stand out for me include Roberto Sierra, Tania León, and Maria Schneider.

> Gyasi: You earned your BA and MA at Humboldt State University. What was it about University of Alberta that made you to pursue a PhD there?

Katz: They offered my wife a very good position. That brought us to Edmonton.

> Gyasi: You recently had a CD come out where you adapted the work of Pablo Neruda into music for voice and piano. Have you read enough of Pablo? What is it about Pablo that made you adapt his work into music?

Katz: Can one ever read enough of Pablo Neruda? Or any author one cares about? He is not, however, my favorite poet. But when I decided to compose a song cycle in the form of German Romanticism—although not in the style of that era—Neruda's lines appeared to most propitiously lend themselves to musicalization. His praises of nature fit into a Romantic conception, and the poetry seemed ready to sing.

Gyasi: Could you name other writers you've worked on their works? I know Gabriel García Márquez is a typical example.

Katz: As a writer of essays and short stories, I have a great interest in others who work with both fiction and non-fiction (even though it usually all seems unreal to me). This semester, I have my students working on an essay and a poem by Lucas Cassidy Crawford, one titled "Transgender without Organs? Mobilizing a Geo-Affective Theory of Gender Modification" and the other "Your Fat Daughter Remembers What You Said." For my doctoral dissertation, I focused on Alejo Carpentier and Zora Neale Hurston. Previously, I had worked on Japanese American writers in Canada, Peru, and the United States for my Masters project. These included John Okada, Joy Kogawa, José Watanabe, and Alejandro Sakuda, all authors I admire. I have published on Watanabe in *Kaikan*, a magazine of the Japanese Peruvian community published in Lima. While in Lima, I had the great pleasure of spending an hour talking with Sakuda, a journalist and author whose work merits far more recognition than it currently receives outside of his country. In my book, I include discussion of the Canadian writer Tomson Highway, the Mexican Mariano Azuela, and the Argentinean Mempo Giardinelli, thus covering the length of our American continent. Recently, I have begun devouring films, stories, essays, and novels by Marcelo Birmajer, Teresa Porzecanski, Sonia Guralnik, and other Jewish authors writing in Spanish from Argentina, Chile, Uruguay, Cuba, Mexico, and the United States. This is beginning to look like a project.

Gyasi: How do you want to be remembered?

Katz: With my name spelled correctly, if possible.

Gyasi: I seem to have asked too many questions. Do you mind asking me just one question?

Katz: Your questions do not seem excessive, but perhaps that has to do with my own self-centered interest in the topic at hand. I hope my answers have not gone on too long. As a writer of essays and poetry, in what ways do you find that interviewing colleagues influences your work? When I read a musical line like "the barking tune of a dog" in "For the Sake of a Dog" and other powerful lines in poems such as "Fighting Spirits," "Supernatural Men," and "Don't Allow Your Mind to Wrestle with the World," I sense that your life experiences, extensive readings, and interactions with other authors all go into your ability to make profound and moving statements with written words. I would like to know more about how you synthesize these elements of your life.

Gyasi: I find your question interesting in as much as you seem to have done a great deal of research on me and my work. Thank you for your kind compliments about my poems. Most of the poems I've written have come from my regular observations of life and the world around me. I often like to think that the best way to take off as a writer is to start from within—writing about your personal life experiences and the things that matter to you most. One of the things I learned from my grandmother when I was growing up was to listen more than to talk. This may have partly influenced my becoming a writer as I channel most of the things I hear and see into writing.

Jessica Goodfellow's books are *Mendeleev's Mandala* (Mayapple Press, 2015) and *The Insomniac's Weather Report* (Isobar Press, 2014), winner of the Three Candles Press First Book Prize in 2011. Her chapbook, *A Pilgrim's Guide to Chaos in the Heartland,* won the Concrete Wolf Chapbook Competition in 2006. Her work has appeared in *Best New Poets, Verse Daily*, and NPR's *The Writer's Almanac.* Goodfellow has received the Chad Walsh Poetry Prize from the *Beloit Poetry Journal,* as well as the Linda Julian Essay Award and the Sue Lile Inman Fiction Prize, both from the Emrys Foundation. Goodfellow has graduate degrees from the University of New England and Caltech. She lives and works in Japan.

Gyasi: You grew up in the suburbs of Philadelphia, Pennsylvania. Could you tell us anything about the place?

Goodfellow: I grew up in the outskirts of Philadelphia, where there is much greenery. Autumns there are stunning. When we first moved there, I was six, and I remember my father driving the car at the same time as taking home movies of all the foliage—that's how impressed he was. This was before cell phone cameras; he had his hands full with a big movie camera and the steering wheel too. When I was in college, a friend visited from Nevada, and she innocently asked me, "Who planted the trees all the way up to the road?"

Gyasi: You currently live in Japan with your husband and sons. My question is, what took you to Japan?

Goodfellow: I left graduate school in the middle of getting a degree, without any plan. Since I had taken a leave of absence, my professors were urging me to get back to school, as were my parents, but I knew I didn't want to do that. I was looking for a job in the classifieds of the newspaper, and found an ad to work in Japan, which seemed about the right distance to be away from people who wanted me to do and be something I didn't want to do and be. I answered the ad, and three weeks later I was in Japan. Within about ten days of arriving, I met the man who eventually became my husband, so almost immediately my life became entangled with this country.

Gyasi: What is the literary scene like in Japan?

Goodfellow: The English-speaking literary scene is largely centered in Tokyo, but I don't live anywhere near there, so my exposure to other writers and readers can be scant. However, in the Kansai area where I live there have been some reading series, including Tracy Slater's Four Stories, and Jared Angel's new Authors Live!

There's also the Japan Writers Conference, which has been running annually for six to eight years or so, and I make a point to get there at least every other year. Occasionally I take the bullet train to Tokyo for an event. Also, my book was recently reissued by Isobar Press, a Japan-based publisher, and that opportunity has introduced me to other poets writing in and about Japan. But I am alone as a writer quite a bit.

Gyasi: When did you actually become a writer?

Goodfellow: Before I could actually write, I followed my mom around and demanded she write things down for me. I would tell her I had a poem, and would she please write it down. In the beginning, I rewrote nursery rhymes, inserting my own ideas. This sounds now far too precious to be true, but it is.

Gyasi: Do you care so much about the place you write?

Goodfellow: I wish I had the luxury of caring about the place I write. I'd dearly love to have a room of my own, even a space of my own, but I live in Japan where homes are very small, so I can't afford to be so choosy. But I have a dream of one day having my own writing space.

Gyasi: Your first book of poetry, *The Insomniac's Weather Report*, won the Three Candles Press First Book Prize. Do you mind telling us something about the book?

Goodfellow: This book has four sections. The first section uses water in its various forms as metaphor for stages of life including young adulthood and early motherhood. The second eponymous section features an insomniac describing the changing weather throughout a year, with the reasons for his insomnia hinted at in his ruminations. The final section is a fugue about marriage, with each poem title linked to the previous and subsequent poem titles in a pattern that can be seen in the first three titles: "Fugue: motion:" "motion: moon:" " moon: map:". The book was reissued this year by Isobar Press, since Three Candles has gone out of business.

Gyasi: What inspired your chapbook, *A Pilgrim's Guide to Chaos in the Heartland?*

Goodfellow: I have a background in statistics and quantitative analysis, and a love for science, so the poems in this chapbook use mathematical and scientific imagery to explore the big questions: belief, randomness, meaning, privilege, impermanence—those sorts of things. When I wrote this book, I was undergoing a radical shift in my worldview, so I took on those topics, which now seem too intimidating to touch. I'm glad I did it when I was younger; I wouldn't dare do it now.

Gyasi: Do you do poetry readings?

Goodfellow: I do, every chance I get. Unfortunately, that's not all that often because of where I live. However, last year I traveled to the Los Angeles area for personal reasons, and was lucky to be invited to read while there. There are opportunities here in Japan a couple of times a year too. 2014 has been my most productive year of readings yet, and I hope it just keeps improving.

Gyasi: Which writers inspire you?

Goodfellow: Anne Carson has been a huge liberating influence because of the way she mixes genres (before everybody was doing it, she did it), and how she juxtaposes different registers and voices. Plus her playfulness when taking on academic topics is delightful. Cole Swensen is another writer whose thoroughness and dedication to exploring a given topic from every angle possible amazes and inspires me. She can write 50 poems on the same topic and it never gets old or trite or repetitive.

Gyasi: Are you an avid reader? Which books are your favorites?

Goodfellow: I am; I read ten or more books a month, which makes naming favorites difficult, but I'll try. The essays of Walker Percy, Annie Dillard, and Lewis Thomas are classics. For fiction, I recommend Jeanette Winterson, Lydia Davis, and David Markson. For poetry, a few favorites are Cole Swensen's *The Book of a Hundred Hands*, Chad Sweeney's *The Parable of Hide and Seek*, Joshua Poteat's *Illustrating the Machine that Makes the World*, and Stefi Weisburd's *The Wind-Up Gods*. Oh, and a new favorite is Sarah Vap's *End of the Sentimental Journey*. And Inger Christensen, anything by her. And now I really have to stop.

Gyasi: Do you ever regret becoming a writer?

Goodfellow: No, do you? I have to be more than a writer to survive financially, and being a writer means that I don't put all my concentration into a career because I have to save time and energy and focus for writing. But I don't regret it. In fact, the years when I did a lot of analytical work professionally and found myself unable to switch from that mode to the more contemplative writing mode, so that consequently I didn't write—those are the years I regret.

Gyasi: Does writing pay the bills?

Goodfellow: No. I teach to do that, and even so, my husband contributes more to the household bill-paying than I do.

Gyasi: How difficult is it to combine motherhood and writing?

Goodfellow: It was very difficult when the children were little, but even then, my husband was quite supportive, so I was able to meet with other writers (we were living in the US then) twice a week. That was a productive time, due to that exposure to other serious writers and their craft. But it was a hard time because of lack of sleep. Even now, I sometimes sequester myself away to write, and I feel torn about it because, though my kids are teenagers (or nearly so) and don't need my constant attention, I know they'll be out of the house one day, and I may regret not spending as much time with them as possible.

I should also mention how good being a mother has been for my work. My kids and my feelings about my kids and my experiences mothering have given me lots of fodder for writing.

Gyasi: At what specific moment did you write the poem "Not Seeing"?

Goodfellow: For the past year I've been working on a series of poems about the loss of my 22-year-old uncle in a mountain-climbing accident on Mt. McKinley. In the midst of this, I happened to hear about poets attending a poetry reading and playing a drinking game in which they took a drink any time the word 'body' came up in a poem. Since my uncle's body was never recovered, I was writing a lot of poems about that fact and what it has meant in my family, so I thought to myself that people playing that drinking game while reading my manuscript would be drunk pretty quickly. And the poem followed from that thought.

Gyasi: What inspired your poem "November Nocturne"?

Goodfellow: I had in mind a specific image about a mother whose child(ren) had inexplicably disappeared in the original version of the poem, and I sent it off to Neil Aitken at the *Boxcar Poetry Review*. He rejected it initially, and told me he thought the poem started after the first four lines, and that I should lop them off. He was right; the momentum began after the poem escaped the initial impulse to write it, so off came the lines containing the genesis (though the lost children are suggested later in the poem). However, I was at that point wedded to the idea of the sonnet-inspired piece, so I added four more lines later in the poem to keep the length to fourteen lines. I sent it back to Neil Aitken, and this time he accepted it.

Gyasi: Could you tell us how "The Beach at Big Salt" came about?

Goodfellow: This poem took longer to write than any other, to date. It took more than seven years. It started with the idea of matter wrapped around space, an idea from astrophysics. And I wanted to write about the ancient geometric problem of squaring the circle. But I got stuck after that and didn't know what to do next, so the poem sat idle for years. I'd go back to it and add ideas, but there's virtually no speaker in that poem, so for a long time it came across as a flat reportage of scientific ideas that interested me, and I didn't know how to salvage it.

Then one day I was at the beach with my family, swimming, and I found a fragment of seaweed in the water that looked like a seahorse and I scooped it up and showed my son. And we suddenly saw that it *was* a seahorse, a very tiny seahorse, and it was alive. I'd never seen a wild seahorse before, and I was astounded. I magically had the ending of the poem—ideas from biology of space curling around emptiness, moving from the macrocosm to the microcosm. And the living beings now mentioned, the babies and the seahorse, solved the problem of the detached or absent voice by giving the poem some reference to life, to movement.

Gyasi: What is the most important feedback you've ever received from a reader of your book?

Goodfellow: After my chapbook came out, I received a lot of interest from people of certain religious traditions about some of my poems. This really surprised me; I thought they were reading my poems differently than I had intended them. But that's fine. From this experience I learned that readers may find things in poems that the writer didn't put there, or didn't put there intentionally. Each reader's experience of a poem combines her own life experience with the words on the page, and it's valid for her. That was useful to learn, that detachment from the finished poem.

Poems by **Bern Mulvey** have appeared, among other places, in *Poetry*, *Agni*, *FIELD*, *Beloit Poetry Journal*, *The Missouri Review*, *Michigan Quarterly Review*, *Cimarron Review*, *The Laurel Review*, *Passages North*, and *Poetry East*.

His first book, *The Fat Sheep Everyone Wants*, won the 2007 Cleveland State University Poetry Center First Book Prize, and his second book, *Deep Snow Country*, won the 2013 FIELD Poetry Prize. He also has published two chapbooks: *The Window Tribe* (White Eagle Coffee Store Press, 2005) and *Character Readings* (Copperdome/Southeast Missouri State University Press, 2012). He lives in Iwate, Japan.

Gyasi: This certainly will sound odd as the first question, but why are you a writer?

Mulvey: I guess I'm a writer because I can't imagine being anything else. And yes, I'm also very lucky in that I can make a living doing what I love to do. However, to be honest, I'd be writing regardless.

Gyasi: How long have you been writing?

Mulvey: I started writing when I was about ten. We had just moved from Brooklyn to Los Angeles, and with my thick Bensonhurst brogue and odd New York ways, I was having a difficult time fitting in with the local kids. Then one day in the spring semester, our teacher announced that he wanted us all to submit creative stories each week, and that he would read one aloud each Friday. Until that point, I had never thought about writing or becoming a writer—heck, the idea that the stories I'd been reading all my life had been "made" by somebody was still beyond me. Well, I wrote this tale about the adventures of a magic popcorn maker. The teacher read it aloud that first Friday, and it was such a hit that I was asked to produce weekly updates for the rest of the semester. Of course, I would only realize much later (2nd year of college) that fiction was not my calling!

Gyasi: What made you realize this?

Mulvey: Strangely enough, this revelation came not in a creative writing or literature classroom, but in a university music class called "Sounds Around Us." As is perhaps apparent from the title, this was an elective class intended for non-majors with particularly limited music ability. I took the class expecting an easy 'A.' What I got instead was a new, extremely dedicated teacher who, among other things, demanded that we prepare, for each class, descriptions of such sounds as "dog nails rubbing against floor tile," "snow falling on wool," "wind blowing through tall grass," and "water flowing over stone." Abstractions (e.g., "It sounded nice") or clichés received a zero. Instead, we were told to describe each sound in such a way as to "recreate the listening experience authentically" for the reader. Time and again, she told us that the only way to do this was to find fresh ways to express things; moreover, she assured us not just that the right words to do this existed, but that it was our job as human beings to find them. Her statements—particularly her belief that finding precise, new language to convey one's experiences authentically could be important enough to be called a vocation (not to mention her absolute confidence that the language to do this existed in each case)—had a powerful impact on me. Indeed, to this day, I continue to see finding the right images to "recreate" experience in my readers as one of my central jobs as a writer. It was also then that I realized that issues of line, sound, rhythm, form, and image were at least as—if not more—important to me than "telling the story." I've considered myself a poet ever since.

Gyasi: You've published poems, articles, and essays in English and Japanese. How did you become interested in Japan and the Japanese language, if I may ask?

Mulvey: I arrived in Japan for the first time in 1989 via Princeton-in-Asia (PIA), a Princeton University-sponsored exchange program that traditionally accepts a number of non-Princeton students as well. I was fortunate enough to be accepted, and scheduled to be sent to China. However, the growing unrest that would lead eventually to the Tiananmen Square Massacre caused Princeton to suspend the China program for that year. And then, just when I'd given up on the whole thing, I received a phone call from the director: PIA had started a program in Japan ... and would I be willing to go (leaving that March)? I said yes. At the time, I knew almost nothing about either the country or the language—my Japanese vocabulary consisted of three words: "arigato" (thank you), "sayonara" (goodbye), and strangely enough "seppuku" (ritual suicide). Still, off to Kyoto I went, arriving at the end of that March. I stayed until December, during which time I fell absolutely in love with the city. Indeed, to this day, Kyoto remains my choice as the most beautiful city in the world. As to learning the language, back then, all street signs, menus, etc. were in Japanese only, and very few people spoke English. Learning Japanese soon became a priority—among other things, I wanted to know where I was and what I was eating!

Gyasi: You currently live in Iwate, Japan. What took you to Japan?

Mulvey: I returned to Japan in 2006. Part of the reason, of course, is the central role Japan has occupied in my writing and research. However, I was also married to a Japanese national, and she wanted to return. Therefore, when I was offered the Dean of Faculty position at Miyazaki International College, I took it (leaving a wonderful situation in the United States at Idaho State University). While I enjoyed the challenges of being dean, I eventually left Miyazaki for my present position at Iwate National University, where among other things, I teach Japanese academic and creative writing. I believe I am the only non-Japanese in the world to be teaching Japanese writing to Japanese students in Japanese at a Japanese university—it's both a challenge and a great honor.

Gyasi: Let's talk about your first book, *The Fat Sheep Everyone Wants*, which won the 2007 Cleveland State University Poetry Center First Book Prize for Poetry. What inspired you to write it?

Mulvey: This is a difficult question to answer, at least partly because I don't consciously set out to write poetry books on a particular topic or theme. Like I believe many poets, my writing each day is dictated mostly by the obsessions of that day—whether they be issues of sound, image, or sense. Instead, the books come together organically, holistically, the sum of the individual poems I write almost daily, with any overall "theme" realized only later, after a critical mass has been achieved and the collection is viewed in the aggregate. Regarding the book in question, at the time, I was living and working in two countries yet feeling at home in neither. Accordingly, the book contains poems that touch on identity, conflict, separation, assimilation, forgiveness, and redemption. However, in a

56

sense, the poems are also an indirect challenge to the "othering" of Japan so often seen in Western creative writing. Though mostly ignored by Western commentators, confrontational themes and dynamic, forceful language have over the last 70 years become a defining characteristic of Japanese poetry (for example, Ibaragi Noriko, Itou Hiromi, Kaneko Mitsuharu, Takamura Koutarou, Tawara Machi, Yosano Akiko, and so on). It is in the flux of Japan's modern styles and themes, in the evolving and often critical dialectic among them, that I see my poems participating.

Gyasi: Did you write "The Korean Youth Choir Visits the Heiwa Kouen at Asuwayama" out of an event?

Mulvey: It's actually a conflation of two separate events, both from the late 1990s. The first was a visit by a Korean youth choir to Fukui City (and the protests by the extreme-right which accompanied this visit). The second event was the time when two foreign friends (one a missionary) and I were interrogated one Sunday afternoon at the Asuwayama Peace Park (Heiwa Kouen). Regarding the latter incident, a neighbor had seen us sitting together "talking in a foreign language" (English), and called the police. Well, the police came, asked to see our IDs, questioned us about our intentions, and then asked us either to use Japanese or to keep our voices down "because there's a graveyard nearby." As it seemed strange for three Americans to speak together in Japanese, and as we were already keeping our voices down, we chose to leave.

Gyasi: Do you have a specific audience you write for?

Mulvey: Yes and no. I think most writers carry within them their own "ideal reader," really that inner voice which keeps them honest, calling them out for any weak images and clichéd language, yet at the same time always getting the puns and noticing, say, that internal slant rhyme scheme you worked so hard on. However, I believe that for poetry to survive, it needs also to be accessible to a wider, more general audience. I try to write for both my ideal reader and this latter audience.

Gyasi: Do you have a specific time you sit down to write?

Mulvey: Mornings … the earlier, the better!

Gyasi: Can you talk about *Deep Snow Country*, your latest book? When was it published? What is it about?

Mulvey: The book was published early last year, after winning the 2013 FIELD Poetry Prize. The title comes from the official government designation for the region where I live—"Gousetsu Chitai," or "the region of deep snows." The epigraph—"The Kingdom of Death lies within a mirror"—was translated from a poem by Terayama Shuuji and underlines one important theme: the idea of self-exploration as a continuing cycle of death and rebirth. Moreover, having directly experienced both the 2011 Tohoku earthquake and its aftermath, continuing as well to contribute to the ongoing (and very slow) rebuilding process, I felt driven to convey through my art form some of what I've witnessed or directly experienced. Accordingly, many of the poems in the book deal with the challenges of living through the devastating earthquake, tsunami, and reactor meltdown that struck northeastern Japan.

Gyasi: Could you explain the title of your chapbook *The Window Tribe* to us?

Mulvey: The title is a direct translation of one of the more fascinating (at least to me) Japanese terms out there: "madogiwazoku." See, Japanese companies rarely can fire full-time workers—for all intents and purposes, once hired you're stuck with that individual until mandatory retirement age. So what do you do with the occasional incompetent worker or slacker? In Japan, you assign them a desk with a nice window view—and as far away as possible from the inner works of the company itself. "The Window Tribe," then, is the Japanese term for these individuals—though in a sense, it also is analogous to the treatment many foreigners living and working in Japan experience. The chapbook itself explores this latter phenomenon.

Gyasi: I am also much interested in the title of your chapbook *Character Readings*?

Mulvey: Something that continues to fascinate me is how "kanji" (the Chinese characters used for writing) came to "mean" what they do. For example, one character for "home" originally was an ideograph depicting a "pig" under a "roof," one character for "beauty" originally depicted "a fat sheep," and two characters used together to convey "truth" really did originally depict "a prisoner hung up by the heels dead" and "a field ready for harvest" respectively. Of course, as in these examples, the characters have become so stylized over time (two thousand years) that their former meanings are not readily recognizable today. The title, and indeed a number of poems in the chapbook itself, address this issue—with, certainly, the additional play on the English meaning of "character."

Gyasi: Which writers inspire you?

Mulvey: Too many to list them all: some specific examples of writers I'm currently reading include Denise Duhamel, Ibaragi Noriko, Mark Doty, Claudia Rankine, Ariel Dorfman, Ellen Bass, Wing Tek Lum, Ann Lauinger, and Steve Gehrke.

Gyasi: Your favorite books?

Mulvey: Again, too many to list. Two relatively recent books that I think deserved more attention are *The White Fire of Time* (Ellen Hinsey) and *Landscape with Silos* (Deborah Bogen).

Gyasi: What does the future look like for you?

Mulvey: I'm working towards completing what I hope will be my next book, including poems with a bit more integration of "West" with "East," along the lines of *Character Readings* and the "dualities" being invoked there.

Henrietta Rose-Innes is a South African writer based in Cape Town. Her novel *Nineveh* (2011) was published by Random House Struik, following a short-story collection, *Homing* (2010), and two earlier novels: *Shark's Egg* (2000) and *The Rock Alphabet* (2004).

In 2008 she won the Caine Prize for African Writing, for which she was shortlisted in 2007. Also in 2007, she was awarded the South African PEN Literary Award.

Her short stories have appeared in various publications, including *Granta, AGNI*, and *The Best American Nonrequired Reading 2011*, and her writing has been translated into German, Arabic, and Romanian.

She was a Fellow in Literature at the Akademie Schloss Solitude, Stuttgart, (2007-8) and has held residencies at the Chateau de Lavigny, Lausanne; the kunst:raum sylt quelle, Sylt; the University of Georgetown; the University of Cape Town's Centre for Creative Writing; and Caldera Arts Center, Oregon.

She is currently Donald Gordon Creative Arts Fellow at the Gordon Institute for Performing and Creative Arts (GIPCA), University of Cape Town.

Gyasi: The Caine Prize has been in existence for a while. Do you think the aim for which it was established has been successful?

Rose-Innes: I think the prize has been very successful in raising the profile of African writing worldwide, and has given a great boost to the careers of several important new writers. The annual workshops have also really benefited many developing writers across the continent. I think the prize has enormous future potential: to bring African writing to a broader audience, to change perceptions and, importantly, to attract more attention (and entries) within Africa and the diaspora.

Gyasi: At what point in your life did you see yourself as a writer?

Rose-Innes: From a young age, I wrote poems and stories, but it was only from my mid-twenties that I started to consider myself a writer. Before that I had thought I would be some kind of scientist. Doing the creative writing MA at the University of Cape Town—when that program was in its very early days—was an important part of that shift.

Gyasi: What is the writing process like? When do you write?

Rose-Innes: I don't have a fixed schedule, but when I'm in the thick of a project I write every day—whether it's dutifully getting down my 1000 words or, in the later stages, putting in hours of revising. I spend an awful lot of time reworking: probably most of the time goes into editing. I'm a slow writer and I probably throw away five words for every one I keep.

Gyasi: Where do you set most of your stories?

Rose-Innes: Almost all of my work so far is set in Cape Town or in the countryside of the Western Cape, which is where I grew up and have always lived, in between traveling. I am not confident of my ability to sense nuance in places that are less familiar to me.

Gyasi: Where do you pick your characters from? Are they from real life? I am, for instance, thinking of Lynn from "Poison."

Rose-Innes: I truly think that each of my characters reflects a part of myself. Where I do draw on other people, I try to mix features up, sneakily, so that nobody's able to recognize themselves too clearly. I haven't yet been busted for identity theft.

Gyasi: How long does it roughly take you to write a short story and a novel?

Rose-Innes: It takes me a long time to mull over ideas and settle on something that could be viable. After that, once I know more or less what I'm doing, I'd say a month is about right for a story; for a novel, maybe two to three years. I'm slow. I can write fast but I take an age to edit.

Gyasi: Most of your stories have been translated into other languages. What does that mean for you?

Rose-Innes: I'm not sure if it is actually "most." Quite a few of my stories have been translated into German, though, largely as a result of a fellowship I held in Stuttgart in 2007-08. It's very exciting to be translated and to find a new readership. I have enormous respect for translators, and it's a strange and flattering feeling to know that someone is focusing careful attention on every word. I was lucky to have sensitive German translators. There is also some anxiety, though: I can read German well enough to see clear errors, but I wouldn't spot anything subtle. I've also been translated into Arabic and Romanian, which was stress-free because these languages are completely mysterious to me. I just had to trust. I think if I'd been less lazy about learning other languages, literary translation is something I would have been happy to do with my life.

Gyasi: Which of the two forms of writing—short stories and novels —would you consider tedious?

Rose-Innes: I think there are always periods where it feels like hard labor. I'm not a writer who burns through drafts in a blaze of passion: I periodically get bogged down and morose about the state of my manuscript. And then it gets better, and worse again, and then better, and then ultimately it gets finished. I have found, though, that the writing that feels "tedious" tends to be the writing that gets deleted. That doesn't mean you don't have to do it, though.

Gyasi: Has Cape Town provided for you that enabling environment to write your stories?

Rose-Innes: There is certainly enough material here, in this complex, old, changeable city, to keep a writer going forever. Practically speaking, we are blessed in Cape Town—and South Africa generally, relative to most other parts of Africa—to have a strong publishing industry, which is also pretty friendly and accessible to young writers. We have some fantastic independent bookshops, a network of writers and writing websites, a number of book fairs and festivals, and creative writing programs at the local universities. It's a very fortunate combination of factors. Of course there is still much that can be done to expand our reading public.

Gyasi: The Nobel Prize winner JM Coatzee actually taught you while studying for an MA at Cape Town University. I am curious to know what it was like studying under Coetzee.

Rose-Inees: It was an invaluable experience: it showed me the level of care and rigor that is required. I think it was also my first experience of being sternly but kindly "edited," and the things I learned have stayed with me ever since.

Jeffrey Alfier is the 2014 winner of the Kithara Book Prize, judged by Dennis Maloney. He has been nominated for seven Pushcarts, and is a two-time nominee for the UK's Forward Prize for Poetry. In 2013 he was selected as a finalist for the Press 53 Poetry Contest. Publication credits include *Spoon River Poetry Review, Arkansas Review, Birmingham Poetry Review, Columbia College Literary Review, Copper Nickel, Crab Orchard Review, Concho River Review, Connecticut Review, december magazine, Emerson Review, Iron Horse Literary Review, Kestrel, Louisville Review, Owen Wister Review, Permafrost, Poetry Ireland Review, South Carolina Review, Southwestern American Literature, Texas Review, Tulane Review,* and *War Literature and the Arts*. In addition to nine chapbooks, he is author of *The Wolf Yearling* (Silver Birch Press), *Idyll for a Vanishing River* (Glass Lyre Press), which won the Kithara Book Prize, *The Storm Petrel—Poems of Ireland* (Grayson Books, 2014), and most recently, *The Color of Forgiveness* (Mojave River Review and Press), co-authored with fellow editor Tobi Alfier (Cogswell). He is an Air Force veteran of 27 years and a member of Iraq and Afghanistan Veterans of America (IAVA). He has written training manuals as a government contractor, and once taught history for City Colleges of Chicago's European Division.

Gyasi: You're an Air Force veteran with 27 years of officer and enlisted service. As a child, did you always want to work in the Air Force?

Alfier: I would say generally yes, though I'd considered other branches of the military as well. But those were usually fleeting thoughts. For some reason the Air Force was utmost in my mind. My dad was also career Air Force, though he didn't influence me one way or another.

Gyasi: You're a member of Iraq and Afghanistan Veterans of America (IAVA). Do you meet regularly and do you have any fond memories of your active days at work?

Alfier: I hold a membership and contribute financially now and again, though I haven't attended any meetings yet. I was in a command post away from the battlefields, but I was in the war's areas of operations. There are indeed a lot of fond memories, most associated with traveling to foreign countries, new jobs, and new assignments. Best times of my life.

Gyasi: How did you become a writer?

Alfier: It was an unwitting thing, really. When I was twelve or thirteen, I began writing a science fiction story called "Lost in Eternity," about a spaceship that could only travel one-way through space, but I gave up the project when I couldn't figure out where the travelers got their food. But when I finished my master's degree in 1990, I found there was a vacancy left by no longer having to write term papers. It was surprising to find myself missing writing college papers! I began to fill that absence within a couple of years when I started writing safety and other professional articles for the Air Force. Then, while traveling once to an Air Force base that had a huge research library, I came across articles on the British trench poets of World War I. I'd never read human language rendered so powerfully before. That was 1997, and it was then that I began to try my hand at poetry. In '97 I was 42, so I came to poetry late in life. It took about five years to find my voice and to write anything worth keeping and seeing through to publication.

Gyasi: Do you remember your first piece of writing?

Alfier: Oh yes—it was horrible. I wrote brief, drunken poems about Greek goddesses and such, and tried to sound high-handed and intellectual. None of that stuff I ever kept.

Gyasi: What was your first ever published work and where was it published?

Alfier: My first credible magazine publication came in 2001, in *Stolen Island Review*, which is no longer around, and in *War, Literature & the Arts*, which still is. The latter was a poem about the loss of a Russian submarine. My first book publication was ten years ago. It was *Strangers Within the Gate*, a chapbook of American Southwest regional poems. It was published by The Moon Publishing & Printing, a one-woman operation in Arizona. The publisher was very kind and ended up publishing a second chapbook of mine a couple of years later.

Gyasi: How did you come to write *The Wolf Yearling*?

Alfier: When I was first assigned to Tucson, Arizona, in 1999, I became more deeply enthralled with American deserts. I always had a fascination with them, but it was mainly through cinema. I'd gone on brief trips to American air bases that were located in deserts and always found the endless vistas enthralling, as I did their stark and sparse flora and fauna. Such fascination blossomed in '99, when I physically resided in a desert area. Everything came to me in a steady stream of images, from picturing the prehistoric deserts to the Ice Age to modern farming and ranching in the desert. As I mentioned, the flora and fauna became fascinating, took hold in my mind for keeps. Again, it took me a while to write anything worth publishing, and that came in 2003 after the two in 2001. From about 2000 onward, almost all of my poems were set in the Southwest and were written in deca-syllabic lines. So after years of continuing to write Southwest poems, I had enough for a manuscript. The title is from one of the poems in the book.

Gyasi: Did you ever struggle seeking publishers for your book *The Wolf Yearling*?

Alfier: Yes. It was initially accepted for publication in 2011 by Pecan Grove Press, based in San Antonio. But after a couple of years it still hadn't been published due to the declining health of the editor. He died in early 2013, and the press began phasing-out manuscripts. Fortunately, I came across Silver Birch Press, based here in Los Angeles, and the manuscript was enthusiastically accepted, and the book was born within a few months. Actually, it had been accepted by three publishers, but I had to turn the others down; Silver Birch Press's terms and conditions for publication were irresistible, and their printing quality was outstanding.

Gyasi: What inspired your book *Idyll for a Vanishing River*?

Alfier: *Idyll for a Vanishing River* is really *The Wolf Yearling*, part two, in that it is also a collection of Southwest poetry that I'd written after *The Wolf Yearling*. I was quite pleased it got accepted, for it was a rather quick acceptance.

Gyasi: What circumstances led you to write *The Torch Singer*?

Alfier: That one is a collection of poems relating to, or touching upon, music, particularly jazz and the blues. After focusing primarily on the Southwest, my mind drifted to other areas that obsessed me—I'm using Richard Hugo's term of obsession here—such as night club singers, bluesmen, jazz players, as well as inner cities, especially as rendered by *film noir* cinema. But the crux of *The Torch Singer* is that woman who sings late at night, that fills not so much a romantic need but rather something in the soul that is elusively defined. Perhaps she is that twin sister that Jungian psychology says every male loses when he is born.

Gyasi: Do you know why you write?

Alfier: Though it may sound clichéd, it seems as natural as breathing to render the world creatively; or, as William Stafford once put it, "So, the world happens twice – / once what we see it as; / second it legends itself / deep, the way it is." So for me, what often results is an invented presence: what my own mind determines as the emotional resonance of a place—what reverberates in image, or emotion, with my readers. I see a place or buildings, whether an abandoned farm in the smallest Arizona town, or a former shipbuilding plant on the coast of California, a New Jersey backwater fishing pier, or downtown Detroit, and I need to render them in verse. Sometimes I do the same just by gazing out over the small valley in front of our house, watching the transit of weather and birds. But it's not a mechanical process; the poem triggers come into the mind's eye, into the poetic vision set deep within us, our imagination. The main thing is that I am a Regionalist, or writer with a sense of Place. I also have a chapbook of Ireland poems, and an unpublished manuscript of Scotland poems.

Gyasi: What do you regard as your best piece of work ever?

Alfier: That's hard to say, but it would be a poem that combines in the best way those elements and techniques I use to write: a sense of concision that results from a strict economy of language that renders sharp images; a key use of metaphors and similes, and an ending that contains at least a subtle sense of what Keats called "negative capability"—uncertainty, obscurity, or doubt without any desperate reaching for resolutions derived from reasoning processes; clarifying moments but not necessarily logical outcomes. A kind of haunting, if you will.

Gyasi: Who are your literary forebears?

Alfier: Well, there are several poets, including Richard Hugo, the British trench poets, Walt McDonald, Philip Levine, Yusef Komunyakaa, Wendell Berry. Joseph Millar is a later one in that he is a poet whom I continually learn from. I didn't earn an MFA and have been in a couple of workshops now and again, but mostly I learn from reading and re-reading those poets above, along with others. That's actually advice I was given early on in my writing life: continually read those writers you admire most. As Nabokov once said, the only true reading is re-reading.

Gyasi: Which book(s) have had great impact on your life as a writer?

Alfier: I would say Richard Hugo's famous little tract, *The Triggering Town*. I go back to it time and again. But it's interesting, because I also love reading how fiction writers create. So much of what they say applies to poetry, such as the intrinsic need to pull the writer into the story, to grab his or her attention and hold it; I mean, that's what we must do as writers, no matter what it is. I also love reading interviews with writers, especially my favorite poets because those interviews often touch on the craft of writing.

Gyasi: What is the best time to write?

Alfier: I don't have a best time, per se, though I find myself writing early morning on into midday, taking a break, then going back to the writing in the early evening. By then I'm sick of what I've been writing and don't want to look at it again till the next day. I guess there's a point where you begin to second guess yourself and at that juncture I think it's good for the mind to go focus on something else so it may more clearly come back to the piece of writing recharged and refreshed. Sometimes I pull off of busy highways because I need to get a line down on paper, and that can come any time of day. Insomnia is also a writing instigator. I know many writers have a set time to write in a set place, but my Muse is just too sporadic or ad hoc for that. Sometimes at the dinner table or in the middle of a clothing store a line comes to me and I have to write it down. I always have my notebook with me, though at times I've written on bar napkins or a paper bag blowing down the street, and once I wrote a word down on the floor, leaning over while in bed. It's not a better way to write, it's just that assigning myself a designated segment of the day wouldn't work in my case. I love writing in greasy spoons, either at the LA harbor areas or downtown, with few customers and low or no music. Part of the reason is that such greasy spoons always show up in my poems.

Gyasi: Do you know who reads your works?

Alfier: Well, the obvious answer is friends and family, the editors that accept me for publication, but beyond that, it's hard to say. I do have fellow poets that read my work and I like to share my books and chapbooks with them.

Gyasi: What is the most boring part of writing?

Alfier: I can't say there are any boring parts, but there are parts that are less captivating or interesting in the process of developing the draft of the poem. I often write about occupations and business I know little or nothing of—such as fishing or blue collar work—and I spend great amounts of time looking things up: raw facts, how engine parts work, job descriptions, terms associated with this or that occupation, and thus I accumulate a lot of data, most of it I don't use because you must filter out what you don't need. Such research—all online—often leads to digressions and I realize I'm bored and need to get back to the poem.

Gyasi: How would you describe your voice as a writer?

Alfier: It varies. Sometimes my voice comes in quieter declarative sentences, sometimes more conversational, though I try not to ramble—which is always a poem-killer (like those poems that shout at the reader). Beyond that, I try to present a sense of wonder without sounding contrived or inflated. I often write in the second person "you," but if the poem sounds better in first-person "I" then that's the perspective I write from. But just because I write in "I" does not mean the poem is autobiographical by any means. I'd say in the aggregate, my poems are semi-biographical at best, save for a few select cases.

Gyasi: What are your main subject areas as a writer?

Alfier: Touching upon an early reply, those areas are deserts, inner cities—mainly cafes, bars, alleys; small towns anywhere, trains and railroads, rural areas, industrial sites, seas, and harbors—basically littoral zones. Sometimes it's sports, though not often. I've written a few war or military poems. But within such physical spaces are humans and the human "mindscape" if you will—the pathos of the human and the human heart.

Gyasi: What legacy do you want to leave behind as a writer?

Alfier: If I can in any way be an example to those who want and need to write with a strong sense of Place, that would suit me fine.

Gyasi: What are you currently reading?

Alfier: I've come across an excellent poetry collection by the late Lynda Hull. I've seen few writers like her who can write extended narrative poems and hold my attention throughout the poem. I'm also reading the Scottish poet John Burnside, as well as the late Frank Stanford. I find all three of them enthralling in the main. Geoffrey Davis has also published an excellent book I've read recently.

Gyasi: Do you mind signing off the interview with anything you want to say?

Alfier: Yes, please. I am very grateful for this interview, Geosi. It has been a pleasure!

Eric Forsbergh was born in London, but raised in Massachusetts and later Tennessee. He wrote poetry in high school and college, but was first drawn into poetry as a child, when his father read to him T.S. Eliot's *Book of Practical Cats*. He attended the University of Tennessee for undergraduate school, double-majoring in Microbiology and Zoology, minoring in English, and graduating Phi Beta Kappa. He attended the University of North Carolina in the School of Dentistry, graduating in 1981. After a 21-year hiatus to attend to family and career, he resumed writing poetry with a 25 haiku surprise presentation to his wife for their anniversary. In 2010, as a first effort, he attended the Hampton Roads Writers Conference, winning their poetry prize. He is currently an active member of the Poetry Society of Virginia, and a regular attendee of their regional salon. He has provided dental care on three mission trips, two to the Guatemalan Mayan Indians, and one in Appalachia. He lives in Reston, Virginia, where he practices dentistry. He is a Vietnam veteran, having served his draft enlistment on an aircraft carrier in the Tonkin Gulf, in Da Nang, Vietnam, and in the Philippines.

Gyasi: Could we begin from your profession as a dentist? What is the dentist doing in the circle of writers?

Forsbergh: Entering college after being in Vietnam, I wanted to be either an English professor or a dentist, for entirely unrelated reasons. I chose dentistry because I enjoy using my hands, am attracted to biology, and enjoy relating to people. But I could not abandon my love of literature. Even though I did not write creatively from 1985 to 2006, I read from famous literary works almost daily. When I began to win prizes, starting in 2010, I joined the Poetry Society of Virginia, and I currently attend its regional monthly salon. As a result, I've met numerous writers. Writers may be interested that I am a dentist, because writers can come from anywhere. However, my dental patients are often quite surprised and curious that I am a published poet.

Gyasi: Do you see writing as a profession? Do you earn anything from writing?

Forsbergh: I don't see writing as a profession, but as a devotion. Or a calling, if you will. For me, writing springs from my broad exposure to life outside the writing community, such as my experiences in the Navy during Vietnam, on a farm, as a dentist, and on medical/dental mission trips to Guatemala and Appalachia. Many writers work full time at writing and the teaching of writing, making that their profession. I admire their knowledge. In fact, the shortcomings of my literary knowledge became evident to me in 2010, after I entered my second contest, with Hampton Roads Writers. I won their poetry prize, and in her comments, the judge wrote that my poem had an "ekphrastic" quality. I'm embarrassed to say it now, but I remember thinking "What does that word mean?" Since then, I've studied poetry steadily, and attended conferences. As for earnings, it's been next to nothing, but I don't care.

Gyasi: How does your work as a dentist influence your writing?

Forsbergh: Dentistry is a highly analytical activity based on diagnosis and treatment. I constantly evaluate and act upon the best available course. But attached to the process is a human being. Frequently patients have fear, anxiety, or pain. I have to respond in a sensitive manner with assurance, and alleviation of pain and infection. Often, patients are masking their feelings, or are unclear at articulating their symptoms. I have to recognize the unspoken elements, and bring them to the surface with open-ended questions. Poetry, in the same way, is about illuminating the hidden central truths in our experiences. A patient of mine once burst into tears over a minor chipped tooth, and when I asked her if there was anything else upsetting her, she responded that her husband had just been diagnosed with cancer. I had to engage her on that level with reassurances about current cancer treatment successes. Fortunately, her husband recovered well. Sometimes a dentist has to respond like a priest or a psychologist.

Gyasi: When did you actually begin to write?

Forsbergh: As a freshman in high school, I wrote a poem about Dylan Thomas and showed it to my English teacher. He gave me great encouragement, but it was the care and attention he gave to editing it that told me he took my effort seriously.

Gyasi: I understand that when you were a child your father read to you T.S. Eliot's *Book of Practical Cats*. Could you say something about books and your childhood?

Forsbergh: I grew up in a house in which books were everywhere, and were often quoted for my personal edification. My mother finished one year of college, but she read all of Shakespeare's works, as well as the works of James Baldwin and Richard Wright, among many others. She frequently articulated her reverence for education. My father had a PhD in physics, and wrote formal verse in English and French. When I was about six or seven, he found and read to me children's versions of *The Iliad* and *The Odyssey*. This explains why I like both military history and verse.

Gyasi: Where do you get the inspiration to write?

Forsbergh: From everywhere, because my mind is always receptive. In fact, I feel pursued by words and language. Often, I hear a personal story that attracts my attention, making me wonder about its unspoken background. At a granular level, phrases and words will often simply appear in my imagination, triggering the idea for a poem. As a result, I leave sticky notes around the house with words written on them so as not to forget. This amuses my wife. Later, I harvest them, to transcribe into a large file called "poetry resources," which I draw from at any time. A lack of self-generated prompts is not my problem.

Gyasi: Do you remember anything odd about your time as poetry editor at UT Creative Arts magazine *Phoenix*?

Forsbergh: Previous to college, I had been to Vietnam in the Navy. At the University of Tennessee, as a 22-year-old freshman, I felt a gulf between myself and the typical freshman. This feeling was based less on age than on experience. The college poems I reviewed most often revealed a narrow self-absorption, even if there was developing talent. In 1977, I won the faculty judged UT prize, for a poem on the meaning of Nagasaki, which I had visited while in the Navy.

Gyasi: Do you have any special ritual you go through before you sit down to write?

Forsbergh: No. I look for extended quiet time, and because there is always something I'm working on in my head, it is just a matter of recording the lines, and the poem grows from there, often quickly. After the first draft, I'll repeatedly grab ten or fifteen minutes to sit and revise. Often, I'll go back 30 or more times for revision.

Gyasi: What is the biggest challenge you've ever faced as a writer?

Forsbergh: The search for nouns and verbs, and the dismissal of adjectives and adverbs. One of my poetry instructors mentioned that instead of using an adverb linked to a verb, a poet should find a better verb. Fortunately, I never experienced the challenge of finding a publisher for my book *Imagine Morning*. After I'd won several prizes with the Poetry Society of Virginia, I was approached by Richer Resources Publications of Arlington, Virginia. They asked if I was interested in publishing a book. This had not occurred to me yet, so I assembled my first book of poems. I am grateful to them for having been given the opportunity.

Gyasi: You were the winner of the Edgar Allen Poe Memorial Prize in 2014. Could you tell us anything about the award?

Forsbergh: This award is the premier award given by the Poetry Society of Virginia, formed over 90 years ago. Poe was a Virginia native, and the annual contest has 25 categories. Usually, there are some 1400 entries, with the Poe award category getting the most entries. I won this prize in 2013 and 2014. Based on my two winning poems, I'd say that gravitas and complexity are important elements for this prize. My two poems were about a medical/dental mission trip to Guatemala, and internet addiction. In my mission trip poem, I wrote about witnessing starvation.

Gyasi: Do you have any favorites among all the poems you've written?

Forsbergh: I'm glad they're not like your children, whom you are required to love equally. In fact, I have several stinkers hiding in my documents file. Actually, I have four favorites which come to mind. From my book, there is "Eleanor," "A Forward Sway," and "Once the Grunt Decides." The first one sat as a chopped up fragment for over a year before I buckled down, and in a good moment, turned it into a coherent piece. The second, on the simple metaphor of an inchworm, seems to be an audience pleaser. It is a meditation on letting go, and I was invited to read it in church. The third, about the grunt, came in a dark moment of contemplating suicides among veterans. In an intense burst, I wrote it in one sitting, with little revision. It won a PSV prize. In a wide reach, it describes our universal tendency to carry out rash actions when we have not adequately weighed the consequences. When I finished reading it at the awards ceremony, I heard several sighs of emotional release. My poem "Under the Influence of Internet," referenced in the previous question, was written in several weeks of steady development around three interwoven themes: internet addiction, strolling in surf at the beach, and Dante's hell. The point is that, for me, a successful creative piece can come into being any number of ways, borne up by any of several attitudes.

Gyasi: Are there times you feel like not writing?

Forsbergh: No, but I get tired of writing if I've been at it awhile without a break. For me, that's an hour. So, writing a novel might be out of the question. I am better suited for the tactile, physically active world, because I grew up on a farm. So after I write, I get relief from that sedentary activity by returning to dentistry, or going to the gym, or splitting firewood, for example. But there are no times when I procrastinate about writing. Also, I don't have the pressure of doing it for a living.

Gyasi: As a dentist, do you get time to read? What books can be found on your bookshelf?

Forsbergh: I have to carve out the time to read and study. My book shelf contains books on poetry, dentistry, history, religion, and neurology. I also have many works of famous literature, from Homer onward. I believe Churchill was right when he said that whenever a best seller comes out, we should pick up a classic. My favorite poets are Homer, Dante, Shakespeare, Whitman, Elizabeth Bishop, and Mary Oliver. Dante's inventiveness amazes me. Growing up in New England, I'm drawn to themes of fish and boats, so I like Bishop's work. And like her, I am drawn to themes of physical labor. I can imagine her with calloused hands, probably because I admire people with calloused hands. Mary Oliver has the ability to calmly put the tip of her finger right onto my deepest notions. Recently, I've been reading *A Poet's Glossary* (Hirsch) and *Functional Occlusion* (Dawson).

I recommend both.

Gyasi: Did your participation in the Hampton Roads Writers Conference ignite your love for writing?

Forsbergh: Not quite. In 2006, I ended my 21-year hiatus in writing poetry by surprising my wife with 25 haiku for our 25th anniversary, describing single moments in our marriage. She was moved to tears, and that got me going. In 2010, I entered the Hampton Roads Writers Conference poetry contest, previously mentioned, and won. My only other contest entry ever had been for the UT prize, which I won in 1977. Batting two for two launched a belief that I could go much further, and the writing followed. Since then, I've attended several workshops for writing, and was told once that I write in the lineage of Roethke. This is unintentional, and I don't carry around his evident misery. The love of writing, though, has always been in me.

Gyasi: Is it easy to write haiku as compared to other forms of poetry?

Forsbergh: It's a game like Sudoku, in a way. It's compact. It needs an exact syllable count, while delivering a message. Then the last line needs a turn of some kind. I find it to be a great exercise in design, precision, and economy of words.

Gyasi: Do you mind telling us anything about the literary landscape in Reston, Virginia, where you live?

Forsbergh: Reston is a suburb of Washington D.C., and as such probably 80% of my adult patients have a college education, and are highly literate. If writing is not their primary profession, then at least they write often for reports, etc. I have found that Reston has many book clubs, and I have a number of patients who have published or are trying to publish their work. Poetry readings are held at various venues, and I have done two readings so far in Reston. So, yes, Reston has a lot to offer for literature.

Gyasi: You served your enlistment on an aircraft carrier in the Tonkin Gulf. Could you tell us anything about Vietnam?

Forsbergh: Between 1969 and 1973, I was on an aircraft carrier for three cruises, totaling 17 months actually at sea. I was an aviation electrician's mate on the flight deck, and flight deck duty has been described as one of the most dangerous jobs, due to the constant movement of aircraft carrying high explosives and jet fuel, and their take offs and landings. Any wrong step or lapse in attention could get you sucked into a jet intake, or blown off the deck. I constantly used to have to scurry under the low bellies of taxiing military aircraft to get around. We worked at supporting bombing runs twelve hours a day, seven days a week for a month at a time, sometimes in the stifling heat. On rare occasion, we would lose a sailor or a pilot. I got an aerial tour of Hanoi once, but considering the fate of John McCain, once was enough.

Gyasi: How do you want to be remembered: as a dentist or a writer?

Forsbergh: Both.

Gyasi: Do you find the art of writing joyous?

Forsbergh: Joyous may not be the word I'd use to describe my response. It's more complex. The art, embodied by the act of writing, seems like being submerged and traveling through an intense daydream. When I come out of that daydream, the reward is that I have something to show for it.

Gyasi: Do you have any questions for me?

Forsbergh: How can I follow your blog, and do you primarily concentrate on poetry?

Gyasi: To follow my blog, all there is to do is to freely subscribe and receive notifications of new posts by email. I do not concentrate mainly on poetry. I cover all genres of literature: essays, fiction, non-fiction, and poetry.

Jack Ridl's latest collection is *Practicing to Walk Like a Heron* (Wayne State University Press, 2013). It was named one of the year's two best poetry collections by Foreword Reviews/The American Library Association. His collection *Broken Symmetry* (Wayne State University Press) was co-recipient of The Society of Midland Authors best book of poetry award for 2006. His collection *Losing Season* (CavanKerry Press) follows a small town through a long winter and a long season with its losing high school basketball team. The collection was named the best sports book of the year for 2009 by The Institute for International Sport and *The Boston Globe* named it one of the five best books about sports. Ridl has been featured on public radio ("It's Only a Game with Bill Littlefield," "The Story with Dick Gordon," and Garrison Keillor's "The Writer's Almanac"). Former Poet Laureate Billy Collins selected his *Against Elegies* for The Center for Book Arts Chapbook Award. He and Peter Schakel are co-authors of *Approaching Poetry* and *Approaching Literature*, and editors of *250 Poems*, all from Bedford/St. Martin's Press. With Bill Olsen, he edited *Poetry in Michigan/Michigan in Poetry* (New Issues Press). Ridl's poetry has been nominated for 18 Pushcart Prizes. He has yet to win. He has done readings in many venues, including being invited to read at the Geraldine R. Dodge Poetry Festival. He was one of twelve people in the arts from around the U.S. invited to the Fetzer Institute for their first conference on compassion and forgiveness. In retirement he conducts a range of poetry writing workshops. For information about them and other information about Ridl, go to his website at http://www.ridl.com.

Ridl taught at Hope College for 37 years. The students named him their Outstanding Professor, and in 1996 The Carnegie (CASE) Foundation named him Michigan Professor of the Year. Nine of his students are included in the recent anthology *Time You Let Me In: 25 Poets Under 25*. More than 85 of Ridl's students are now published authors.

Gyasi: Can we begin this way? The cover design of your book *In Practicing to Walk Like a Heron* features artwork by your daughter, Meridith Ridl. My question is, is there any major difference between an artist and a writer?

Ridl: The only major difference that I'm aware of is that my daughter and I use different media and different created results. Our vision, the sensibility we bring to what we do, is pretty much shared, as is what we believe to be the importance of creating for everyone.

Gyasi: How did you become a writer?

Ridl: I like your saying "become" because I didn't set out to be a writer and I sure couldn't simply go to school, learn about poetry, and declare myself a poet. It's been a process. In fact, after college, I apprenticed myself to the poet Paul Zimmer. He said that he would read my drafts, critique them, and added that he would tell me when I had written a poem. Two and a half years later he said, "That's a poem." Even then I, of course, could not call myself a poet. It's always a becoming. One must become able each time to be able to serve the next appearance of a possible poem.

Gyasi: What sort of diction do you often use in your poetry?

Ridl: I have a very small vocabulary. My diction is pretty much confined to particulars, good ole Anglo-Saxon diction and images. If I use conceptual language, it is usually within the context of a particular or an event or a person or a place.

Gyasi: Does the place where your poems are set matter to you?

Ridl: Yes. I always hope that the reader feels at home within the context of the poem. I usually signal something about place and/or context in the title or early in the poem. I try to keep the poem on the ground and/or in the affect of the speaker.

Gyasi: You've been named as one of the 100 most influential sports educators in America by the Institute for International Sport. What kind of sport do you love most?

Ridl: My father was the basketball coach at Westminster College and then at the University of Pittsburgh. I grew up loving the game and still do. I have only a couple teams, college teams, that I pull for. I simply love watching most any game. I also love baseball. I was a shortstop from Little League. During the season, I watch most any game although I do follow the Pittsburgh Pirates. I'm learning about hockey, am dazzled by the skaters, and I actually like to watch golf. I know a lot about it, and watching it is also kind of meditative.

Gyasi: Did your love for sports influence your book *Losing Season*?

Ridl: Not so much a love of sports, but a knowledge and understanding of the world of sports, especially basketball. In the book, there is no poem about a game. The book explores the life around the game and those involved with the game as well as asking why the U.S. is a sports-centered culture, why so many people's emotions are tied to sports at any level.

Gyasi: Were you surprised when your book *Broken Symmetry* was selected by the Society of Midland Authors as the best book of poetry for 2006?

Ridl: Yes, very surprised. And of course, thrilled, delighted. It helped me believe that I was okay at doing this art.

Gyasi: Your books *Broken Symmetry* and *In Practicing to Walk Like a Heron* were both published by Wayne State University Press. What sort of relationship do you have with Wayne State University Press?

Ridl: A deep, lasting, wonderful relationship. My editor, Annie Martin, "parents" my poems. She cares and her insights are penetrating in their intelligence. Also everyone there is both professional and personal, a rare combination, a rare ability. I love those people.

Gyasi: In 1996, The Carnegie Foundation named you as "Michigan Professor of the Year." Why do you think you were named for this award?

Ridl: I don't know how to answer that. I suppose the judges were taken with the letters written in my behalf.

Gyasi: What is it about your style of teaching that would make your students select you as the "Favorite Professor" in 2003?

Ridl: My guess is that they appreciate that I don't teach a class as a whole, don't teach "how to write poetry" as a given thing that applies in the same way to everyone. I always try to guide each student to her/his own vision and make sure each student has learned the art itself so that each student can bring his/her vision to fruition in a poem. I learned from my father the coach that each player plays differently even though the rudiments of the game are the same for everyone. Maybe that's why they selected me. Or maybe it's because I didn't/don't believe in grades. Or maybe I'm just so damn nice.

Gyasi: What is the first thing that comes to mind when you sit down to write?

Ridl: Nothing

Gyasi: Did you write "Hands" out of a personal experience?

Ridl: Yes. I wanted to celebrate my grandfather. However, one can't just sit down and write about the "whole person." So I decided to concentrate on one physical part of him that would, I hoped, bring out the "essence" of who he was.

Gyasi: Permit me to put you to test: which of your books is your favorite?

Ridl: Our daughter when she was seven asked us if we "could have a rule for the whole family." When we asked what that would be, she answered, "Never use the word 'favorite.'" We have kept that promise ever since.

Gyasi: Could you tell me the inspiration behind your poem "After Spending the Morning Baking Bread"?

Ridl: Like a lot, most?, of my poems, it was elicited by noticing our cat and realizing that there are reasons to wish one were a cat. I wanted to celebrate Hattie not the way Christopher Smart did his cat, Jeoffry, but nonetheless a quiet celebration with a twitch of longing.

Gyasi: Can we describe "Scrub Dreams of Taking the Last Shot" as a prose poem? In your view, what is a prose poem?

Ridl: Yes, it seems to land in that category, although poetry is what a poem offers so all poems are, to me, formal. That poem is for me simply a poem without lines because when I wrote it in lines, the energy needed was not there.

Gyasi: How would you like to be remembered as a writer?

Ridl: As a father, husband, teacher.

Gyasi: Do you have any questions for me?

Ridl: Nope. Just enormous gratitude for what you are doing and for your intelligence, which shines in your questions. And a wish for all that can be good to arrive again and again.

Keith Taylor has authored or edited some fifteen books and chapbooks, including his most recent small collection, *Fidelities* (Alice Greene and Co., 2015). His last full-length collection was *If the World Becomes So Bright* (Wayne State University Press, 2009). He has also co-edited several collections of fiction and non-fiction, including a recent collection of contemporary Michigan ghost stories. His poems, stories, reviews, and translations have appeared widely in North America and in Europe. He has received fellowships from the National Endowment for the Arts and the Michigan Council for Arts and Cultural Affairs. He teaches at the University of Michigan where he also serves as Associate Editor of *Michigan Quarterly Review* and director of the Bear River Writers' Conference.

Gyasi: You were born in 1952 in British Columbia but spent your childhood in Alberta and Indiana. My question is, what accounted for the move to Alberta and Indiana?

Taylor: Oh, I was very young. Maybe 11 years old. My father got a new job teaching at a small religious college in Indiana. We moved. Years later all of my family moved back to the west, but I stayed in Michigan.

Gyasi: Your name is often associated with Canada and America. Could you explain why this is so?

Taylor: I have tried to make a distinction that some people do not feel is a difference. I say I am an American writer (most of my influences have been American; I live in the States and am shaped by the demands of this culture and this political environment), but I remain a Canadian citizen and only a Canadian. It does seem clear to me that Canadian literature is a different thing than American literature, although I am not sure I can articulate that difference yet. Margaret Atwood has made the case that American literature focuses on conquering or being conquered, but Canadian literature focuses on surviving or not surviving. It's an interesting idea.

Gyasi: Besides being a poet and professor, you're also a translator. How many languages do you speak and which of them do you feel more inclined to?

Taylor: I know French better than any other language, but I worked quite hard in middle-age learning at least some Modern Greek. The only book of translations I've published is from Greek (*Battered Guitars: The Poetry and Prose of Kostas Karyotakis*, with William W. Reader). I can make my way through Latin and Spanish, but they are difficult for me.

Gyasi: Among the many jobs you've been engaged in are a house painter and a freight handler. Could you narrate how you earned a living as a house painter?

Taylor: I started painting houses when I was 12, shortly after my family first moved to the States. My father was very involved in the religious life, and we had very little money. As I got older and wanted to travel and buy books and write poems, working as a house painter fit my schedule. I could do it anywhere and I could do it when I wanted to. If I needed to stop and take a nap or read a book, I could. Of course, I had only myself to support, so it was almost ideal. I painted my last house when I was 27, so that means I did it on and off for 15 years.

Gyasi: You also worked at Shaman Drum, a leading independent bookstore for twenty years. What accounted for the long years you worked there?

Taylor: I worked at Shaman Drum for 10 years, and in other bookshops before that. It was a great job for me, as I think it has been for many writers over the centuries. I was around books all day, and I could talk to customers and my co-workers about them. Everyday was an education in the bookshop—and it was a broad education. Literature, history, philosophy, the sciences. Children's books and art books. Everything. Teaching has better vacations, but working in a bookshop might be better for a writer.

Gyasi: Your poems have appeared in many journals including *The Los Angeles Times*, *The Ann Arbor Observer*, *Michigan Quarterly Review*, *The Detroit Free Press*, and a host of others. Have you ever been rejected for your work?

Taylor: Oh, Geosi, I was rejected hundreds of times! I still get rejected regularly. I even get rejected by journals that solicit work! It is in the nature of what we do. I try not to let it depress me.

Gyasi: As a professor in the creative writing program at University of Michigan, do you think it is worth it for a budding writer to study writing?

Taylor: Absolutely. Young writers need to take the time to do the work and do the reading that shapes the work. Studying the process in a university setting helps focus the mind. But it is certainly not the only way of becoming a writer. Perhaps the school of the streets might lead to more interesting writing, or perhaps it may simply lead to an early death.

Gyasi: How did you come to write "Sea and Rain: Lake Michigan"?

Taylor: At the University of Michigan Museum of Art, which is right next to the building where I work and where I go often to unwind, there is a lovely painting by Whistler called *Sea and Rain*. There is a very ill-defined figure that looks very hazy in the left foreground. People have often referred to the figure as someone fading away. I see him as important to the painting. He defines it. And in my imagination, I have the recurring image of a dancer at water's edge. She too provides focus. Could I pack all of that into 9 lines? I'm not sure I succeeded.

Gyasi: Is *Learning to Dance* your first poetry collection?

Taylor: Yes, it is. It is a chapbook that was published by a small press here in Ann

Arbor that existed long enough to publish three little books.

Gyasi: The sound of your book *Weather Report* is quite interesting. What inspired it?

Taylor: I have kept a journal for many years, indeed for most of my life. Sometimes I wonder if I'm doing anything other than simply recording the weather in it (which is, by the way, the kind of thing my farmer-ancestors did more than a century ago). Of course, I think the weather is important. So when I put that tiny collection together 25 years ago (or more), I used that as a title. It is also the title of a poem in that collection, which was a kind of political protest poem, too, so that was part of it.

Gyasi: Do you mind telling us about your book *If the World Becomes So Bright*?

Taylor: To date, this is my favorite of my books. There is work I like in others, but as a whole book, this is my favorite. It includes many of the poems I wrote when my daughter was very young, when it was more difficult to find the time to write poems, and they are meaningful to me. It was also the place where I tried almost explicitly to write about my connection to the natural world. This is central to my life as a writer—the effort to find the words to reconnect to the natural world. That process is clearest, right now, in this book.

Gyasi: What is the biggest motivation for why you write?

Taylor: It's odd, Geosi, but at some point—now a point quite a ways in the past—this became the way I am, the way I define myself to myself. I can't imagine not writing now. I'm certainly not as prolific as some people, and perhaps I am a bit unfaithful to "the habit of art," at least on a daily level, but I can't go more than a couple of days without doing something that engages me with the search for words. If I weren't trying to write something, I'm sure I would lose my sense of myself. I really don't have a choice about it anymore.

Gyasi: As a well accomplished poet yourself, I'm not sure if it is worthy to ask if there are any writers you admire?

Taylor: Absolutely, although I read widely and enjoy many different kinds of writers. As a poet, I have been most moved by Americans James Wright, William Carlos Williams, Denise Levertov, and Philip Levine. More internationally I have been absorbed by the modern Greek poets, particularly Cavafy, of course, and by Kostas Karyotakis, whom I spent a decade translating. French poets have been important to me, particularly the exquisite miniaturist, Jean Follain. In prose I have been most involved with Barry Lopez and, of course, Ernest Hemingway. Canadians Margaret Atwood and Michael Ondaatje have been very instructive as examples of poets who have moved into prose in very interesting ways.

Gyasi: Could you share with us the work you do as the Director of the Bear River Writers' Conference?

Taylor: I have tried to keep this conference going, and so far I've been able to do it for fifteen years. The biggest problem with this kind of thing is always finding the money to attract the best writers I can as teachers while not making it too expensive for the attendees. So far, I've been able to juggle that, but the search for money is always going on and does get tiring.

Gyasi: Among all the books you've written, which one is your favorite?

Taylor: Right now *If the World Becomes So Bright* is my favorite. The next full length collection of poems that I'm working on now, which doesn't have the right title yet, will definitely be my favorite when it comes out, but I'm not sure when that will be.

Gyasi: Do you see yourself writing more poetry books? When do you hope to retire from writing?

Taylor: I will retire from teaching, even in the next three or four years, but I can't even imagine stopping to write. If I can keep my wits about me, I hope to write up to the day before they lay me down for the final time.

Gyasi: Do you belong to any group of writers?

Taylor: I was involved with a bi-weekly writing group for a decade back when I was in my thirties. It was a very helpful group, and I probably got three books out of it. I had to stop because I was imagining that small group as my only readers. Sometimes I still miss those meetings.

More generally I am associated by others with different groups or categories of writers: nature writers, Great Lakes writers, Michigan writers, Ann Arbor writers, University of Michigan writers. Those are all "groups" that have been important to me and that I am proud to acknowledge, even if I sometimes bristle at the regional dismissal that can come by being associated with them.

Gyasi: Do you want readers to like your poems?

Taylor: Yes, I would like readers to engage with my poems as deeply as I have engaged with some poems by other people. On the other hand, if I were told I would never have another reader of any poem I wrote, I would probably still keep at it. Like I said before, I really don't have a choice anymore.

Gyasi: I just can't end the interview without you asking me any question you want?

Taylor: I know from your web site that you are a West African writer most interested in fiction. Yet you have also been very generous to contemporary American poets, some of us not very well known in the larger world. I often worry that we are far too "culture bound" and insular in our attitudes to find international readers. I'm very curious how you managed to connect with the contemporary American poetry scene and what you really think of it.

Gyasi: When I first started blogging, I wanted to concentrate mainly on African books and writers. However, with time, I realized that the majority of visitors to my blog were Americans and a few from other continents. So I found it worthwhile to research into American poetry. The American magazine *Rattle* was instrumental in connecting me with contemporary American poetry. I am not sure if there's anything to add beyond what you think about American poetry; I could possibly use a preferable synonym "parochial" in place of "insular" in describing how I see the contemporary American poetry scene.

Cecilia Woloch is a poet, writer, teacher, and traveler based in Los Angeles but "on the road" across the U.S. and Europe six months each year. She has published essays, reviews, and six award-winning collections of poems—most recently *Earth* (Two Sylvias Press, 2015) and *Carpathia* (BOA Editions, 2009). Her second collection, *Tsigan: The Gypsy Poem*, was published in French translation (*Tzigane, le poème, Gitan*, Scribe-l'Harmattan, 2014) and has been adapted for multi-media performances in the U.S. and Europe. Woloch is also the author of *Narcissus* (Tupelo Press, 2008), *Late* (BOA Editions), and *Sacrifice* (Cahuenga Press, 1997/Tebot Bach, 2006). Her honors include fellowships from the National Endowment for the Arts, the California Arts Council, Chateau de La Napoule Retreat for Artists, and the Isaac W. Bernheim Foundation. She has been awarded the Indiana Review Poetry Prize and the New Ohio Review Poetry Prize. She collaborates regularly with musicians, dancers, visual artists, theater artists, and filmmakers, and conducts workshops for writers around the world. The founding director of Summer Poetry in Idyllwild, The Istanbul Poetry Workshop, and The Paris Poetry Workshop, she has also served on the faculties of a number of graduate and undergraduate creative writing programs. Her new novel, *Sur la Route,* will be published by Quale Press.

Gyasi: You're a poet, writer, teacher, and traveler. How do you manage to combine all?

Woloch: Well, these things are so inter-related in my life that I don't know how I'd separate them. My teaching and travel feed my writing; my writing—my familiarity with the writing process and with the craft and with literature—is what qualifies and enables me to teach others to write; my teaching takes me all over the world; my travels provide me with experiences and challenges that feed into and enrich my writing.

Gyasi: Could you tell us what you actually do as a traveler?

Woloch: Hmm, I'm not sure I understand what you mean by "actually do." I get on planes, trains, buses and go places. I generally prefer to spend a substantial amount of time in any place I go—anywhere from a few weeks to a few months—to establish a more or less "normal" life for myself in that place, and a community, if only temporarily. Since I return to the same places pretty regularly, I arrive in those places already having certain things in place, certain relationships and routines, ready to slip into that particular life. Wherever I go, I do many of the same things—I read, I write, I talk to people, I walk around, and I usually also give readings and lead workshops.

Gyasi: At what point in your life did you see yourself as a writer?

Woloch: I remember always wanting to write, wanting to craft stories and tell stories, and also wanting a sort of secret life that I felt I could have in imagination and in language. I started keeping a journal—not as a diary but as a writer's journal—when I was in high school, because my creative writing teacher insisted her students do that. I've never lost that habit. My first poems were published when I was in college. I think I wrote what felt to me like my first 'real' poem when

I was nineteen. It won a prize from the Kentucky Arts Council and my name was in the newspaper. So I might have started to see myself as a writer at that moment—as a "real" writer, if that's even possible for any writer. And my parents saw that newspaper article—they saw it before I'd even had a chance to tell them I won the prize—and I think they started then to see me as a writer, too, which helped me to see myself that way.

Gyasi: You were born in Pittsburgh, Pennsylvania, and grew up in rural Kentucky. Do you have any fond memories about your childhood?

Woloch: I have both very fond and very unhappy childhood memories. The fond memories center around my family and extended family—I was born into a large, wild, closely-knit tribe—and my unhappy memories have mostly to do with people outside the family circle, and with institutions such as school and church. But when my family moved from Pittsburgh to rural Kentucky, it was like when Dorothy goes over the rainbow in *The Wizard of Oz*: the world went from black-and-white to color. I felt more accepted in Kentucky. I was happier in school and had more friends. We built a big house out in the country. I think my whole family was happier, though life in the country was in some ways harder.

Gyasi: You are the author of six acclaimed collections of poetry. Do you feel you've written enough books?

Woloch: There are definitely at least a few more books I want to write, though not because I feel it's important to have written any certain number of books. I love the writing process and hope to write for the rest of my life. There are also stories I still want to tell. I've just published a novel and I'm working on a long nonfiction project in prose, something I've been working on for a decade now; so I'm feeling more drawn to writing prose these days. I also feel that I've now served a fairly long apprenticeship as a writer of prose.

Gyasi: Take us through how you wrote *Sacrifice*.

Woloch: *Sacrifice* collected poems I'd been writing for ten or fifteen years; it was my first collection, and wasn't published until I was forty years old—which, really, seemed about right to me. I needed that time to mature as a poet, and for the poems to mature. I think some younger poets are in too big a hurry to publish these days. Learning to revise effectively was difficult for me; you really have to understand and respect your own process to revise effectively, and also to have gained a certain mastery of the tools of craft—how grammar and syntax work, and line breaks, and how its music moves a poem forward—without losing touch with the mystery and magic of the poem. Most of the poems in *Sacrifice* were critiqued in a workshop led by Holly Prado, who also advised me when it came to putting together the manuscript, as did the poet Bill Mohr. At that point, it was mostly a matter of finding a shape that would hold the poems I'd already written, discovering the ways they related to one another, and putting them into a sequence that created a kind of narrative arc.

Gyasi: What inspired your book *Narcissus*?

Woloch: Here again, I'd been writing the poems that went into the manuscript over a number of years, so it was a matter of shaping them into some kind of whole. To be honest, I heard about a chapbook contest and wanted to submit a manuscript, so I looked at the poems I had that seemed finished and started to weave them together. Most of the poems were inspired—if "inspired" is the right word—by the shattering of a relationship and the after-effects of that, the shattering of some illusions about romantic love and desire, and moving past that shattering, reassembling a sense of self and reemerging into a more "real" kind of love.

Gyasi: How do you often start a poem?

Woloch: Almost all of my poems begin in my journal—that is, they begin as journal entries, which are often experiments in free-writing triggered by an image or phrase or a sort of melody I'm beginning to hear in my head. It may be a memory or image that leads me into the poem, or it may be language itself, some mysterious combination of words that I want to follow to find out what they're going to say.

Gyasi: Do you ever get writer's block?

Woloch: Not really, because I have such a bad writing habit—I mean, by that, that I write in my journal very habitually, maybe a little obsessively. So I'm always getting something down in language, even if it's just a recounting of the day's events, or a random memory. There are times, of course, when I feel as if the writing isn't going anywhere, isn't moving—maybe that's a kind of being "blocked"—and while that's frustrating, I try to take the long view and remind myself that it's just a phase. Also, I've learned that, sometimes, when I think I'm not writing, or that I'm just spinning my wheels, I may actually be getting some productive writing done. Of course the opposite is also true: sometimes I think I'm on some kind of roll or have had a kind of breakthrough and written something good, only to discover that's not the case.

Gyasi: How long did it take you to write *Earth*?

Woloch: It depends on how you calculate. One of the poems in *Earth* is a poem I began to write in 1994, twenty years ago. Other poems in the book were written much more quickly and recently. Putting the manuscript together didn't take that long. Maybe you're asking these questions about "how long" it's taken to write a book of poems because some poets work with a notion in mind that they're writing poems for a particular book, that they're in the process of writing a book of poems. For the most part, I work on individual poems and work poem by poem, then I try to see where I've been, where the poems have taken me, and make a kind of map.

Gyasi: How different is teaching from writing?

Woloch: Teaching and writing are very similar, at least for me, in that I do my best work as a teacher and as a writer when I work intuitively. It's not that I don't plan my classes and workshops—I do—but that I try to listen to students' work in the same way I try to listen to my own, to find out where the poem wants to go, where the power and magic lie, and to apply the tools of craft in the service of that. I try to teach my students to pay attention—to the world around them, to their own inner urgencies, to the ways that language works—and that's also what I'm trying, always, to teach myself.

Gyasi: Do you know who reads your work?

Woloch: Well, I know who some of the people are who read my work—friends and colleagues and students and family members. But there are always surprises, too, like when I find out that someone I've never met, or haven't seen in decades, has been reading my poems and finds in them something that moves her or him in a very personal way.

Gyasi: What has been your greatest challenge as a writer?

Woloch: Sitting still. That's getting easier as I get older. But really, so much of being a writer is being able to sit down and sit still long enough to get something down, to be able to concentrate and to be patient.

Gyasi: You seem to have won prizes for most of your books published. How much value do you place on awards and prizes?

Woloch: Prizes and accolades are nice, but I don't think they're that important, or necessarily indicative of the quality of the work or its value to the world. We all know that certain prizes are decided in advance, that there are cliques, that there is corruption, even in the world of poetry, though one hopes that's the exception and not the rule. Prizes and the kind of status they confer matter some if you're trying to climb the corporate ladder of academia, of course, and they might help when it comes to getting teaching gigs and such. But I've read unpublished or self-published work that I've found more moving and well-crafted than work that's been awarded "major" prizes, so I don't set much store by such things, especially as a reader.

Gyasi: Did you struggle coming up with a title for your book *Carpathia*?

Woloch: I always struggle to come up with titles. I think I'm just no good at titles, which is why I try to keep them very simple, so as not to embarrass myself. I was desperate for a title for the collection that ended up being called *Carpathia*, and it was my friend Collin Kelly (another poet) who read the manuscript and came up with the title. I knew as soon as he suggested it that it was right. And once I had the title to work with, it helped me to finalize the manuscript, so I owe a big debt to Collin.

Gyasi: Do you feel fulfilled as a writer?

Woloch: Well, today I'm feeling hugely fulfilled, because yesterday was the "launch" of my novel, *Sur la Route*, and it was a very successful launch and a very happy day in celebration of something I didn't ever really believe I could do! I wrote the first draft of that book 20 years ago, and put it "back in the drawer" so many times. So having it come out now is really a wonderful surprise. And the lesson is that patience can pay off, just keep doing your work, give it time; this isn't a sprint, after all.

Gyasi: What do you regard as your greatest achievement as a writer?

Woloch: Well, I hope my greatest achievement as a writer will be my next book—the book I've been working on for at least a decade and think of as my true life's work. But what I feel is my greatest achievement thus far—or the book I'm most proud of—is my second book, *Tsigan: The Gypsy Poem*. It's a long poem that, when I was writing it, I thought wouldn't be of interest to anyone but myself and my family, so I was writing it for us. It was published in a small edition by Cahuenga Press, a small cooperative press in Los Angeles. But it turns out that that little book has a life of its own, and wings. It's shown up in places I never expected it to go, all over the world. The book has been included in exhibitions in Europe. The text has been used in multi-media performances and film. It was translated and published in French in 2014 and, this past January, sections of the text were translated into Polish for a bilingual, multi-media performance at the Museum of the History of Polish Jews in Warsaw. I'm immensely proud and, really, amazed by the response to it. It was also my mother's "favorite" of the books I'd published before she died, and that's gold to me.

Gyasi: What are you currently working on?

Woloch: I guess I'm working on several things at the same time, always, even when I think I'm only doing one thing. (Or sometimes I think I'm working on one thing, and it turns out that I've been working on another thing!) Anyway, the main focus of my writing for the past ten years has been a long work in narrative and lyrical prose, a kind of travel memoir and family history and geopolitical murder mystery. It centers on my paternal grandmother, who was "disappeared" before I was born. I think I wasn't prepared for all the research I've had to do to get the material for this book. It's been pretty all-consuming for the past ten years. But it's the book I think I was born to write, if there's any such thing as being born to write anything, and the reason I became a writer, in the first place—so that I could tell this story.

Gyasi: Do you have a specific audience you write for?

Woloch: No, not at all. I think it's dangerous to write for an audience. I think it can make a writer self-conscious in all the wrong ways. I think if you write what you feel most deeply compelled to write, for yourself, and write as best you can, your writing stands a chance of touching people you never dreamed of touching. I like what Cyril Connelly said, "Better to write for yourself and have no audience than to write for an audience and have no self." That said, I strive to be as clear as I can be in my writing; because, while I honor mystery and love the mysteriousness of poetry, I hate the arrogance and cowardice of willful obscurity and don't want to keep anyone out of my poems. One of the happiest moments in my life as a writer was the night I walked through the screen door of my mother's house and came upon my oldest sister, a beautician, reading my book, *Tsigan: The Gyspy Poem*, out loud to my mother and teenaged niece. When I started to say something, my mother shushed me and said, "We're listening to this." I don't think it gets much better than that.

Gyasi: Do you write on a computer or notebook?

Woloch: Both. First drafts are mostly written by hand, often in my journal, and then typed into the computer, but I go back and forth between the two modes.

Gyasi: What do you think of Natasha Trethewey's review of your book: "This is a gorgeous book by a poet who is passionately alive in the world."

Woloch: I'm deeply flattered, of course, and I hope it's true.

David James has published three books and five chapbooks. More than thirty of his one-act plays have been produced from New York to California, including five of them off-Broadway. He earned his B.A. from Western Michigan University, his M.A. from Central Michigan University, and his doctorate from Wayne State University. He teaches writing full-time at Oakland Community College in Michigan.

Gyasi: Beginning, you teach for Oakland Community College. How do you manage your time between teaching and writing?

James: It's tough, as always. For 21 years, I worked as a director of admissions and dean of academics for three colleges and I still found time to write. As a faculty for the last thirteen years, I feel like I have more free time than I did as an administrator. I have to make time to write. Sometimes it happens as a reward after grading a group of papers. The old adage says we find the time to do the things we really want to do. I really want to write.

In between teaching full-time, reading and grading student work, caring for my aging parents, spending time with my family, I'm always trying to carve out time to find poems and plays in my daily life.

Gyasi: Do you believe the opinion that teachers are great writers?

James: I've had great teachers who were great writers (Stu Dybek, John Woods, Herb Scott) and I've had great teachers who were not great writers. I don't think writers are, by nature, better teachers. Teaching is one of the most difficult tasks possible and it takes inspiration, motivation, skill. Writers can bring personal experiences into the classroom that can certainly help students understand the writing process, but that alone does not make them better teachers.

Gyasi: What do you do when in the middle of teaching you get an idea for a story?

James: I simply write a note to myself. It takes ten to twenty seconds and is not a problem.

Gyasi: Do you have any literary influences?

James: All writers have literary influences, whether they admit to them or not. My influences are varied and changing. My early influences are the poets Galway Kinnell, Pablo Neruda, Richard Hugo, Anne Sexton, James Wright, Richard Shelton, Ira Sadoff. More recently, I find my work being influenced by James Tate, Wendell Berry, Billy Collins, Sharon Olds, and probably every poet I read. In fact, every great poem I read, regardless of who wrote it, influences me, and I'm so thankful for that.

Gyasi: Do you think of yourself as a poet or writer? Can you distinguish between the two?

James: I see myself primarily as a poet since I've written that the longest. But I also write fiction and plays and essays. All writing feeds on itself, so any manipulation of language strengthens my skills as a poet. What you call yourself, a writer or poet, is inconsequential: it's what you write that counts.

Gyasi: Could you describe your beginnings as a writer?

James: I wrote my first despairing love poem as a 10th grader to an ex-cheerleader girlfriend. Once in college, though, I was planning to be a physicist and scientist. I took one creative writing course in my freshman year and decided that was the route for me. Ever since, I've been trying to learn how to write.

Gyasi: Speaking of your recent publication in *Rattle*, you wrote that, "writing poems, and maybe all writing, is a spiritual activity." Could you elaborate on this statement?

James: If you're a spiritual person, you believe in something you cannot see or know. You take that "leap of faith" into the darkness and believe someone will catch you, eventually. A writer mirrors that process. He cannot see or touch his imagination or intuition: he must trust that it will lead him somewhere. He begins with an urge or an image and starts writing with the faith that his imagination will lead him to a discovery of sorts. Writers travel into the unknown the way prophets tap into the spirit.

Gyasi: Your book *She Dances Like Mussolini* won the 2010 Next Generation Indie Poetry Award. What is it about this book that impresses you?

James: The fact that it took me 25 years to publish this second book after my first book in 1984. I love the humor and craziness in *She Dances Like Mussolini*. I admire Russell Edson, Billy Collins, and James Tate, all writers with a funny bone, and like to think my book is a minor tribute to their work and influence.

Gyasi: Is there more to the title of your book *A Heart Out of this World* than what readers encounter as the content of the book?

James: The title is a metaphor for poetry—"beating a heart out of this world." That's what I try to do in writing: find the 'heart' of the matter and shine a little light on it. My first book, like all of my books, is an eclectic collection. I have difficulty following a theme or motif, so my poems go all over the place.

Gyasi: You've had quite a number of your plays produced off-off-Broadway, in Massachusetts, and in Michigan. Do you think plays have more audience than poetry?

James: I started writing plays because I was interested in the genre and because I thought I might have an audience. The idea that someone else (actors) would say my lines instead of me was intriguing. The idea that people would attend a play was also an incentive. So far, I have to admit that my plays have provided me with joy beyond compare. When I'm in the audience, watching my play with everyone else, it's an out-of-body experience. It's hard to believe I wrote the piece. I tell people that writing a play is like giving birth. After writing, you give your baby to the director and actors, and they make it walk.

Gyasi: Is poetry hard to write?

James: No, poetry isn't hard to write. In fact, anyone can do it. But good poetry is very hard to write, and great poetry is nearly impossible. I like John Ciardi's quote: "Failure is the writer's only real business. The one hope is for a better and better failure." The longer I write, the closer I'm getting to creating a better failure.

Gyasi: This may sound silly to ask, but how much money do you make from writing?

James: In 40 years of writing and publishing, I can account for about $4,000 directly from poetry (or $100 per year). Few people do this work for money. One writes poetry out of a passion and urge and pleasure that can't be measured by conventional methods.

On the other hand, I'd have to say my publication credits have helped me receive every academic position in my career, so it's paid off in that way.

Gyasi: What do you do when you receive unfavorable reviews?

James: I have to admit I'm not "big or famous" enough of a writer to merit negative reviews. I'd appreciate ANY review of my work. I'm one of the thousands of poets in the U.S. writing in relative obscurity, plodding along, publishing here and there, coming out with an occasional small book from an independent press, working a full-time job to make ends meet.

Gyasi: What are you working on right now?

James: Speaking of publishing, my third book, *My Torn Dance Card*, is forthcoming in spring 2015 from FCNI Press, a new start-up press in Michigan. This is a book of poems about aging, loss, and mortality—poems in stark contrast from the poems in my second book.

Gyasi: Do you come from a family of readers? What books did you read growing up?

James: I did not come from a family of readers, but from a family who valued education. On both sides of my extended family, I was only the second person to attend college. The trickle down effect of this is amazing. Three of my four siblings have degrees and all thirteen of our collective children either have degrees or attended college.

Gyasi: You probably have something to say to end the interview.

James: I want to thank Geosi for asking me to do this interview. I want to thank all of the people who read and value poetry. And I especially want to thank all of those who write poetry. It's one of those sacred human acts, like smiling or hugging someone that, in its own small way, makes the world a better place.

Andrew Blackman is the author of the novel *On the Holloway Road* (Legend Press, 2009), which won the Luke Bitmead Writer's Bursary and was shortlisted for the Dundee International Book Prize.

His second novel, *A Virtual Love*, (Legend Press, 2013) deals with identity in the age of social networking.

Blackman has lived in London, Barbados, and New York. His work has been published in *Monthly Review*, the *Cincinnati Post, Pittsburgh Post-Gazette, Seattle Times,* and a host of others.

Gyasi: The first time I heard your name and nationality I was a bit confused. Why Blackman? On a lighter note, which part of you is black?

Blackman: This question made me laugh! I don't know the exact origin, but apparently Blackman is an Old English name meaning someone with dark hair or dark skin. It does cause confusion sometimes!

Gyasi: You attended some of the best well-known schools in the United Kingdom: Dulwich and Oxford. Did you know at the time that you were being prepared to be a writer?

Blackman: I did want to be a writer at that time, but it felt like an impossible dream. We were being prepared for high-paying, high-status jobs, and creativity was not on the curriculum. So I wrote a bit in my spare time, but I didn't consider the possibility that I could do it as a career.

Gyasi: At a point in your life, you quit the highly paid corporate banking job to become a writer. For Christ's sake, why would you do that?

Blackman: It always felt dishonest to me, and I hated who I was becoming. Day to day it was not too bad, but when I thought about doing it for the rest of my life, I felt as if I'd made a terrible mistake. Things reached a head when I was working on Wall Street and saw the World Trade Center buildings collapse just down the road from my office. I walked home covered in the ash of several thousand dead people, and decided that I didn't want to die doing something I hated.

Gyasi: Is your writing career paying the bills? Are you satisfied as a writer? Do you ever regret quitting the banking job?

Blackman: Just about! It's a constant struggle to pay the bills, especially because my wife is an artist so her income is pretty erratic as well. I don't make a full living just from my novels, but when I add in short stories, freelance writing, and journalism, I can just about cobble together enough to get through the month. We have to be very frugal and can't do a lot of the things we used to do when I was a corporate banker, but I don't ever regret it. I'm so much happier now, and am doing what I wanted to do with my life.

Gyasi: You enrolled at Columbia University's Journalism School. Do you see any influences of your journalistic background in your writing?

Blackman: Yes, it was great training. First at university and then as a reporter for *The Wall Street Journal*, I learned how to write quickly, how to write under pressure, how to write when I didn't feel like writing, how to grab readers' attention quickly and then fight paragraph by paragraph to stop them from drifting away to something else, how to accept seeing my writing ripped apart by editors, and how to put readers' needs above my own at all times. I also learned a lot about editing by seeing what experienced editors did to my writing. I saw that a piece can almost always be made better by deleting rather than adding words.

Gyasi: You were the first winner for the Luke Bitmead Award in 2008. As a writer, do you ever experience depression?

Blackman: I often experience despair and hopelessness, and struggle to keep writing and putting myself out into the world. But I hesitate to use the word 'depression,' because clinical depression is something very different from day-to-day woes. I've never got close to what Luke Bitmead experienced, being hospitalized several times and eventually committing suicide at a very young age. Since winning the award, I've got to know Luke's mother, and learned more about his life, and I'm grateful never to have experienced those depths of depression myself.

Gyasi: How much of an impact did your winning of the Luke Bitmead Award have on your writing career?

Blackman: A huge impact. Before that, I didn't really have a writing career! I'd had one short story published, and that was it. Winning gave me a £2,500 cheque and a publishing deal, which was just a massive break for me. It felt as if my life had changed overnight. Six months later, *On the Holloway Road* came out, and the 'impossible dream' of being a writer had come true. I also got an agent on the back of that, and had the confidence and the credibility to take my writing career seriously. Now I have a second novel published, and feel as if I am on my way. None of it would have been possible without the Luke Bitmead Award. Perhaps I'd have found another way, but I just don't know—it's so competitive, and there are many talented writers who never get a publishing contract.

Gyasi: From *On the Holloway Road* to *A Virtual Love*, a gap of four years between the two books! Why that long?

Blackman: I wrote *On the Holloway Road* very quickly—I completed the first draft in a month. But *A Virtual Love* is quite a different book, with a more complex plot, and I needed to take more time over it to get it right. My agent was very helpful with suggesting changes at various stages, and so the rewrites took time. And then there's the simple fact that the publishing cycle is quite slow: I signed the contract with Legend Press a year ago, but the book only came out at the beginning of this month!

Gyasi: Much of *A Virtual Love* takes place online. How obsessed are you with social media in this modern age of Internet?

Blackman: I think it's a very interesting time. Whenever human beings create a new technology, that technology also shapes us in ways we don't always realize, and the Internet is no different. I'm interested in the profiles that we create online and how they differ from our real selves. I find that they're often more like advertisements for ourselves, editing out all the boring or embarrassing stuff and presenting an idealized version for public consumption. And because everyone else is doing this too, it's easy to feel inadequate or anxious about how people view you, and how many friends or followers you have. Some of the ways we behave online are simply extensions of what we've always done, but some I think are quite new.

Gyasi: I read online that you wrote the last chapter of *A Virtual Love* in a cemetery. How much does place/environment factor into your writings?

Blackman: Yes, that's true! Usually I am more boring and simply write at my desk, but sometimes I like to mix things up. It was a bright spring day, and I had gone out around north London looking for a café to write in, but came across a beautiful old Victorian cemetery and went for a walk. Then I found ideas coming into my head, and I sat on a log with a notebook and pen and the whole chapter just came to me. The environment I was writing in gave the chapter a mournful, contemplative tone, which is exactly what I was looking for.

Gyasi: You've dabbled in several kinds of jobs: banking, journalism, writing, and blogging. Did your life as a blogger influence you to create a Jeff Brennan who was a reclusive famous blogger?

Blackman: Ah, I wish blogging was a job, but I haven't made any money from it! I started my site as a place to write book reviews—I have a terrible memory, and wanted to keep a record of the books I'd read, as well as perhaps understand them better by analyzing them as I wrote the review. I still do book reviews, but have branched out to talk about the writing process and literary events, and to give updates on my latest writing. My own blog didn't really play a part in creating Jeff Brennan. My fictional character's blog is much more popular than my own, for one thing! And he's a political blogger too. So a lot of the things he experiences are quite different. My own blogging life has been much more pleasant and less dramatic than his.

Gyasi: Besides London, you've lived in Barbados and New York. Could you discuss any striking experiences in these places?

Blackman: In Barbados I was quite struck by the effects of tourism. Essentially the main national industry is the production of a fantasy for foreign tourists. The tourists want a tropical island paradise, and so that's what they get. It's so important for the economy that the needs of local people often seem secondary to the needs of the visitors from Europe and North America. In the US and UK I have also noticed that fantasy plays a large part in the construction of national identity, but at least it's the fantasies of the country's own citizens, not those of outsiders. Barbados is a tiny island that was left with a lot of problems after centuries of British colonialism, so it's remarkable how far it's come in the short period of independence, but there have been significant costs to that rapid development as well.

Stephen Kampa was born in Missoula, Montana, in 1981 and grew up in Daytona Beach, Florida. He received a BA in English Literature from Carleton College and an MFA in Poetry from the Johns Hopkins University. His first book, *Cracks in the Invisible*, won the 2010 Hollis Summers Poetry Prize and the 2011 Gold Medal in Poetry from the Florida Book Awards. His poems have also been awarded the Theodore Roethke Prize, first place in the *River Styx* International Poetry Contest, and two Pushcart nominations. His second book, *Bachelor Pad*, appeared this spring from The Waywiser Press. He currently divides his time between teaching poetry at Flagler College in St. Augustine, Florida, and working as a musician.

Gyasi: For some fifteen years, you've been playing the harmonica. How did you start playing?

Kampa: When I was a teenager, I lived in Brazil for a year as an exchange student. A big part of the culture, or at least of my host family's life, was music: I can remember us visiting the family farm in Perdões, Minas Gerais, and gathering on the porch to sing while my host uncle strummed an acoustic guitar. I also remember the time another host uncle took me aside and let me know that, judging by my porch singing, I couldn't carry a tune in a bucket. Of course, I resolved to prove him wrong, and when I returned to the United States, I happened upon a little basket of harmonicas while wandering through the local bookstore. I've never looked back except to wish the bookstore had put out a basket of pianos.

Gyasi: When did you acquire your first harmonica?

Kampa: The first was that bookstore harmonica, and I was probably sixteen years old; however, I date the beginning of my serious harmonica playing to my seventeenth birthday, when I bought myself my first *real* harmonica, a Hohner Special 20. I chose that model because my hero, John Popper, played Special 20s.

Gyasi: Which of these types do you play—the diatonic, the chromatic, or the tremolo? Could you explain your choice?

Kampa: I play diatonic harmonicas. The diatonic is generally the harmonica a person thinks of when thinking of harmonicas at all, the pocket-sized ten-hole job most commonly used in blues, rock and roll, and folk music. When Sara Bareilles plays harmonica on "Basket Case," it's a diatonic she's playing.

They're rather ingenious little instruments. At a basic level, they are *designed* to sound good because they're tuned to play in one key, so any of the notes you play will more or less fit the music as long as said music is in the key stamped on the harmonica; thus, a total beginner might sound aimless, but he won't sound out-and-out *wrong*. (Of course, that all goes right out the window if there are complex chord changes.) At a more advanced level, diatonic harmonicas are capable of great expressiveness and musical surprise, but you have to know what you're doing, and it rarely involves playing in the key stamped on the harmonica at that point. The harmonica has its own bizarre logic, which is quite interesting, but something to save for the rainiest rainy day.

I don't own any tremolo harmonicas—in fact, I'm not sure I've ever even played one—and the same could be said for the other more orchestral harmonicas: the chord harmonica, bass harmonica, octave harmonica, and so on. I do play a bit of chromatic, and although I'm hardly a virtuoso on it, I'm pleased to say that this year should see the release of an album for which I contributed some session work, including my first recorded chromatic work.

Gyasi: I've watched you play the harmonica a couple of times. From where do you get the energy to play?

Kampa: Whiskey.

That's not true, of course, or only a little. I think the answer might be *joy*. I believe artistic creation comes from a deep and abiding sense of joy in the possibilities of the medium and in the intelligence that discovers them. This runs counter to the culturally accepted stereotype of the artist as a tortured soul, a loner, an alcoholic manic-depressive who amidst the destruction and subsequent wreckage of his own life manages to create a few glittering monuments. (Kierkegaard: "What is a poet? An unhappy man who hides deep anguish in his heart, but whose lips are so formed that when the sigh and cry pass through them, it sounds like lovely music. ... And people flock around the poet and say: 'Sing again soon' ..." Notice the role of the people in that little parable.) I'd argue that even when artists are dealing with grief-riddled material—when they're singing the blues—their creative response to it is part of what makes art redemptive, if art is.

That is perhaps an elaborate answer to a straightforward question. I should add that when it comes to playing music, many things contribute to the performance: the energy and responsiveness of the crowd, the friendship and mutual admiration I share with my bandmates, and that blessed moment when one stops regretting the past and worrying about the future and simply inhabits the present moment, which is where the music is.

Gyasi: You currently front your own band, Stephen Kampa & the Pickups. Could you tell us what this band is about?

Kampa: This band is about making money. Although I enjoy music and know that it is an art form, for me it has also been a way to make a living, and where I am, one has to seek out as many opportunities as possible for making that living. As much as I enjoy my band, and as much as I have learned about music, my voice, and the challenges of being a front man and bandleader, I put together Stephen Kampa & the Pickups because I needed more gigs than I could get as a sideman. That said, I think there are some things that make the band pretty special. Obviously, at the top of the list are the first-rate musicians who have contributed their talents to the music-making. I also think that we tend to defy expectations. When people see the band is built around a harmonica player, they expect a blues band, but we actually do very little straight-ahead blues: more often, we're drawing from the soul, funk, and R&B traditions. Harmonica tends to get pigeonholed when it comes to repertoire, but there's no reason we can't do songs by Marvin Gaye, Marshall Tucker, Herbie Hancock, or the Box Tops, and we do. I like to believe that when we're playing, we're helping people reimagine how the harmonica can sound. I suppose, then, in all honesty I should say that in addition to being about making money, the band is about getting to play the music I want to play.

Gyasi: Is there any relationship between music and poetry?

Kampa: There are many, but I think the interesting analogies leave aside the question of song-writing and poetry—something Glyn Maxwell discusses concisely and persuasively in *On Poetry*— and focus instead on the relationship between an art form that has no semantic content and one that, despite the best efforts of the avant-garde, simply buzzes with semantic content. I'm particularly fascinated by the way vowel pitch affects the movement and feeling of individual lines, but that is only one example.

Gyasi: When did you first realize that you wanted to be a poet?

Kampa: I'm still not sure I want to be a poet, given all the baggage that word carries: the foppish outfits, the little twiddles of cigarette smoke, the visionary gleam. I guess I think of myself as a writer who mostly ends up writing poems, possibly because I lack the attention span to write short stories or a novel, possibly because poems afford me the kind of concentration, flexibility, associative logic, and musicality that I need to do my kind of thinking.

Gyasi: If for some fifteen years you've been playing the harmonica, how long have you been writing?

Kampa: I've been writing since I was a child, but in high school I had a teacher who sentenced me to a life of poverty by introducing me to poetry. Truth be told, I've been in her debt ever since. So, I've been writing for as long as I can remember, but I've been writing poetry for about as long as I've been playing harmonica.

Gyasi: How do you split your time as teacher, writer, and musician?

Kampa: It can be difficult. I can say with certainty that when I'm teaching, my students are my priority; in fact, this summer I've been working on an essay about teaching, love, and Theodore Roethke. On the whole, though, I'm still trying to find a balance when it comes to the time each of those roles demands, as well as a way to harmonize those parts of myself into a single coherent identity.

Gyasi: Your first book, *Cracks in the Invisible*, won the 2010 Hollis Summers Poetry Prize and the 2011 Gold Medal in Poetry from the Florida Book Awards. Your poems have also been awarded the Theodore Roethke Prize, first place in the *River Styx* International Poetry Contest, and two Pushcart nominations. Do you feel fulfilled as a writer?

Kampa: When I was a high school student, I won an award for a poem I'd written, and I got to go to Miami. There I had a bracing conversation with Mike Raymond, a writer who taught at Stetson University and whom I'd met only once. Professor Raymond looked at a small sheaf of poems I'd brought for him to read, then leaned back and said, "Stephen, when are you going to stop playing around and start writing poetry?" It was chastening; I felt taken aback, perhaps even a little humiliated, not least because I was there to accept an award for my poetry. Later, during the ceremony, I was called up to the front of a small room and given a certificate or some such, and when I got back to my seat, a woman came up to me—presumably because she'd read my poem—and said, "Thank you." That was it. She left. Mike Raymond leaned over quickly and said, "*That's* why you write." I tell this story for two reasons. First, that day was formative for me: although I may still argue with Professor Raymond about the place of play in poetry, I value that he took whatever talent I had seriously enough to challenge me to make more of it, and the moment when a woman I'd never met simply *thanked* me for a poem taught me something important. Second, I tell this story because it comes to the heart of your question: How do we as writers understand fulfillment? What is the measure of one's success?

What I tell my students is that you have to love the act of writing itself, the process, if you hope to be a writer. When it comes to publication, recognition, prizes, fame, fortune, and eventually owning your own little island empire where everyone acknowledges you are the greatest writer ever, the sad truth is that one day soon after arriving on your island, you're going to start to think it's just a little bit *small*. Anne Lamott has words of wisdom here:

"All that I know about the relationship between publication and mental health was summed up in one line of the movie *Cool Runnings*, which is about the first Jamaican bobsled team. ... The men on his team are desperate to win an Olympic medal, just as half the people in my classes are desperate to get published. But the coach says, 'If you're not enough before the gold medal, you won't be enough with it.'"

W. S. Merwin has a beautiful poem about meeting Berryman that also speaks to the issue, but with a different emphasis:

I asked how can you ever be sure
that what you write is really
any good at all and he said you can't

you can't you can never be sure
you die without knowing
whether anything you wrote was any good
if you have to be sure don't write

If, then, we can find no satisfaction in plaudits before the enormous maw of the ego, and we can't trust our own sense of whether work is any good, all that remains is the doing of the work itself. In that sense, I feel very fulfilled: I've structured my whole life around writing, and for the most part, I am grateful, knowing how lucky I am to be able to do that.

Still, I'm waiting for my island. Even a small one would do. For a while.

> Gyasi: This happened to be one of my favorite lines in *Bachelor Pad*—"He worried that he lived his whole/Life in his notebook, and he wondered why/That didn't seem so bad." How and when was the whole idea of *Bachelor Pad* conceived?

Kampa: I noticed at some point that I'd been writing a number of poems on the same themes—relationships, love, the life of the single man—and when you realize that about your own work, you've got two immediate choices: you can either work against the tendency and break through to something new, or you can acknowledge that you've got something on your mind and make a project out of it. I opted for the latter.

> Gyasi: With all honesty, which of these two do you spend most of your time on: playing the harmonica or writing poetry?

Kampa: At this point, writing. When I was a young man and learning my instrument, I practiced harmonica incessantly—hours every day—as is customary for anyone learning to play an instrument. The writing, however, has always been my priority; if I had to pick between the two, I would always choose writing. I always have, in fact. Happily, for now, I don't need to choose.

Amit Majmudar is a novelist, poet, essayist, and diagnostic nuclear radiologist (M.D.). He writes and practices in Dublin, Ohio, where he lives with his wife, twin sons, and baby daughter.

Gyasi: You practice full-time as a Diagnostic Radiologist and you are also a poet. How do you combine the two?

Majmudar: I guess the correct way to think of it is that I *split* the two, rather than combine them. I split the two roles the same way people split roles in everyday life—the way a young man can behave one way with his buddies from college, and quite another way around his parents. When I am at work, I speak and think in a medical way. When I am writing, my language and my thought patterns alter drastically. But I do not think this ability to toggle in and out of either mode is all that unique; we do it naturally in our various social roles.

Gyasi: Your approach to your poetry is quite refreshing—for instance, your "Rune Poem" has a unique style. From where did you acquire your style of writing?

Majmudar: I think I am, more than most of my contemporaries, oriented toward poetic styles of distant antiquity from a variety of cultures. I am more likely than other poets to take a bygone form or mode of poetry and try to make it work in a modern context; or rather, I am more likely to believe, in the face of all evidence to the contrary, that there is no such thing as a historically antiquated poetic form or mode, only poets inadequate to meet their challenges.

Gyasi: Can a writer learn style?

Majmudar: A writer can learn not to make obvious mistakes. That is a crucial part of style. But it is, alas, also a form of caution. And caution never accomplished anything of worth in literature. This paradox, coupled with the institutionalization of the teaching of writing, accounts for the unprecedentedly high level of technical competence in American writing—and for its stubbornly unchanged percentage of dross.

Gyasi: When did you first start writing?

Majmudar: In one of my past lives.

Gyasi: When you're writing a book, do you look back on your previous works?

Majmudar: With disgust and contempt.

Gyasi: Your poetry and prose have been published in a number of venues including *The New Yorker*, *The New York Times*, *The Best American Poetry*, *The Atlantic Monthly*, *Granta*, and other places. What is the best response you've ever received from a reader?

Majmudar: I once wrote a novel called *The Abundance*, and a woman wrote me from New England, and her story was, uncannily, almost identical to the fictional one I created. Even her voice, in the email, was similar. It was like hearing from the character herself.

Gyasi: Have you ever received a negative review? How do you react to negative reviews?

Majmudar: The first review I ever got as a poet, in a UK journal called *The Dark Horse*, and the first review I ever got as a novelist, in *Publishers Weekly*, were both very negative. I reacted to them with a mixture of disbelief and anger; I felt that I had seen far inferior writing routinely praised to the skies, and I was frankly astonished that mine should be singled out for insult. I promptly used that anger to fuel more writing.

Gyasi: You are a blogger for *The Kenyon Review*. Do you think there is a relationship between blogging and writing?

Majmudar: It is a form that has existed for centuries, I suspect, just never in public; the blog is a sort of diary or notebook, only opened to the world. In a hundred years, I predict, one or two blogs from our time will have been elevated to literary status; in the manner of the diary of Samuel Pepys, or the notebooks of Dostoevsky.

Gyasi: How much emphasis do you place on rhyme? I am actually thinking of your poem "Pattern and Snarl."

Majmudar: I think it is good for what it is good for, and not good for everything. It is unnecessary; but so is every other kind of fun.

Gyasi: How much of your writing comes from your own personal experiences?

Majmudar: 23.3%.

Gyasi: What do you mostly read?

Majmudar: I mostly read the beginning of anything at all, and then get bored and abandon it. I listen to audiobooks more than I read; I listen to books during my work commute. Only great poetry keeps me awake. Reading prose puts me to sleep within a few pages; I simply operate on too great a sleep deficit to sustain wakefulness for more than a couple of pages of low-intensity or diffuse writing. My desert-island reading list would consist of classical heroic epics in translation, the *Bhagavad-Gita*, McCarthy's *Blood Meridian*, Oswald Spengler's *The Decline of the West*, and Shakespeare.

Gyasi: What poets among your contemporaries do you admire?

Majmudar: Don Paterson, Kay Ryan, A. E. Stallings, Joshua Mehigan ... But I confess I regard Cormac McCarthy (author of *Blood Meridian* and *The Road*) as the greatest living poet in the language; he just happens to write in the form of the prose narrative.

Carol V. Davis is the author of *Between Storms* (Truman State University Press, 2012). She won the 2007 T.S. Eliot Prize for *Into the Arms of Pushkin: Poems of St. Petersburg*. Twice a Fulbright scholar in Russia, her poetry has been read on NPR, Radio Russia, and at the Library of Congress.

She teaches at Santa Monica College and Antioch University, Los Angeles. Her poems have appeared in *Ploughshares, Prairie Schooner, Mid-American Review, Bellingham Review, Verse Daily,* and Ted Kooser's *American Life in Poetry*. She is poetry editor of the Los Angeles newspaper the *Jewish Journal*.

Gyasi: You seem to have some sort of affinity for languages. Is/Are there any circumstance(s) that influenced you to study Russian?

Davis: I fell in love with Russian literature early on at university. There were family ties, but that really didn't influence me. My paternal grandparents were from Russia and Ukraine, but once they came to the U.S., they didn't want to speak Russian. They spoke Yiddish in the home, but I didn't grow up with it. My parents were born in New York, but their first language was Yiddish for both of them. I don't think I have an affinity for languages; living in a country certainly helps in fluency.

Gyasi: This may sound somewhat unimportant, but is the Russian language difficult to study?

Davis: Yes (laughing) it is if you are a bad language student, as I was. I was always off reading a novel instead of studying my case endings. Russian grammar is difficult in that each word changes depending on what case it is (genetic, dative, etc.).

Gyasi: You earned an MA in Slavic language and literature from the University of Washington. Is there any special thing you remember about your days as a student?

Davis: I struggled with the language. I have fonder memories of my undergraduate days, as I went to what was called an experimental college, very small classes, and the chance to do lots of independent study. I was the only one studying Russian literature there, but it was a college with a lot of freedom and it suited me well.

Gyasi: Did you know that you would one day become a writer?

Davis: No, though I was always in the arts. I trained as a dancer from a young age, though I decided to go to university and also studied art at first at university. I was always a reader. In some ways I think being a reader and certainly studying literature is good training for becoming a writer. Now it is common for writers to study creative writing at university and graduate school. This was not common when I went to university, and though I teach creative writing, I have mixed feelings about it as an academic subject. In graduate school I imagined I'd go on for a PhD and teach Russian literature. I left after my MA and soon after started writing seriously. Very quickly then I knew that was what I wanted to do with the rest of my life.

Gyasi: Your book *Into the Arms of Pushkin: Poems of St. Petersburg* won the T.S Eliot Prize in 2007. How much effort did you put into the writing of the book?

Davis: I'm not quite sure how to answer that. I wrote the book actually over a 10-year period, so I guess a lot of effort. I first went to live in Russia in 1996, finished the book in 2005, and it won in 2007. I was very lucky as it won the first year I submitted it to a competition. There were about 550 manuscripts submitted to the

T.S. Eliot Prize that year, so I was very, very lucky to have won. I had published a book in Russia in 1997 in a bilingual English/Russian edition, but *Into the Arms of Pushkin* is considered (by many) as my first book. The part I found most difficult was the ordering of the poems. Also, since the manuscript was in some ways a record of this time period, I initially had the poems more or less in chronological order. I was later advised (by a poet who read the manuscript) not to keep that ordering. I'd published a lot by the time the book came out, but as a friend put it, "After 27 years you are an overnight sensation." I was not at all expecting to win and was stunned when I got the call.

Gyasi: You've said somewhere that you explore faith and doubt and superstition in your poetry. I am wondering about the link between faith and doubt and superstition.

Davis: First faith and doubt. Many of us go through periods of more intense religious beliefs and practice at certain times in life than at other times. As for superstition, well there is a certain level of suspension of disbelief in religion. There are religious events and experiences that are hard to accept if one believes them as historically true. I suppose all cultures (if not religions) have some superstitions. My grandparents (on my mother's side, since they were the ones I knew more) certainly adhered to certain superstitions. These were culturally based. My parents were vehemently opposed to these. Some of this was the difference between an immigrant generation (my grandparents) and an American-born generation, my parents. Yet sometimes I saw my mother continuing these superstitions, for example, not buying a baby stroller or baby clothes before the birth of the baby. Many superstitions, I think, came about because of the frailty of life, the danger of disease. Many superstitions cross cultures varying slightly. I also became interested in Russian superstitions and how they were different from the Jewish or American ones I knew. I'm now working on a new manuscript and one of the themes I am exploring is Jewish superstitions.

Gyasi: Do you mind sharing your views on the political situation in contemporary Russia?

Davis: I lived in Russia through many different administrations: Presidents Yeltsin, Putin, Medvedev, and Putin again. Over the years Putin has shut down much of the free press and taken away freedoms. It is alarming. My friends there are mostly in the arts, academic and Jewish communities, so I see Russia through those eyes as well. I'm hoping still to go back in early 2015. The undeclared war with Ukraine is terrible and the rise of fascism in Eastern Ukraine among the separatists also. Many people in Russia (as in other countries) are more concerned with a rise in quality of life than in politics. There is a striking difference between life in the major cities, St. Petersburg where I lived and in Moscow, than in the provinces and rural areas.

Gyasi: Is there any special link between teaching and writing?

Davis: Several: a chance to do close reading of texts. There is the hope for time off (summers mostly) and the stimulation of working with students, but it is draining too, of course. I am now teaching both literature (mostly American) and creative writing (poetry).

Gyasi: Your grandparents are Jewish immigrants from Russia. My question is, are you a practicing Jew? If so, what does it mean to be Jewish?

Davis: Yes, from Russia and Ukraine on one side and Germany and Austria on the other. When my parents married, this match was considered an intermarriage. I think it was class differences, as the German Jews were middle class and the Russian Jews peasant/working class. The term intermarriage has a very different meaning now. Yes, I am a practicing Jew. Being Jewish is complicated, as one can be a Jew and not be religiously observant at all, as Judaism is a religion, a culture, a history; some Jews are purely gastronomic, some socially active in causes. I have gone in and out of observance and belief, but have always identified as Jewish. The past few years I have reconnected more strongly as far as observance goes. My children, nor husband, are. A few weeks ago the portion (chapter) read in the Torah was about arguing with God. That is a strong tradition as well. I don't believe there is only one way of being Jewish. I'm in the more liberal branches of Judaism, so I believe in women rabbis and full participation for women. I have friends in various movements in Judaism. One legacy that I was strongly brought up in and is one strain of Jewish tradition is *tikkun olam*, literally repairing the world, giving back to society. That was very strongly preached in my family. One must make a contribution to society in order to have a fulfilling life.

Gyasi: How does your family feel about your books?

Davis: My mother passed away young so only was alive at the beginning of my career. My father was an academic so was pleased when I got my first Fulbright scholar's grant, but he didn't read poetry. My kids don't read my books, though my oldest son is a visual artist and my 2nd son works in the art world. I think my kids are happy we didn't pressure them to become accountants (laughing), but they are not interested in poetry, or at least my poetry or books. Of course I hope that will change at some point.

Gyasi: What things are often found on your writing table?

Davis: Lots of print outs of drafts of poems, poetry books, a notebook where I record submissions. It's a mess.

Gyasi: Do you keep a strict writing schedule?

Davis: I do try to devote at least a morning a week to poetry, whether writing, revising, sending out work, but time is always an issue during the academic year. I try to get to an artist's residency when I can, where I can have two or three weeks of uninterrupted writing time. That is wonderful and terrifying (without distractions). I like going to different parts of the country (America) and find I see more clearly being in a new place. A few years ago I spent a cold, snowy January in rural Wyoming, and two summers ago I had a National Parks residency in Nebraska, on the Great Plains. Russia isn't exotic for me, but rural Wyoming and Nebraska certainly were! I got lots of writing done in Russia too as I was more isolated (not so many friends, home more).

Gyasi: Do you show your work to others before it is published?

Davis: The question isn't so much before it is published as before it is ready to send out for submission. I have a friend I often show a poem to, especially if I have uncertainty about it or it feels not quite right. I have another friend I sometimes email poems to. It can be a long time (years sometimes) between initial submission of a poem to when it is published. Sometimes I feel like a poem is good, but it takes a long time to find its rightful "home." Not all the poems that end up in a book are published in literary journals, but I do try. And I want to be in the top-tier journals, so it's a long process. It can take years between when a poem is written to when it is published, and it can be rejected many, many times first. Getting published in good journals is harder and harder now, as well as getting a publisher. I think there are 350 university writing programs in the U.S. now. Last year when I attended the AWP conference (the large yearly creative writing conference), there were 13,000 people in attendance. That's a lot of writers. Many people in the U.S. are writing poetry, but I wonder how many read it. I also do not teach in a university. It's a little harder getting a book when one is outside the "academy."

Gyasi: Do you remember these lines: "This is the new Russia/of suntans from Egyptian holidays/gated houses with security cameras/foreign cars and chauffeurs waiting at the curb." What inspired "The New Russian"? Did you struggle choosing the title for the poem?

Davis: I struggle with titles a lot. For me titles are one of the hardest parts of a poem. Ironically that poem was not hard to title. The term New Russian is a quite pejorative term meaning a Russian who has made a lot of money but is not very cultured or sophisticated. There was such a big difference in Russia between when I first went to live there in 1996 and when I last lived a long stretch there in 2005. Oil money has arrived and more conspicuous consumption. I had visited the Soviet Union in the 1970s when I was a college student, and it was very, very different. Russia, like other countries, but not the U.S., has a long history with poetry and the role of the poet is/was central to the identity of the country. In the Soviet days it was not unusual for a book of poetry to sell out overnight. Poetry was central to the country's identity and conscience. That's not so any more, but it was wonderful living in a country which still has respect for poetry. No one in Russia ever asked me, "What do you really do?" And everyone there can recite Pushkin from their school days.

Gyasi: Do you feel you're trapped between two worlds—thus, the United States of America and Russia? Which of these two worlds are you most attached to?

Davis: I would say I was for a long time. It was hard to come back to the U.S. after Russia. I had more freedom to teach interesting things in Russia. I was the first person to teach various subjects in Russia and that was very exciting. Ironically it took living in Russia to seeing how American I really am. I never felt very American before. I grew up partially in Europe, but when I lived in Russia I saw how much I am a product of my own society. It showed in ways like my independence. I had a hard time asking for help. People were fine about helping me (computer problems, for example) but I had a hard time asking and accepting it. On the other hand, I was and will always be a foreigner in Russia, even though

I (more or less) speak the language and know the culture. I was always considered an outsider. That is one of the themes of that book. It was painful at times. The book that came out in 2012, *Between Storms*, is not about Russia, nor is the one I am now working on. So I have moved on thematically.

William Trowbridge's latest collection, *Put This On, Please: New and Selected Poems*, was published in March by Red Hen Press. His other collections are *Ship of Fool*, *The Complete Book of Kong*, *Flickers*, *O Paradise*, *Enter Dark Stranger*, and the chapbooks *The Packing House Cantata*, *The Four Seasons*, and *The Book of Kong*. His poems have appeared in more than 35 anthologies and textbooks, as well as in *The Writer's Almanac* and in such periodicals as *Poetry*, *The Gettysburg Review*, *The Georgia Review*, *Boulevard*, *The Southern Review*, *Plume*, *Columbia*, *Rattle*, *The Iowa Review*, *Prairie Schooner*, *Epoch*, and *New Letters*. Trowbridge lives in the Kansas City area and teaches in the University of Nebraska Low-Residency MFA in Writing Program. He is currently Poet Laureate of Missouri.

His website is williamtrowbridge.net.

Gyasi: What do you do to relax besides writing and teaching?

Trowbridge: I like to watch film classics, which I've always drawn from in my poems. I especially like the silent comedies and especially the ones of Buster Keaton. I'm also a big fan of the Laurel and Hardy talkies. And I've written a whole collection of poems narrated from the point of view of King Kong. I also like to ride my Triumph Sprint ST motorcycle, travel, dine out with friends, and tend to the landscaping in our yard. And, of course, I enjoy giving poetry readings around the country.

Gyasi: Teaching and writing—which of them do you enjoy doing most?

Trowbridge: That's a tough one; each activity offers its own rich rewards. I'm having an especially fulfilling experience in my present teaching post in the University of Nebraska Low-Residency MFA in Writing Program—wonderful students of all ages and a first-rate group of colleagues. But I must say that I enjoy writing even more—though not by much.

Gyasi: Have you ever encountered any student who is frustrated about writing?

Trowbridge: I think everyone gets frustrated about his or her writing once in a while. Sometimes a poem just won't come out the way you'd hoped. William Stafford had some refreshing advice about one kind of frustration: "There is no such thing as writers block for writers whose standards are low enough." I don't think he meant to just start writing bad poetry. Rather, he was suggesting a strategy for avoiding the feeling of anxiety people suffer from having overly-high hopes for an early draft and giving up on it too soon. As Stafford said, "If I waited for perfection, I would never write a word." When one of my students gets frustrated, I try to listen to what the worries are and try to address them. I find that sometimes assigning a poetry exercise helps get things going again. One of the best exercises I've ever run across is "20 Little Poetry Projects," by Jim Simmerman. It asks you to do the twenty projects the exercise calls for in the order in which they're listed. They are very little projects. For example, one of them asks you to "use an image in such a way as to reverse its usual associative qualities." You can start this exercise without having any idea what the poem is going to be about or where it will go, and you almost always wind up with a poem worth keeping. I've found that it works for students from junior high to graduate school, as well as for established poets. There's an anthology consisting entirely of poems written from this exercise. It ranges from works by kids to ones by poets like Robin Becker, Allison Joseph, and Michael Waters. It's called *Mischief, Caprice, & Other Poetic Strategies*, ed. Terry Wolverton (Red Hen Press).

Gyasi: How long have you been writing?

Trowbridge: If you mean writing poetry, I started later than most. I was going to be a scholar, specializing in the American novel. My doctoral dissertation was on the novels of William Faulkner. But while I was studying modern poetry to prepare for my Ph.D. comprehensive exam, I came across some poems by Howard Nemerov that seemed to cast a spell on me. So I decided to write a poem, imitating his style. Then I wrote another and another, and finally I had enough to take to a trusted professor to find out if they were any good. He liked them enough to recommend I enter the Academy of American Poets competition at Vanderbilt, which I wound up winning. I think from then on, that encouragement and, even more, the lift I got from writing poems carried me into a new vocation, though it took me a number of years to shift from Faulkner scholar to poet.

Gyasi: Do you remember your first piece of writing?

Trowbridge: No, thank goodness.

Gyasi: What interests you about the writing process?

Trowbridge: I think the most interesting part is the series of discoveries you usually make while writing a poem. I tell my students to "listen" to what the poem says to them about where it wants to go. When a poem begins to steer you away from your original conception, it's time to follow it instead of enforcing that old rule about "sticking to the subject" we're given in early prose-writing classes. In most cases, following where the poem takes you will yield delightful and necessary surprises—necessary because, as Frost famously said, "No surprise for the writer, no surprise for the reader." I love those surprises.

Gyasi: What do you remember most about your days as a student at Vanderbilt University?

Trowbridge: I have good memories of many of my professors and fellow students. My dissertation director, Thomas Daniel Young, was one of the best teachers and best people I've ever encountered. I wasn't alone in that opinion: a fellow grad student named his first child after Dr. Young. I'm still in contact with some of my grad student pals. And I also recall the lingering aura of the Fugitive Poets, a Vanderbilt group that included the poets John Crowe Ransom, Robert Penn

Warren, and Allen Tate. The English department was then located in Old Central Hall, which was the original farmhouse on the property purchased with money Cornelius Vanderbilt gave in 1873 for the founding of the university. In the entryway was a plaque that read, "Through these doors passed the Fugitives daily."

Gyasi: Is poetry hard to write?

Trowbridge: I guess my answer would echo Woody Allen's reply to the question "Do you think sex is dirty?" He answered, "Only if it's done right."

Gyasi: So what makes a poem "right"?

Trowbridge: My answer was "only if it's done right." Whether a poem is "right" or is "done right" are two different issues. What I meant by "done right" has to do with devoting maximum and sustained attention to the elements of craft, including form, word choice, line breaks, accentual stresses, sound, sentence structure, use of tropes, and use of detail. All should work together toward the final version of the poem. Of course craft isn't the only element at work in composing a poem. There are also those less definable ones some call "inspiration," "insight," and "emotional truth." At any rate, writing a good poem almost always takes a lot of hard work, a lot of drafts before the poem is finished. Though once in a great while a poem will develop very quickly, with little revision, I'm not a believer in "first draft, best draft." As to a poem being "right," the finished poem may end up "right" to varying degrees, from generally right to exactly right. Which degree applies must be decided ultimately by the reader, whose decision I don't think is entirely subjective.

Gyasi: You've won a host of awards including the Academy of American Poets Prize, a Pushcart Prize, a Bread Loaf Writers' Conference scholarship, a Camber Press Poetry Chapbook Award, among others. Which one of them are you most proud of?

Trowbridge: The Academy of American Poets prize was my first award, one that contributed to my decision to become a poet. The Bread Loaf scholarship and the Yaddo fellowship were other early contributors. And the Pushcart is certainly a source of pride: there were over 8000 nominations the year I won one and only 67 winners. I'm also proud of being appointed Poet Laureate of Missouri.

Gyasi: How do you get along when a poem isn't going well?

Trowbridge: Like most writers, I usually put it aside for a while in order to later look at it without the tunnel vision that sometimes happens when you're working and working and the poem still won't come to life. When I put it away for a couple of weeks and then come back to it, I usually discover a strategy for making it work—though in a few cases I've just had to send it to an early grave.

Gyasi: You were once an editor of *The Laurel Review*/GreenTower Press from 1986 to 2004. What's your observation about editing and writing?

Trowbridge: Two colleagues and I took over *The Laurel Review* in 1986 and edited it till 1998. None of us had any idea how much work must go into editing a good literary magazine.

I was a smoker most of those years, and I hate to think about how many cartons I went through per issue. But the rewards are also great. A great feeling of pride comes from holding a new issue you know contains some first-rate writing. I also enjoyed the contact the magazine gave me with other writers, some of whom are now old friends. And, of course, it was always a thrill to discover a writer who hadn't yet been published. Though publishing established writers is important to the life of a literary magazine, perhaps its main function is to discover and encourage new talent,

Gyasi: You have about five poetry publications. Do you fill fulfilled as a writer? Does the number of books one writes matter at all?

Trowbridge: Actually, I've published six full collections and three chapbooks. However, I find the writing of poems, rather than their publication, to be the most fulfilling. As long as I'm writing new poems, I feel fulfilled. Certainly publication is an important element of being a poet, but I think that, if it's the main motivation, the actual writing is likely to become just a task. When that happens, you should find a different task, one that pays better.

Gyasi: Could you tell us about the writing of *Ship of Fool*?

Trowbridge: The book consists mainly of poems about a character named Fool. At first I wasn't clear on exactly who Fool was—other than an interesting figure to write about, one who seemed connected to the fool figure in silent and standup comedy (e.g. Keaton, Pryor, Woody Allen). But now I've gotten to know him better, I see him as connected to the fool archetype that appears not only in silent and stand-ups but also in tales running back to the beginning of storytelling. To borrow from Yiddish comedy, he is a combination of *schlemiel* and *schlimazel*. The difference, as you may know, is that the *schlemiel* is a bungler who's always accidentally breaking things and spilling stuff on people and the *schlimazel* is a sad sack who's always getting his things broken and getting stuff spilled on him. My Fool is both. He is often treated harshly, which seems to come simply from his being a fool. Most fool figures, though "comic," are subjected to a great deal of violence. The very term "slapstick" derives from this. In her book *The Fool: His Social and Literary History,* Enid Welsford concludes that the Fool's essence is expressed in St. Chrysostom's phrase "he who gets slapped." The fool's vulnerability and "foolishness" are seen by the non-fool population and perhaps by the fates as an invitation to take a shot—or at least be amused by watching someone or something else do so. The fool becomes a kind of scapegoat. Nathanael West, in *Day of the Locust,* discourses briefly but memorably on the clown's tendency to create a thirst for violence—usually mirthful but sometimes not—in an audience. People laugh when he gets slapped or slips on metaphorical or literal bananas. Keaton discovered this as a child when he was in his parents' vaudeville act. When the acrobatics began to feature little Buster taking what looked like and often were hard falls, the audience roared. The Keatons became a hit. I touch on the violence motivation fairly directly in several of the Fool poems.

Gyasi: What inspired your book *Enter Dark Stranger*?

Trowbridge: Well, of course, my interest in the dark strangers in film, fiction, and poetry. The book contains poems about dark strangers like King Kong, Karloff's Frankenstein monster, and Jack Palance's hired killer character in the movie

Shane. The ones most effectively portrayed in literature and film elicit at least some empathy, however uncomfortable, as well as disapproval. And quite often they're more interesting than whatever hero they're in conflict with. Milton was accused by some of being a Satanist because of his riveting portrayal of Satan in *Paradise Lost.*

Gyasi: Which of your books stands out best for you?

Trowbridge: Just as my latest poem is always my favorite, so is my latest book.

Gyasi: Do you feel poetry has a place in modern world?

Trowbridge: It certainly does. The problem is getting people in America to realize that. Right now, there's considerable effort being put into making that happen, but many other countries seem to have much larger audiences. But when poetry no longer has a place in the world, we will have lost our collective soul.

Gyasi: What's the most difficult part of writing?

Trowbridge: The most difficult for me, due to it's tedium, is the clerical part: keeping book and individual poetry manuscripts circulating to magazine editors, book publishers, and contests, though I don't spend much time on the latter. It involves a lot of record keeping, as well as envelope stuffing and stamp licking. Ugh. Online submission, when a magazine will allow it, has made things a little easier, but I still to do a lot of the work the old fashioned way. Habit, I guess, and fear of pushing a button that will send my submission into a web black hole.

John Philip Johnson lives in Lincoln, Nebraska, with his wife and some of his five children. He has recently started a new career, teaching English at a local college. He publishes literary and genre poetry, and is at work on a book of graphic poetry with Bob Hall, a Marvel Comics illustrator, and other artists. He is running a Kickstarter campaign for his graphic poetry book, running from October 24 through November 23 at https://www.kickstarter.com/projects/1528463848/stairs-appear-in-a-hole-outside-of-town. His poetry can be found at the Poetry Foundation http://www.poetryfoundation.org/poem/246744, and on his own website http://www.johnphilipjohnson.com/Publications.html.

Gyasi: Is there any personal story that led you to write?

Johnson: A really good high school teacher, Kerstin Vandervoort, showed me how enjoyable poetry could be. I read it on my own after that, and one day in college I was reading Byron's "Don Juan," and he had rhymed 'gunnery' with 'nunnery.' I was shocked he would do something that corny, and then I realized, anybody can write poetry. That's when I started.

Gyasi: Do you have any formal training in writing?

Johnson: I was mostly self-taught, but recently went back to school and got a master's degree in English, at age fifty-four, with an emphasis on poetry writing. I think years of working out my own weird ideas helped me stay unique, but without the help I got at school, I would have no polish. The faculty and fellow graduate students at UNL were hugely helpful to me.

Gyasi: Do you keep a strict work schedule?

Johnson: I wish. I used to. I hope to get back to that soon.

Gyasi: Your poem "Bones and Shadows" had me thinking after reading. Is there any relationship between the two?

Johnson: I wanted a spooky title for the poem and one that pointed to the theme. Bones and shadows are two pretty spooky things. Also, the poem is about the two lives, here and hereafter. Since I'm a Catholic, I believe in body and soul; bones are like the body, shadows are like the soul.

Gyasi: You were the first editor of *Laurus*, the UNL undergraduate literary magazine. Could you share some of the work you did there?

Johnson: If I remembered that far back! Actually, one thing stands out; we didn't want it to be a club that published our friends, we wanted it legitimate. So we did all the editorial decisions blind, without knowing the authors, and the whole editorial staff, about ten people, voted on each submission. The quality we ended up with was really high, and it was a good start for the magazine.

Gyasi: How often do you revise?

Johnson: Until it sounds right. I've got a poem I was working on the other day I started fifteen years ago, but that is an extreme example. Most poems probably get revised five to ten times, usually within a month or two of the first draft. Often I revise from start to finish, to make it seem like a moment's thought.

Gyasi: Tell me about the literary landscape in Lincoln, Nebraska, where you live.

Johnson: It is great! From London or wherever, you might think of Lincoln as a simple farmer's town, but it has a big university and lots of smart people in it! The local poets, both in and out of university, are very talented! I'm lucky to be in such a lively place! It's a peaceful city, too, prosperous and clean. And we have farmers who write incredible poems. One of my all-time favorite poetry books is called *Alvin Turner as Farmer*, by a guy who was raised rural named William Kloefkorn. Your readers should go buy it.

Gyasi: Did any of your children take after you—writing, I mean?

Johnson: Three of my five little darlings write poetry, but I never, ever pushed it on them. But they're painters, too—my wife makes her living as an artist—so eventually they took up Daddy's art. And they're not so little anymore; they are all in their late teens and early twenties. They're good poets, and good artists, too. As for lessons, I'm constantly talking to them about composition and artistic effect. I'm surprised how much I have to say and how interested they remain. It's really a beautiful atmosphere to be in, all these artists. Paintings leaning against the walls, poems on the dining room table. I'm very blessed.

Gyasi: What do you make of the current explosion of technology? Do you use a Kindle or iPad or Nook, or some other electronic gadget for reading?

Johnson: I love technology. I do read on my Kindle and on a tablet, and, yes, I prefer a paper book, but technology has some advantages, and it is just going to speed up. You'll be able to read on a Google Glass, and then with light sprayed directly on your retina, and then they'll hook it up even deeper than that. I even have some doubts about the future of language as we know it, although I'm sure it has thousands of years left.

Gyasi: Have you ever had a hard time writing about sex?

Johnson: No, no hard times, but the only time my writing on sex has been any good is when it is indirect and psychological.

Gyasi: Do you have a specific reader for your work?

Johnson: No, but I try to write them so anybody who can read English might be able to enjoy them. This is not the way most poets are trained. Lately I've been trying to make them like little *Twilight Zone* episodes, but I also do stuff with no weirdness in it. Ted Kooser told me that, ideally, you should be able to take a poem to the guy working at the convenience store, and he would give you a pack of gum for your poem. That's the ideal. Of course, a pack of gum is a buck, so good luck.

Gyasi: Do you ever bother about literary critics?

Johnson: About as much as they bother about me. Since I've started writing again, I'm getting a little attention, and so far it's favorable, but I suppose a real thumping is coming at some point.

Gyasi: The imagery in "Stairs Appear in a Hole Outside of Town" is quite superb. How do you start a poem?

Johnson: Thank you. I'm glad you like it. A graphic version is coming out soon by Julian Peters, and I'm really excited by it. On how I start a poem, I usually have some inspiration, some idea or image that seems to weigh with some portent in me. I can just tell there is some richness in it, some depth. I mull it around for a while, and then a first line comes to me. Sheila Finch told me the same thing, that the writing starts when that first sentence occurs to her. Often I drop the first sentence later on, but it is the launch pad for the rest.

Gyasi: Do you write lots of long poems?

Johnson: No, very few. Rarely over 30 lines. Long poems bore me.

Gyasi: My very last question. Is your poem "There Have Come Soft Rains" written from a personal experience?

Johnson: Yes! Annette, the girl in the poem, was a friend of mine in grade school. I really did have a crush on her in kindergarten. And happily we found each other on Facebook, after not seeing each other for forty years. We're friends again! So, yes, that is an autobiographical poem, whereas poems about, say, giant ants, are mostly in my imagination. Thanks for interviewing me! Blessings on you and your readers!

Born in Accra, Ghana, **Benjamin Kwakye** attended the Presbyterian Secondary School (Presec), Dartmouth College, and Harvard Law School.

His first novel, *The Clothes of Nakedness*, was published in 1998 by Heinemann as part of its African Writers Series. It won the 1999

Commonwealth Writers Prize for Best First Book (Africa Region) and has been adapted for radio as a BBC Play of the Week. His second novel, *The Sun By Night* (Africa World Press, 2005), won the 2006 Commonwealth Writers Prize for Best Book (Africa Region). His third novel is *The Other Crucifix* (Ayebia Clarke, 2010).

Gyasi: Thank you very much for accepting to be interviewed here considering your busy schedules as a legal practitioner and a writer.

Kwakye: Thank you! I admire what you're doing here, Geosi Gyasi. Keep it up.

Gyasi: From the brief biography I have said about you, is there anything else that has escaped me? Would you like to add anything?

Kwakye: I like it. It is succinct and to the point. The only thing I'd like to add is that at some point I also dabbled in journalism when I reviewed African titles and interviewed African writers on Window to Africa Radio in the Chicago area.

Gyasi: In fact, you really amaze me. I think all your fans and daring readers are also equally amazed. You are a legal practitioner and at the same time an award winning writer. E-h-m, E-h-m, how do you combine these two professions?

Kwakye: The way you phrase this question makes me smile, but I don't think it's as difficult as it may seem. If you have a passion for something, you strive to find the time for it. Of course, it requires some sacrifice. But my point is, people find time for all kinds of hobbies. Some play golf or watch television, for example.

Gyasi: Your first book, *The Clothes of Nakedness,* won the 1999 Commonwealth Writer's Prize for First Book for the African Region. In addition, your second book, *The Sun by Night,* won the 2006 Commonwealth Writer's Prize for Best Book for the African Region. Now, has being published and winning all these accolades changed your life in any particular way?

Kwakye: I don't think so—not in any significant way. You do get some more attention and invitations to speak here and there, and it's always gratifying and humbling to receive such recognition. The greatest reward for me, however, is the process of writing itself. It's absolutely joyous to take a blank piece of paper or computer screen and transform it into a work of art. That is what girds me and keeps me focused.

Gyasi: Most writers face a great deal of difficulties getting their first book published. Would you put yourself as part of these writers? In any case, were there any challenges faced with the publication of your first book, *The Clothes of Nakedness*?

Kwakye: Yes. *The Clothes of Nakedness* was rejected by a number of publishers. I did a lot of rewriting and submissions before it was accepted by Heinemann. My word of encouragement to unpublished writers is to persevere and never give up hope. Many writers, even those that go on to achieve success later, have had to deal with rejection at some point.

Gyasi: Have you always wanted to become a writer? What must have inspired a legal practitioner to enter the world of fiction?

Kwakye: I was a writer before I became a lawyer, so I suppose the question should be what inspired a writer to become a lawyer. I can't pinpoint the exact time when I decided to be a writer. I think it was a process. My love for reading began at an early age, as I was surrounded by books at home. I devoured as many books as I could. And then I started reading African writers like Achebe and others who inspired me to pick up the pen myself. I started writing in secondary school and continued from there on, culminating in the publication of *The Clothes of Nakedness* many years later.

Gyasi: You live abroad, specifically the United States of America, yet you write thought provoking books rich in African content, and you often explore themes relevant to African society. How do you achieve this, considering the fact that you live and work abroad?

Kwakye: Don't forget I grew up in Ghana, went to primary and secondary schools there, and even finished a year's national service before coming to the US. You never forget the place that gave you grounding. Additionally, I visit Ghana often and maintain my connectedness to the country. I love Ghana. Given this, it's not difficult to write vividly about Ghana or, for that matter, Africa in general.

Gyasi: Let me shift to your books for a while. In your first book, you draw heavily on a typical Ghanaian proverb for the title of the novel. How relevant was this proverb to the content of the book?

Kwakye: It is very germane. The proverb you're referring to is, "If Nakedness promises you clothes, hear his name." What is "Nakedness" referring to here? How can anyone give you something he or she doesn't have? In the context of the novel, you realize that the morally bankrupt are not able to deliver anything worthwhile, despite what may appear to be great promises, except moral bankruptcy and its agents of destruction. This theme is at the center of the novel.

Gyasi: A major theme that runs throughout your first book is the portrayal of man's injustice against man, and this we see in the character of Mystique Mysterious. Who is Mystique Mysterious? Is the name reflective of his character? How should your readers approach him?

Kwakye: Great question, Geosi Gyasi. I often say that a key to understanding the novel is how each reader answers the question: "Who and/or what is Mystique Mysterious?" I don't think it's my place to answer this question for the reader. The beauty of literary appreciation is what the reader brings to a particular work. Therefore, each reader's answer is as good as mine. Yes, the name is reflective of his character, given his chameleonic approach to things and how he manages to bedazzle the unwary. If I may offer a clue, I'd say that perhaps readers should endeavor to see Mystique Mysterious as something other than a mere human being.

Gyasi: In the same book, we notice by the end that despite all Mystique Mysterious's sinister acts, he is left unpunished. In fact, we see him as a free man harboring in the same society. Should we see this as a kind of metaphor?

Kwakye: A lot of readers have expressed dissatisfaction with the ending of the novel precisely for the reason that you articulate. But as I tried to hint in the previous answer, we should perhaps see him as more than a human being. What is he? For example, is he a metaphor for evil? If so, does evil completely disappear or does it lurk in the background, waiting to pounce and wreak destruction if we let it? I think a critical reading of the novel suggests that it is how we react to phenomena that we can't necessarily control that determines our fate.

Gyasi: Not so many writers have had their books turned into a different medium, say for radio or motion pictures, yet your first book was adapted by the B.B.C for radio. How did you feel as a writer seeing your work translated into another form?

Kwakye: It was exciting for me to see another person's interpretation or reinterpretation of the novel. Again, it was gratifying to see this happen.

Gyasi: Let me move on to your second novel, *The Sun by Night*. This is a book that involved murder and its subsequent court case. How much of your legal profession influenced this book?

Kwakye: I can't say that it had no influence at all, but not so much in the large scheme of things. The kind of law I practice is usually transactional in nature. I think it will be more appropriate to say that I was more influenced in my general observations rather than in my narrow focus as a lawyer. I like to say that I harvest a lot from my day to day experiences and observations outside of my work as a lawyer.

Gyasi: By the end of reading *The Sun by Night,* the reader comes to appreciate the title of the book. In fact, the titles of your books seem to be very appropriate and exact. How do you choose titles for your books? How much effort goes into choosing your titles?

Kwakye: In general, I try to pick titles that capture the essence of my novels. I play with a lot of titles until I find one that I think fits perfectly. Sometimes, I even change titles a number of times.

Gyasi: In *The Sun by Night* the language at some point in time seems to be high for the normal and average reader. Was this as a result of the voices of the major players like the rich businessman, the politician, and the lawyers who all played a part in the development of the plot?

Kwakye: Yes. I was telling the story from multiple viewpoints, with each major character telling a part of the story in his or her own peculiar voice that illuminates that narrator's character. You will notice that one character speaks in very short sentences and another speaks in highly bombastic language. Why? Is one constricted by his circumstance and the other bent on a language that others can't understand but still admire? I hope readers consider these questions as they read the novel.

Gyasi: Your third book, *The Other Crucifix,* was released this year and covers the African American immigrant experience. With respect to your first two books, which were all set in Ghana, do you intend to gradually shift the focus of the settings of your books to abroad?

Kwakye: I have no such intention. I will continue to set other novels in Ghana or other parts of Africa. In fact, my next novel, which I hope will be out next year, is set in Ghana. At the same time, having lived and worked in the US for a long time now, the migrant's story is important to me, and I think to many Ghanaians. So, other novels in progress aim to continue from where *The Other Crucifix* ended.

Gyasi: Do you somewhat envisage that the frequent coups and their aftermaths that have hampered the growth of Ghana for many decades could be the reason why most Africans living abroad would not like to resettle back in their home country?

Kwakye: A migrant's decision to migrate is often complicated. That said, I think it's true that instability and sometimes persecution prompts many Africans to leave their homelands. I have no doubt that we will see a reversal of the "brain drain" if conditions are stabilized. In fact, I think that is already beginning to happen in Ghana, as many who left are returning home.

Gyasi: You often have political and historical themes running through your books. How much research goes into these aspects of your writings?

Kwakye: It depends on the novel. *The Clothes of Nakedness* did not require a lot of research. I wrote mainly from my memory and imagination. *The Sun by Night* and particularly *The Other Crucifix* required a lot of research. As you know, *The Other Crucifix* is set in the US in the 1960s and 1970s, when I was either not born or living in Ghana. Although it's a work of fiction, such research lends context and texture.

Gyasi: Being an accomplished writer yourself, do you have any writer(s) or people you look up to for inspiration?

Kwakye: There are too many to name them all. Let me just mention a few who inspired me to believe that I too could become a writer: Ayi Kwei Armah, Chinua Achebe, Ama Ata Aidoo, Wole Soyinka, etc. These are the pioneers that paved the way.

Gyasi: Do you have any favorite book(s) you've read and still linger on in your mind?

Kwakye: This is another question that I find difficult to answer because there are many.

Gyasi: You are a legal practitioner and then a writer. Would you one day lay down your legal tools and turn to writing full-time? Is there any possibility?

Kwakye: There is a possibility, given that I enjoy writing so much. However, as it's very difficult to make a living solely from writing, it is not an option for me at this time. Perhaps, some day, I will have the option.

Gyasi: It has often been said that Africans (and in your case, Ghanaians) do not read. Do you believe in this statement? Can you share with us your thoughts on this?

Kwakye: I think we could improve on our reading culture. We tend to be distracted by so much that reading often takes a backseat. Perhaps books are also too expensive. Unfortunately, it seems that, even among those who read, there is a general preference for foreign writers.

Gyasi: There is a gradual penetration of electronic books in the publishing industry. There have been mixed feelings among writers and publishers alike. Do you think physical books would one day disappear? What is your take on electronic books?

Kwakye: I think electronic books will take greater space in the future. In fact, that is probably a fait accompli. Especially among the youth, electronic books are gaining greater ground. Readers and publishers will adjust. But I don't foresee paper books disappearing entirely. Personally, and perhaps this is "old school," I prefer that tactile feeling and experience of paper books, although I do own a Kindle and occasionally read electronic books, which I find are good for travel. When all is said and done, I think it's good to have the choice and I see both coexisting, at least in the foreseeable future.

Gyasi: Do you have any online presence where your fans and readers can read news, updates, and new releases of your books? Where can readers get copies of your books to buy?

Kwakye: I do have a website (www.benjaminkwakye.com), where readers can read about me and my books. They can also email me from that website. My books are available on the Internet (e.g., Amazon). In Ghana, *The Clothes of Nakedness* and *The Other Crucifix* are available in a few bookstores. I am trying to make the books more available.

Gyasi: Your last words?

Kwakye: Thanks for this interview. I really enjoyed it. I am also impressed by the number of reviews and interviews you have undertaken. This is really remarkable. I also thank my readers for their patronage. To budding writers, never give up the dream. Read, write, and persevere. Above all, stay positive.

Rewa Zeinati is the founder and editor of *Sukoon Magazine*, an Arab-themed, online literary journal in English. She is the author of the creative non-fiction book *Nietzsche's Camel Must Die: An Invitation to Say 'No'* (xanadu*, 2013) as well as the poetry chapbook *Bullets & Orchids* (Corrupt Press, 2013). She lives and works between Beirut and Dubai.

Gyasi: I feel I ought to begin from where I ought to—tell us how you started *Sukoon*?

Zeinati: I started *Sukoon* two years ago, but I'd been thinking about the concept or idea behind *Sukoon* for years. The truth is, it was only during the time that I moved to the US in 2002, to study and live, did I begin to become familiar with literary journals; those incredible little worlds where so many literary voices come together in one place, to find each other, and to be found.

Over the years, I started doing my own research, online and offline, to purchase, subscribe to, and attend the readings that some journals held. But with time, I began to realize something; I realized that the Arab narrative was absent, or not as available as I'd liked it to be. The Arab narrative in English, I mean. Sure, there are wonderful journals like *Mizna*, based in the US, that tackle the Arab-American narrative, and there are various journals that invite the Middle Eastern story or that of the Mediterranean, or some that are more specific to place, like Egypt, for instance, or Lebanon-relevant, like the journal *Rusted Radishes*, for example. Some journals invite translations of Arab literature. But I couldn't (and maybe I'm wrong) find the Arab story (in all its diversity) in English. In other words, I couldn't find what reflected "me."

I wanted a more inclusive journal, one that combines East and West, but in the most unconventional sense; one that embraces not only the Arab-American, but the Arab-Irish, or the Bolivian who lives in Arabia, or the Turk who lives in Yemen. I wanted the Iraqi artist who lives in Australia, or the Saudi poet, or the Lebanese storyteller who lives in Spain. I wanted the Indian poet who's based in New Mexico, but who's lived in Ramallah for some time too and has a story to share about it. The Arab element had to be present, but I wanted to show how diverse, distinct, and rich this Arab-ness can be, whether through the artist or the art itself. I want to include the story of the Christian Arab and the Muslim Arab, the Sufi, the Buddhist, the indifferent, and the atheist Arab, the Arab Jew, the homosexual Arab, the modern, the confused and the traditionalist, the uprooted and displaced, the controversial and the conformist, and everything in between, and I want them all in one place. Mainstream media tends to clump Arab with Islam, or to use the terms interchangeably, and to really narrow down the idea of "Arabness" for the world. I wanted to speak to that, and keep speaking to that. With every issue I am amazed by the submissions I receive from all over the world; the diversity of the contributors—the new and established voices all coming together in one space.

Gyasi: What is the actual meaning of the word "sukoon"?

Zeinati: Sukoon means "stillness" in Arabic. It's also a phonetic symbol in the Arabic language (check the logo!). But to me, it is the "stillness" that the artist feels when he/she is in the midst of the creative process. There is a certain kind of "sukoon" that occurs when you're right there, in that moment, in the muddled storm of your craft, and that is the reason I chose the name.

Gyasi: What were some of the challenge(s) you faced starting *Sukoon*?

Zeinati: Deciding on how the journal will look online. I did some research and decided that the pdf format works best, because there's also a lot of visual art involved, not just text, so I wanted to see it all in one space. To look and feel like one magazine. And for the reader to at least be exposed to everything in the issue at once, instead of just clicking on one story or one poem at a time.

Gyasi: Has the vision for which *Sukoon* was set up been realized?

Zeinati: I don't know if it's been realized. I mean, vision is a big word. But I do know that I've been receiving a lot of positive feedback from people telling me that they are pleased that I've filled a gap, and that I've started a necessary outlet that's been missing for so long. It makes me happy to know that I haven't just been imagining this absence all along!

Gyasi: How do you know when a piece of work submitted by a writer is right for *Sukoon*?

Zeinati: It depends if I've had my coffee. Okay, that's not true at all. Coffee is essential, but there are many boxes that need to be ticked. The Arab element is important, but of course that is the least important part. The poem or story needs to be engaging, to play with language, to be intelligent, to introduce something new, memorable, surprising, uncomfortable, amusing, painful. It needs to feel real and ordinary. I steer clear of poetry that rhymes, or archaic language, not my cup of tea. Or coffee. Or existential poetry or poetry that discusses angels. Those poems sometimes show up in my inbox.

Gyasi: How do you find time to run *Sukoon*?

Zeinati: It's a challenge.

Gyasi: Was *Sukoon* set up for only Arab writers? In other words, is it only Arabs who can submit to *Sukoon*?

Zeinati: No. The writers of, and contributors to, *Sukoon* need not be Arab. If the artist is American, for instance, then something in the work itself needs to relate to the Arab experience. If the poet is Syrian, then the work itself can either be related to the Arab experience or not, since the "Arab" element is already covered by the artist being Arab.

The "slogan" for *Sukoon Magazine*, you'll see it on the cover of every issue, on the bottom right hand corner, is: *To get to know each other from the outside in, and from the inside in.*

Wait a minute, I suppose that's the vision!

Gyasi: You are often referred to as a Lebanese-American poet and writer. My question is, where do you actually belong—Lebanon or America?

Zeinati: Neither. I don't know. I belong to both and neither. I belong to Dubai, since I now live here, been living here for years, but I also don't. This whole globalization business seems to have messed things up, huh? Which is why I like to keep *Sukoon Magazine* so open, but with one anchoring factor, although at first glance you might feel that it is restrictive. Actually, it is not. Anyway, enough about *Sukoon*!

Gyasi: How did you come to write *Bullets & Orchids*?

Zeinati: Some of it began as separate poems to be included in a longer collection. Then at one point, I found myself writing this one continuous sequence poem, and while I was writing it, I realized that I've already written some segments of it before realizing what I was doing. So I began to meditate on the idea of a single poem that is many pages long, piecing old and new segments together like I was sewing together a quilt. It just began to make sense to me. And then I started sending it away into the big and scary world to get published.

Gyasi: Was it easy finding a publisher for *Bullets & Orchids*?

Zeinati: It wasn't difficult. Relatively. I sent it away and then forgot about it and then heard back from one Anglophone publisher in Paris who thought it was worth his time. That was nice.

Gyasi: What do you think is the main difference between fiction and non-fiction?

Zeinati: Well, the line is a bit blurry isn't it? Fiction can be based on a big chunk of reality, taken and reimagined, and offered back to us. And nonfiction is supposed to be based on what we call reality, but that easily becomes memory, so then is it "real" anymore, and is it accurate? Or is it just what we think is real? I don't know if I answered your question. Did I?

Gyasi: What is your creative nonfiction book *Nietzsche's Camel Must Die: An Invitation to Say 'No'* all about?

Zeinati: It's a series of personal essays/notes that started online and completely unintentionally became a book. It's a very personal, "non-fictional," account of my life, memories, thoughts, surroundings, musings, silliness, pain, readings, interpretations, identity, and imagination over the course of about a year.

Gyasi: What inspired your poem "Of a Summer Three Years Later," published in *Blood Lotus Journal*?

Zeinati: The 2006 war between Israel and Lebanon. The poem was written three years after that summer war.

Gyasi: You grew up in Abu Dhabi, then moved to Beirut for your higher education. Do you mind telling us a little about your education?

Zeinati: I finished high school in Abu Dhabi, then I attended the American University of Beirut where I majored in English Literature. I earned my MFA in Creative Writing, with a focus on poetry, from the University of Missouri-St. Louis, USA.

Gyasi: What actually took you to the United States of America?

Zeinati: My first marriage.

Gyasi: Is there something in particular that inspires you to write?

Zeinati: Years ago it would have to be some sort of negative situation that would ignite a wave of emotion and response. Over the years I've learned not to wait for the inspiration; I've learned that I need to keep at it, to be there, ready all the time, before the inspiration decides to show up, late and hung over. I need to be writing every day. To be reading every day. All the time. And out of all that rubbish, sometimes something good comes out.

Gyasi: Could you name just one writer who has had greater impact on your writing?

Zeinati: Just one?? I am a loyal admirer of the wonderful Etel Adnan, above all. I've read many of her books, but I find myself going back to her book *In the Heart of the Heart of Another Country*, many times over the years. I love the rawness and truth of Charles Bukowski, Kim Addonizio, and Cecilia Woloch, the beauty in the words of Naomi Shihab Nye. Nawal El Saadawi's mere existence and life is an inspiration. She is a phenomenal woman. I always go back to Mahmoud Darwish in Arabic, probably read most of his collections. Hanan Al Shaikh, Ahlam Mustaghmni, Naguib Mahfouz, Adonis, Qabbani. Too many wonderful poets and writers to choose from.

Gyasi: Are there times you feel bored when writing?

Zeinati: Yes, when I'm being false. And of course that's different from being "fictional."

Gyasi: What are your future literary plans?

Zeinati: Write more, publish more. Read more. Focus on taking *Sukoon* to the next level. I'm moving to Beirut soon, which I think is good for my literary plans!

Gyasi: What do you think of the future of Arab literature?

Zeinati: I'm not sure about Arab literature in Arabic. There's always a sense that no one reads in the Arab world. I don't know how accurate that is. Maybe it is. I guess it depends where in the Arab world. I think Arab literature by Anglophone writers is alive and kicking. So many great new voices everywhere. I keep hearing that a new Arab Anglophone writer just got published! I'm optimistic about that.

Zeina Hashem Beck is a Lebanese poet with a BA and an MA in English Literature from the American University of Beirut. Her first poetry collection, titled *To Live in Autumn* (The Backwaters Press, 2014), won the 2013 Backwaters Prize, judged by esteemed poet Lola Haskins, was a runner up for the Julie Suk Award, and has been included on *Split This Rock*'s list of recommended poetry books for 2014. She's been nominated for two Pushcart prizes, and her poems have been published in various literary magazines, among which are *Ploughshares*, *Nimrod*, *Poetry Northwest*, *The Common*, *Mizna*, *The Midwest Quarterly*, *Mslexia*, *Sukoon*, and *Magma*. She lives with her husband and two daughters in Dubai, where she regularly performs her poetry and hosts the open mic show PUNCH. Her website is http://www.zeinahashembeck.com, and you can follow her on Twitter (@zeinabeck) and Facebook (https://www.facebook.com/zeinahashembeck).

Gyasi: Let's begin from your first poetry collection, *To Live in Autumn*. Where did you get the idea from?

Beck: *To Live in Autumn* is a collection of poems inspired by Beirut and Lebanon. I left Beirut in 2006 and felt nostalgic for it, so I started writing poems about the city, as a way of summoning it back to me in writing. I didn't realize, at the beginning, that this would turn into a whole book about Beirut, but it eventually did. The poems went beyond mere nostalgia, of course, and into a portrayal of *my* Beirut—its streets, clubs, buildings, taxis, people, and the love/hate relationship one could have with it.

Gyasi: Did you struggle coming up with the title?

Beck: I didn't worry much about the title at first. My working title was, for years, *Re-Membering Beirut*, because the book deals with memories of a city that I had moved away from, a city that was probably changing in my absence. Years after working on the manuscript, some of my Lebanese friends said they were tired of seeing the word "Beirut" in book titles, that it was becoming a bit clichéd, and I felt they were right. So I came up with another title, *We Who Have Decided to Live in Autumn*, which is also the title of one of the poems in the book. This particular poem portrays the city as some sort of a limbo space between war and peace, tolerance and intolerance, secularism and sectarianism, etc. The manuscript I had submitted to the Backwaters Prize was in fact titled *We Who Have Decided to Live in Autumn*, and poet Lola Haskins, who judged the contest, advised me to shorten it to *To Live in Autumn*.

Gyasi: How long did it take you to write *To Live in Autumn*?

Beck: Around seven years.

Gyasi: What was the most difficult part of writing *To Live in Autumn*?

Beck: Writing *To Live in Autumn* was an enjoyable process. I loved working on the book so much that after I launched it, I felt as if I had the baby blues. One challenging aspect of the writing was probably figuring out the manuscript's organization. The order of the poems and the different sections in a book matter a great deal to me; I had to have some kind of structure early on, and I kept changing it as I went. Other challenges were finding variation in content, perspective, and tone (since the book is heavily focused on one city), and making sure that I was writing about a city that I loved and missed without being too sentimental.

Gyasi: Did you ever anticipate that *To Live in Autumn* would win the 2013 Backwaters Prize?

Beck: Not at all. I think the best thing a writer could do is actually do the work and keep submitting, and try NOT to anticipate anything (although I'm preaching a little here, because I often get restless, and I keep checking my submissions). I found out that, as long as you are doing the work, good things tend to happen when you least expect them. I received an email from Greg Kosmicki, my publisher, around midnight, telling me I had won. I remember I was sitting on the balcony, and I had to make my husband re-read the email for me to make sure it was real. Then I started screaming and literally jumping up and down. I'm never "cool" about these things.

Gyasi: Are you comfortable with the label Lebanese poet?

Beck: I don't see it as a label. It is part of who I am.

Gyasi: Do you mind telling us anything we ought to know about Lebanon?

Beck: I don't like telling; I like showing. That's why I wrote a whole book about Beirut. Read the book!

Gyasi: Sure! But at least tell us something to make a reader want to pick up your book?

Beck: Alright, some shameless self-advertising then: the book has won the Backwaters Prize and was runner-up for the Julie Suk Award. It was included on *Split This Rock*'s list of recommended poetry books for 2014. The poems are carefully crafted, yet also authentic, accessible, and unpretentious; you don't have to be a poetry expert in order to understand and enjoy them. You also don't have to have visited Lebanon in order to identify.

In terms of subject matter, *To Live in Autumn* is inspired by the streets, bars, friendships, neighbors, strangers, taxi drivers, cafés, dances, explosions, languages, meetings, and separations that I've known. It's inspired by a city (and a country) that has, and continues to attract/repel/soothe/scare me. If you know

114

Beirut, I hope you will find part of *your* Beirut in there. If you don't know Beirut, I hope this book will take you to mine, and that you will carry it with you for some time because

We carry cities, instead of angels,
on our shoulders, we trail them
behind us like old hurts.

Gyasi: Have you ever thought about why you write?

Beck: Yes, I've thought about it because I've been asked this question many times. And my answer is always that writing is stronger than me. I simply can't not write. It's an obsession, a calling, and I think it has to do with a strong urge to tell stories, a love for language, and a fascination with the power of words.

Gyasi: Do you remember your first piece of published work?

Beck: Yes. It was the poem "To Hamra," which is the second poem in the book. It was also the poem that made me begin to realize that I wanted to write a book about Beirut.

Gyasi: Do you perform your poems?

Beck: Yes, every time I get the chance. Poetry should be read out loud, and I've always enjoyed performance; I believe it breathes more life into the poem, both for the audience and the writer.

Gyasi: You're the founder of PUNCH, a Dubai-based poetry and open mic collective. Could you spend sometime talking about what you do at PUNCH?

Beck: Because performing poetry is important for me, I started PUNCH almost two years ago in order to create a platform where people could simply sign up and read their work. I try to host it every six weeks to two months (depending on how busy and energetic I'm feeling), and it's usually a mixture of regular poets and newcomers, of experienced and new performers. I believe it's important for writers at all stages of their careers to share their work with others.

Gyasi: What is the greatest challenge you've ever faced as a writer?

Beck: To answer the question, "What do you do?" with "I'm a writer." To keep believing in your writing, to keep writing, to keep submitting and having faith that you will eventually get published.

Gyasi: Could you please break down your poem "After the Explosions"?

Beck: "After the Explosions" is a tribute to my hometown of Tripoli, Lebanon, and to my cousin. In August 2013, my cousin was shot dead on the street, in Tripoli. Two days later, there were two massive explosions that targeted two mosques in the same city. I was on vacation in Lebanon at the time, and the poem deals with both of these tragedies.

Gyasi: What inspired your poem "Ya'aburnee"?

Beck: I wrote the poem in July 2014, after the shelling of Shujaiya in Gaza. The images from that bombing kept haunting me all day, even when I was playing with my little girls. The poem also refers to ISIS forcing Christian families out of Mosul. I remember holding all this terrible knowledge with me all day, and then my daughter telling me "*ya'aburnee*," which is an endearing term that Arab parents use. It literally translates as "may you bury me," and implies the parents' wish of dying before their kids. When my daughter repeated that term that she often hears from me, I felt terrified. I wrote on *Rattle*, which is where this poem was published, that this was a poem written for the parents who had to bury their children, and for those fighting against the burial of identity.

Gyasi: Are you working on any new projects?

Beck: I'm in the process of working on my second collection.

Gyasi: What is the most difficult poem you've ever written?

Beck: "We Who Have Decided To Live in Autumn" (from the book) took years of revision. "After the Explosions" was difficult to write, because it deals with both a communal and a personal loss. I've recently written poems about my youngest daughter's pre-term birth and my oldest daughter's severe pneumonia when she was two, and these were tough to write as well. But I think I have yet to write my most difficult poems, and they will probably go places that I have been avoiding so far.

Gyasi: What is the best time to write?

Beck: For me, it's usually in the morning, when my kids are at school and my energy levels are highest.

Gyasi: Do you have any secret ritual you do before you write?

Beck: It's not a secret, really, and I think many writers do this. I read. I read to get as much beautiful writing as possible under my skin before I begin writing. Coffee is also essential for me (I'm trying, and so far failing, to quit smoking). And more recently, I've been listening to Arabic music. And sometimes, I dance.

Sefi Atta was born in Lagos, Nigeria. She was educated there, in England, and in the United States.

A former chartered accountant and CPA, she is a graduate of the creative writing program at Antioch University, Los Angeles. Her short stories have appeared in journals like *Los Angeles Review* and *Mississipi Review* and have won prizes from *Zoetrope*and Red Hen Press. Her radio plays have been broadcast by the BBC. She is the winner of PEN International's 2004/2005 David TK Wong Prize and in 2006, her debut novel, *Everything Good Will Come*, was awarded the inaugural Wole Soyinka Prize for Literature in Africa.

Her short story collection, *Lawless*, received the 2009 Noma Award For Publishing in Africa. *Lawless* is published in the US and UK as *News From Home*.

She lives in Mississippi with her husband, Gboyega Ransome-Kuti, a medical doctor, and their daughter, Temi.

Gyasi: You write in many different genres: short stories, radio plays, novels. Could you discuss the different genres? Which one do you enjoy doing most?

Atta: I enjoy writing plays most. I haven't written a radio play in a while, and I don't write short stories anymore because the process of submitting them depressed me. I really enjoy revising novels, but drafting them can be a pain.

Gyasi: Were you a keen reader growing up? Which book(s), if any, had the most influence on your becoming a writer?

Atta: I don't remember being a keen reader, but apparently I was. My aunt told me that whenever I was teased for reading, I would say, "To each his own." I read *Macbeth* as a secondary student in Nigeria and it was like an African play to me. It had all the right elements—witches, kings and assassinations. I was my class playwright and I wrote plays set in villages with kings and chiefs. My plays were about treason and betrayals. If they were influenced by *Macbeth,* they were also influenced by Nigerian plays I had seen and *Village Headmaster,* a television drama series I had watched as a child. Later, as a student in England, I studied French and English literature. I read *L'Etranger* and the rhythm of the novel felt familiar to me—very African. Camus was so different from Shakespeare, Dickens, Moliere, Maupassant and other writers I was studying. I had stopped writing plays set in villages because they were not relevant to my experiences and I knew my English classmates wouldn't appreciate them. I can't say *L'Etranger* influenced me to write, but for the first time I considered the possibility of telling a story that resembled my own experiences in my own voice.

Gyasi: Do you ever mind what people say about your writing?

Atta: Only when they are rude, but I no longer read reviews so it doesn't matter.

Gyasi: Are you rigid about your writing schedules?

Atta: I have to be because I don't know when to stop. I'm addicted to writing.

Gyasi: Do you remember an exact moment when you decided to become a writer?

Atta: I never wanted to be a writer; I just had stories I wanted to share, so I learnt how to write and kept going. If I could sing or paint, I would.

Gyasi: Do you ever have writer's block?

Atta: Yes, whenever I write non-fiction. I fall asleep and eat a lot of chocolate cake.

Gyasi: Is the process of writing a novel very different from a play?

Atta: Absolutely—the visual possibilities of a play, the sheer number of words you have to write in a novel. But I have to say that writing about my writing process is more daunting than writing non-fiction.

Gyasi: Your debut novel, *Everything Good Will Come,* won the inaugural Wole Soyinka Prize for literature in Africa. *Everything Good* must have been a big success.

Atta: I don't think of my work in that way. For me it's always been about developing and trying something new.

Gyasi: Your short story collection, *Lawless,* which received the 2009 Noma Award for Publishing in Africa, was published in the US and UK as *News From Home*. Were you worried about the change of title?

Atta: No, but it was confusing for a while. People thought I had a new book out.

Gyasi: You seem to play with words when it comes to titles of your books: *Everything Good Will Come, Swallow, News From Home, A Bit of Difference*. Do you engage in a conscious exercise in "fishing out" words for your titles?

Atta: I couldn't decide on a title for my first novel and my editor came up with *Everything Good Will Come*. After that, I thought I should name my own books. *A Bit of Difference* seems just right.

Gyasi: Which of your own books would you say stand up best?

Atta: Again, I don't think about that. You have to understand that I'm always working on something new and while I'm working, I'm absorbed with my characters, their conflicts, my language, and settings. I'm in another place and it is a shock to come out and consider my previous works. Of course once in a while I do, for example at literary events, but for the most part I am focused on my next work.

Gyasi: Will Sefi ever return to her profession as an accountant? Or, is she happy as a writer?

Atta: No, but my accountancy experience could come in handy if ever I find myself in the right position. For now, I'm very happy to write.

Frank Dullaghan lives in Dubai. He holds an MA with Distinction in Writing (University of South Wales). He co-founded the *Essex Poetry Festival* and edited *Seam Poetry Magazine*. He has three poetry collections (*On the Back of the Wind*, 2008; *Enough Light to See the Dark*, 2012; and *The Same Roads Back*, 2014, Cinnamon Press) and two haiku collections published. He has been a children's poetry judge for the Emirates Airline Festival of Literature since 2013. His screenplay *Melody* was featured in the best short films Dubai 48 hour Film competition 2012 and in the Mumbai Women's International Film Festival 2013. His short stage play, *Crossing the Road*, was featured at the Short & Sweet Festival 2013, and he has had various other short plays performed. In 2014 he was commissioned to provide the final English translation of the poetry of HH Sheikh Mohammed (Ruler of Dubai and PM of the UAE). It is published as *Flashes of Verse*.

Gyasi: Are you comfortable with the label Irish writer?

Dullaghan: I have no problem with the label. I am Irish and a writer. But foremost I am a writer. That said, I believe there is an Irish idiom in my work. That's both a positive and a negative thing. There is a long history of great writers coming out of Ireland: there is this to fall back on; there is this to live up to.

Gyasi: Could you give us a brief background into Irish literature and writing?

Dullaghan: Oh that would take far too long and there are many great books about it. The shortest history ever would include:

- When what was known as the *Dark Ages* in Europe and most of classical literature and knowledge from Rome and Greece etc. was lost, Irish monks kept it alive and later reintroduced it to Europe.
- There were a great number of bardic poets (*na fili*) writing in Gaelic who's

work passed down the generations and informed the many great writers and poets who followed.

- Some of the great writers would include Raftery, Yeats, Synge, Shaw, Joyce, O'Connor, Kavanagh, Heaney, to name just a very few of the greatest names.

Gyasi: You hold an MA with Distinction in Writing from the University of Glamorgan, Wales. Did you know as a child that you would one day study writing?

Dullaghan: No. But I always liked reading, and to be a writer you need to be a reader, you need to be able to live in your head.

Gyasi: Do you remember your first day in the writing class?

Dullaghan: They weren't classes so much as workshops and critical feedback sessions. The easiest way to learn is by doing. Of course there were technical classes as well and discussions, but the main focus was on developing one's own craft.

Gyasi: Are there any teachers who have affected your life as a writer?

Dullaghan: I had an English teacher when I was sixteen who introduced me to Kavanagh's poetry. It was like an electric shock ran through me. The work was about ordinary day-to-day things but made surprising and bright through the use of imagery and language. He had a line in a poem to his mother about watching her piling ricks of hay up against the moonlight. I could see it. At that moment I was hooked.

I also had some great tutors at Glamorgan, now the University of South Wales. And I have kept in touch with most of them. I think the most important thing about doing the MA was that it focused me, it made me serious about being a writer.

Gyasi: While living in the UK, you were the co-founder of the Essex Poetry Festival. Could you tell us a little about the Essex Poetry Festival?

Dullaghan: The Essex Poetry Festival started as a coming together of local poetry groups to share their work. But I wanted to bring national poets to Essex so we could hear work of quality and learn from it. So together with some colleagues, I hired the local theater, approached a number of well-known poets and persuaded them to come and read for us for next to nothing (we had no budget). Some of the early poets included Andrew Motion and Carol Ann-Duffy, both of whom would later become poet laureates of the United Kingdom. That was back in the 1980s. The festival is still going strong. I read at it in 2014.

Gyasi: What are your interest areas as a writer?

Dullaghan: Mainly poetry. I have three collections published by Cinnamon Press in the UK. I have also had two collections of haiku published. In addition I write short stage and screen plays and am working on a novel. My short screen play *Melody* has been screened in Dubai and has won the audience award at the Mumbai Women's Film Festival. The other thing I have found interesting of late is working with literal English translations of Arabic poetry and rendering it into something closer to western poetry. I was commissioned in 2014 to do this for Sheikh Mohammed's latest book of poetry. This was published as *Flashes of Verse* in Nov 2014.

Gyasi: Could you share something about your time as editor of *Seam Poetry Magazine*?

Dullaghan: Being on the other side of the table, as it were, was certainly an experience. The big thing I learned was that editors also have off days, make mistakes, but also can receive some extraordinary work (which makes it all worthwhile). Small press editors work hard for no other reward than the love of writing, the opportunity to play a small part in it. We need to remember this when we send work off and are waiting for a response. The editor most likely has a day job and is dealing with our submissions in his evenings.

Gyasi: What do you regard as good writing?

Dullaghan: Writing that is fresh, surprising, that finds new ways of telling the old stories, that opens up the world for us, making it personal, particular, and unputdownable.

Gyasi: I am wondering if you could define haiku?

Dullaghan: Haiku is a Japanese poetic form that provides a moment of insight. It's about the thing itself, not allusion, not analogy and should be without poetic device. Haiku should be subtle. They will often invoke the response "so what." We must be quiet and let the haiku moment inhabit us to appreciate the aesthetic. Often we are told that it is a short poem of 17 syllables in 5-7-5 shape and then anything that fits this shape is considered a haiku (particularly if it includes a "season word"). But this is wrong! It's more important to meet the aesthetic requirements of the form than a Western imposed syllable count. By way of example, here's one of my own haiku:

only myself

in the train window

these dark evenings

Gyasi: Could you compare the literary scene of Dubai to that of the United Kingdom?

Dullaghan: The UK is a much larger place with a long and established literary tradition. Dubai is young and, excepting its native Bedouin literary traditions, only beginning to grow a literary scene. When I arrived in 2006, there was a performance poetry collective—Poeticians, run by the charismatic Hind Shoufani (still going strong) and the Dubai Writers Group. But very little literary work was happening.

All of that is changing. There are a number of strong writers now: there's the poet Zeina Hesham Beck for example, who in my opinion will become a major literary figure from this region. It is heartening to see other poets and writers of quality coming through. As with much of the arts in Dubai, it is growing and growing fast. It is a wonderful time to be part of it. I imagine it is like what "the village" in New York was like in the '60s. We even have our first literary magazine now—*Sukoon*—edited beautifully by the writer Rewa Zeinati.

Our crowning glory is the Emirates Airline Festival of Literature, which is quite probably one of the best of its kind in the world. Not only does it attract writers from across the globe, Eastern as well as Western, Arabic as well as English, but it also has an outreach program which involves placing those writers in local schools and universities to help develop a love of literature early on; to raise awareness and excitement about the writing process in our youth.

Theatre too is developing fast here. And, of course, some very good writing is emerging from this as well.

Gyasi: How did you come to write *On the Back of the Wind*?

Dullaghan: *On the Back of the Wind* is my first poetry collection, so was many years in the making. It collects together the best poems that I had from 15 years of writing. Getting a poetry collection published by a literary press is very hard—there are lots of poets and very few presses. I could have self-published, but I value the affirmation and quality control aspect of an independent press. So I waited a long time for my first book to come out. I'm going through the same process now with my first novel.

Gyasi: How do you start a poem?

Dullaghan: There isn't a formula. There are many ways to start a poem. It depends on the poem. Perhaps open with an original image, a surprising or arresting line that takes the reader into the poem. I suppose you just have to pick up a pen and write. You can come back and cross most of it out later. Here are some examples of opening lines from my poems:

His death is curled beside him in his bed

Each evening now your pain goes out

It was too late to be young

Gyasi: How do you end a poem?

Dullaghan: Again, there is no magic formula. The end line in some way needs to complete the poem. It could be a twist, an insight; it could be an appropriate image. I suppose, as with all writing, there's a feel to it. You know it when you read it. Hopefully, you will also find a way to write it. Here are some examples of closing lines from my poems:

and all of his words taking flight.

Then I remembered—he was always good at beginnings.

emptying their hands of the one glove left to them.

Gyasi: At what stage in your life did you write *Enough Light to See the Dark*?

Dullaghan: This is my second collection and I had been living in the Middle East for over four years by then. So this collection begins to show some of this in terms of subject matter and imagery. The writing of it seemed a progression from my first book. It is also probably true to say that following the publication of the first book I was more comfortable in my role as a poet/writer and more confident. So the writing also came out of that place.

Gyasi: Do you have a favorite among all the poems you've written?

Dullaghan: I have a number of favorites. Here's one from my latest collection, *The Same Roads Back*. It is also a formal poem, which is unusual for me:

On This Dark Night

What small uncertainty triggered you afraid?

That dark stairwell that never was a thought,
possessed now with something close to dread
and nothing to tell what brought this all about.

It's as if the shadows are woven in a braid
of darker stuff just there, as if it's wrought
of something that was flesh but now, instead
of substance, an essence casting doubt

on all that's solid, safe. Now the dead
are finding a way back to hand, to mouth—
whisper, touch. Regardless of your creed
don't unwrap the mirror from its cloth.

Gyasi: Is it true that poetry is no longer relevant in modern world?

Dullaghan: Of course it's not true. Poetry is always relevant. It puts us in touch with the reality of our lives and the world around us in a way that is both necessary and true. It has that ability to put into words those things we have locked up inside us which are indescribable. It's done through image and metaphor, often using the simplest words. But we have to listen. And that's the part that is happening less often. We are losing our ability to touch the world, and be touched, in this way.

But poetry will always be alive. One of the things you find is, that despite the seeming neglect of poetry, people still turn to poems in times of great emotional need—death of a loved one, marriage, falling in love, catastrophe. We who are poets must not abuse this. We must remain true to our art and continue to find ways to keep it fresh and relevant.

Gyasi: What is your writing schedule like?

Dullaghan: My day job is working as a business consultant, so I often work long hours. It is hard to find time to write, and I have learned to do it in small handfuls of time snatched from my busy schedule. It works for me, probably because it has to. Some weekends, though, I have the luxury of longer, more concentrated writing time. This is usually when I will write plays, short stories, or work on my novel. Poems are small little animals that you can carry around in your pocket and work on, on-and-off, during the day.

Gyasi: You have the last words to end the interview?

Dullaghan: Perhaps just to say, if you want to be a writer, then write. You can't learn to ride a bike without getting up on it. But, of course, you can't write in isolation. Read, read, read. Read good books, challenging books. Associate with other writers, preferably ones that are better than yourself.

Anne Simpson is a Canadian poet and novelist who has written seven books, including two novels. Her most recent novel, *Falling*, won the Dartmouth Award for Fiction. She also won the Griffin Poetry Prize for *Loop*, one of four books of poetry she has published. She has been a Writer-in-Residence at universities and libraries across Canada. In 2012, she volunteered at the Osu Children's Libraries in Ghana.

Gyasi: Perhaps we could begin from your poetry collection *Is*. Could you give a brief background to why you chose this title?

Simpson: *Is* has to do with the beginning of life in terms of cells dividing and then becoming a human being, or at least that was what I had in mind for the first long poem. I kept thinking about the strangeness and wonder of something coming into being that hadn't been there before. And so, throughout, I think all the poems have to do with existence (or the verb "to be," from which we get "is"). Towards the end of the book, there are poems about a man with Alzheimer's, so I was thinking about both the beginning of life and the end of life, and how birth and decay could be conveyed in language. But really, my main concern throughout the book is this: What does it mean to be alive?

Gyasi: The first poem we encounter in the book is "Book of Beginnings," which stretches over several pages. How much time do you spend on structure and/or style of your poems?

Simpson: I believe that content and form are very connected. It may look odd to see so much white space on the page, but it allows for time to pass between poem sections, and so it allows for breathing space. In "Book of Beginnings," my idea has to do with the intersection between creation and time. Once something comes into being, it comes into time. A story can be told about it. So I went back to Genesis for inspiration. And if there could be a creation story told about anyone's life, how would it start? That was what I was thinking about.

When I read "Book of Beginnings" out loud, it's like a long chant. I love the way some poems have the potential to be incantations. They're like songs, if you see what I mean. Perhaps this helps to describe the structure of "Book of Beginnings." The structure of it is like a long creation song.

Gyasi: How does your profession as an artist affect your writing?

Simpson: I am very visual. I painted large canvases (oil paintings) for years before I started writing poetry and fiction full time. Now I always think about how something sounds—how a poem sounds, for instance—and how it appears on a page. The words on the page, and the white space around the words, or how a poem looks on a page—all these things are fundamentally important to me.

Gyasi: Did you intentionally set out to end the book with the poem "Double Helix"?

Simpson: Yes, I wanted to end with "Double Helix" because I wanted to tell the story of ordinary people. Our DNA tells our story. So I thought: "What if I wove together the stories of two people—a woman and a man—who decide not to have a child because they know they could pass on a defective gene?" I wanted the poem to have several strands, just like DNA, and yet to be one long, constantly turning narrative.

Gyasi: How long did it take you to complete *Is*?

Simpson: I don't write poetry every day, but *Is* took me about two years. I often stopped to do some work, and then I'd start again.

Gyasi: You've often been described as a poet, novelist, and essayist. Do you have a special preference among the three genres of literature?

Simpson: I love all three genres. Poetry isn't as taxing to write (as fiction can be). I'm struggling to revise a novel right now, and it's an overly ambitious book, so I have to try and simplify it and settle down with the characters to find out what they're thinking. Fiction allows a writer to stay in an imagined world for a very long time, but it also allows a writer to delve into social and moral issues. When a character makes a mistake, for instance, it's my job to see how that mistake affects other characters. I like the fact that fiction lets me look at the world from a different perspective. What is it like to be the characters who inhabit the world I've created? These are not always good characters. They are often flawed. So I have to try to stand in the shoes of the characters and yet try to stand outside them at the same time.

Poetry allows for some story, but not to the same degree, since it's not necessarily about a narrative arc (think about haiku, for instance, that merely sketches a moment in time, but makes that moment seem eternal). Yet some poetry does have a strong story to tell, but it is not the same as fiction. Sometimes my poems start with an image and go from there, but I'm usually trying to find the answer to a question of some sort. So poetry is also a form of meditation on a question. It has a deftness about it. It can be brief, yet say so much about longing, for instance, or loss.

As for essays, I like the way I can think about a question long enough to understand why it interested me in the first place! I can think about the question of climate change and our responsibility to the environment, but I can turn around and discuss why we look at paintings and what happens to us as we look at paintings. The essay is a wonderfully malleable form: it can stretch out as far as we want it to stretch. But essays are also hard to write, because it's not easy to gather a lot of rambling ideas into a coherent shape!

Gyasi: When did you actually become a writer?

Simpson: I became a writer when I started taking it seriously.

Gyasi: Are you happy as a writer? Do you earn a living out of writing?

Simpson: I'm happy as a writer and not happy as a writer: it's always an up and down thing! But when you ask yourself what you'd do if you couldn't write or if you weren't allowed to write—that's when you know you're meant to write.

I make part of my living as a writer, part of my living as a writer-in-residence or as a teacher, and part of my living as an editor. Writers are multi-taskers.

Gyasi: You studied at Queen's University and the Ontario College of Art. Can I assume that your study in art and design is the very reason you work as an artist?

Simpson: I did academic studies in literature at Queen's and fine art studies at the Ontario College of Art (now called OCAD University). I guess I've always been interested in art and in making art. Writing is another form of making art.

Gyasi: You've lived in France where you worked in a L'Arche

residence. Did you learn how to speak French when you were in France? Could you tell us about some of your experiences in France?

Simpson: I bought a second-hand bicycle in England and went all over the countryside on that bicycle. I got as far as Inverness in Scotland. When I went to France, I was still traveling by bicycle. I have no idea how I found my way to Trosly-Breuil in France, though I had wanted to go there. It really seems a little crazy when I think about it now, because I was traveling alone and I was only nineteen years old. Anyway, I arrived in Trosly-Breuil, and although I spoke imperfect French, I stayed for a few months, working in the home community for L'Arche that had been started by Jean Vanier. I was drawn to working as a volunteer among people with disabilities.

Gyasi: You also studied art in Italy. Why Italy? How long was your stay in Italy?

Simpson: I was in Italy a couple of times. The second time I was there with the Ontario College of Art and I stayed there about eight months. It's a lively culture, and so it's a very interesting place to live.

Gyasi: Is it appropriate to say that Nigeria was your first introduction to Africa? What took you to Nigeria?

Simpson: I went to Nigeria as a CUSO volunteer teacher on a two-year contract. I was new to the teaching profession, so I had a steep learning curve about learning to be a good teacher! I was also adventurous and I traveled a lot. It wasn't always easy to live there, because I missed Canada. But I was so heartened by my experience with people there: they were invariably generous. And so my two years there broadened and enriched my life much more than I knew at the time.

Gyasi: You were the writer-in-residence at Osu Children's Libraries, in Ghana. Do you mind sharing some the things you did at the libraries whilst in Ghana?

Simpson: I was so happy to be in Ghana. At the Osu Children's Libraries I did a couple of workshops on poetry and it was a lot of fun, I hope, for everyone involved. At the library in Goi, we made a poetry tree and the children made poems on paper leaves to put on the tree. Those were just a few of things I did there.

Gyasi: I'm not sure why I'm asking this, but could you educate us on the importance of libraries?

Simpson: Well, I think it begins with books, and loving books. To be in the presence of a lot of books, if you love them, is like being in the presence of family and friends. You want to spend time with them. The American writer, Ray Bradbury, said that he didn't go to college, but that after he graduated from high school he spent ten years, on and off between jobs, I guess, at his local library. He said that he "graduated" from the library.

What you'll find with any writer is that he or she loves to be inside a library. It's not because the library has a computer; it's because the library is a place to read and think. We don't have enough spaces to read and think now, and so we should regard libraries as precious places.

Gyasi: How vibrant is the literary scene in Antigonish, Nova Scotia, the place where you live? Do you belong to any community of writers?

Simpson: I live in a very small town in Nova Scotia. There are a few writers here, and we get together often. I'm not involved in a writing group, though. And yes, I belong to several provincial and national groups of writers.

Gyasi: Why do you think the judges chose your poetry collection *Loop* as the winner of the 2004 Canadian Griffin Poetry Prize?

Simpson: Well, it's hard for me to say what the judges saw when they read it. I know that I put everything I had into *Loop*. There's a way in which writing can span the world; it can stand apart and look at what happens in the world and bear witness to the joys and tragedies people experience. I look at the events of history, very often, but I also look at ordinary events in ordinary places.

Gyasi: Do you continue to teach at St. Francis Xavier University? If so, how do you combine teaching and writing?

Simpson: I teach a course in the English Department now and then, but I don't do this as much now. I love to teach individuals who care about writing, so I have been a writer-in-residence in many universities and libraries. But I am doing this work less and less. I guess I know that time is short. I need to write what I can in the time I have left in my lifetime.

Gyasi: Could you tell us something about the Writing Centre at St. Francis Xavier University?

Simpson: The Writing Centre at St. Francis Xavier University is an academic writing centre. We found that students needed help with writing assignments and essays, so the centre was established to assist them.

Gyasi: Who is your all-time favorite poet/writer?

Simpson: I don't have one writer I would put above other writers. There are so many who have influenced me. I've always loved the American fiction writer Marilynne Robinson, and Jack Gilbert, an American poet. Alice Munro, a Canadian short story writer, Michael Ondaatje, a Canadian poet and novelist, and Anne Carson, a Canadian poet—all of these writers have influenced me. This is only the beginning of a long list: Toni Morrison, Chinua Achebe, Gabriel Garcia Marquez. And this doesn't begin to cover some of the great writers of the past, like George Eliot, Leo Tolstoy, Virginia Woolf. ... You see, there is no way I could stop at just one writer.

Gyasi: How would you like to be remembered?

Simpson: I don't know what I'll be remembered for, if I am remembered! But I know that all writing comes out of our lives—we live our lives first and writing comes second. So being a mother, raising a family with my husband, that comes first. My books, somehow or other, come out of the spirit of living my life, and trying to do that as lovingly, and as wisely, as I can possibly do it.

Gretchen Hodgin was born in South Carolina but resides in Maryland, where she has become enamored with the local deer. Her poems have been published in a variety of magazines, including *Gargoyle*, *Magma Poetry*, *Measure*, *Rattle*, and *Tar River Poetry*. She's currently making steady progress compiling her first book of poetry, half of which she is striving to write in terza rima.

Gyasi: Help me begin the interview with any word or sentence in Russian.

Hodgin: Привет!

Gyasi: Which means?

Hodgin: Hi!

Gyasi: You graduated cum laude with a Bachelor's in Russian from the University of South Carolina. What influenced you to study Russian?

Hodgin: I read Dostoyevsky's *The Brothers Karamazov* as a teenager, and it literally changed my brain. I've been interested in Russia ever since. The program I was involved in does a very comprehensive major, so I studied culture, history, language, and literature. My main focus was literature. I taught myself first-year Russian; however, whatever part of the brain responsible for language and mathematics had some kind of power outage, so I never learned Russian the way I wanted. It's a shame, too, because it's such a beautiful language. It's still a goal, though.

Gyasi: Has your study in Russian benefited you in any particular way?

Hodgin: I think it has enriched my overall perspective. When I visited Russia, I learned that the onion domes on top of the churches were meant to symbolize candles during the harsh winters.

Gyasi: Moving on, it appears you ditched the Russian somewhere and opted for a Master's in writing. What happened?

Hodgin: "Ditched" sounds so harsh. I don't think I'm capable of ditching Russian because Dostoyevsky and Tolstoy are probably infused in my blood at this point. Charles Bukowski wrote a fantastic and articulate poem about Dostoyevsky's effect on him. It's aptly titled ... "Dostoevsky."

Gyasi: When did you actually begin writing?

Hodgin: I started writing poetry at around 10 or 11, and even then it was about the natural world and existentialism, so I'm not sure what that says about me.

Gyasi: Which writer has influenced you most?

Hodgin: Probably writers like Anne Sexton who have that whole, "I'll invite you into my home, but I'm gonna take you into the basement, too" thing going on. I like my art raw.

Gyasi: You work as a writer and editor. How does your editorial work influence your writing?

Hodgin: I edit a lot of transcripts these days, so I pay a lot of keen attention now to the way people actually talk. I try to make my work sound as natural as possible, and being made acutely aware of people's speech habits is helpful.

Gyasi: Do you edit your own writing?

Hodgin: It would be such a hot mess if I didn't. I also have a few close friends that read some of my work. It's easy to get all excited about new stuff after writing it, but you have to learn to simmer down and come back to it. After some time, I'll read stuff I initially thought was AWESOME and bang my head on the desk because I realize how much work it actually needs.

Gyasi: Tell me about how you got the inspiration to write "To Myself When I Am Sobbing to Pachelbel for the Fiftieth Time in One Night."

Hodgin: I struggle pretty often with severe bouts of clinical depression. So a lot of what I write is just basically me talking myself down from the ledge. But there's this particular piano version of that song I found on YouTube that always makes me cry. I was listening to it one night on loop and realized how it was *physically* affecting me. I wrote that poem to convince myself that if I can write even one thing that helps somebody get through the night, it would mean that my life would not have been lived, as Emily Dickinson already perfectly wrote, "in vain."

For those who are similarly battling, there is a book called *Lincoln's Melancholy* that argues that Abraham Lincoln's depression drove him to achieve rather than cripple him because he wanted to make his life useful. I subscribe to the notion that life is bigger than any of us individually, so I strive to devote my life to improving the world in whatever way I can. It just so happens that writing is just about the only thing I'm any good at.

Gyasi: You are originally from South Carolina. What took you to Baltimore, Maryland?

Hodgin: A writing program at Johns Hopkins. I like Maryland because it's still southern enough to sell grits at the grocery store, but it's slightly more liberal.

Gyasi: Do you mind telling me about reading and writing during your childhood?

Hodgin: Around high school I started collecting and memorizing poems. I would stumble across something that I really liked and would add it to a little scrapbook. One of my favorites from those days was Sara Teasdale's, "There Will Come Soft Rains." I also had a lot of Dorothy Parker poems dog-eared.

Gyasi: What do you do when not writing or editing?

Hodgin: I love nature walks, taking pictures of wildlife, swimming, reading, dancing, and watching tennis and documentaries. I'm also learning how to draw. Sometimes I post my stuff on Facebook and people make fun of me because a third-grader could have done better, but I like monitoring my progress and being able to have visual proof of improvement.

Gyasi: Did you write "To Bitterness" from a personal experience?

Hodgin: I did. It's kind of embarrassing and pathetic, but, fortunately, I don't have any shame, so I don't mind talking about it. I was sick and went to the doctor. I had been single for a while and was feeling especially out of touch with the world. Then he put his fingers on my throat as part of the exam, and I think all the hair on my body stood up in shock. I didn't have an epiphany sitting there, but I realized later that that was the first time I'd been touched by another human being in a while. A doctor's job is to care about you, so it was this gentle connection where my life was confirmed by a heartbeat, and I felt like a part of humanity again.

Gyasi: Could you explain what influenced the use of Afanasy Fet's quote in writing "To The Bird Trope"?

Hodgin: I collect quotes the way I collect poems. Sometimes somebody else just kind of beats you to the punch and writes what you wanted to write. Most of the poems in my scrapbook, for example, are poems I wish I had written—the kind I want to eat.

"To the Bird Trope" was written for a friend who was scared to open up her pain and write about something deeply tragic.

Gyasi: Are there any benefits one gets from studying creative writing at the university?

Hodgin: Writers write, with or without formal training. But meeting and growing with a community of other people pursuing your passion is pretty valuable. I was also introduced to things I doubt I would have come across on my own.

Gyasi: Again, I want to make use of your study in Russian. Do you mind signing off the interview in Russian?

Hodgin: Спасиьо! Это было весело!

Gyasi: I'm eager to know what it means in English!

Hodgin: Thanks! It was fun!

Robert Fanning is the author of *American Prophet* (Marick Press), *The Seed Thieves* (Marick Press), and *Old Bright Wheel* (Ledge Press Poetry Award). His poems have appeared in *Poetry*, *Ploughshares*, *Shenandoah*, *The Atlanta Review*, and other journals. Recent work has also appeared on *The Writer's Almanac* with Garrison Keillor on NPR, and Fanning was interviewed at the Library of Congress for the nationally-syndicated radio program "The Poet and the Poem." A graduate of the University of Michigan and Sarah Lawrence College, he is an Associate Professor of Creative Writing at Central Michigan University. He is also the founder and facilitator of the Wellspring Literary Series in Mt. Pleasant, Michigan, where he lives with his wife, sculptor Denise Whitebread Fanning, and their two children.

To read more of his work, visit www.robertfanning.wordpress.com.

Gyasi: It wouldn't be bad if I begin with your book *American Prophet*. It has an interesting title. What inspired the book?

Fanning: *American Prophet* was inspired by the passing thought of a rather brooding, grave man in a black suit standing on the diving board during a pool party. He tries to bring dire warnings to the people in the pool, but everyone ignores him. This became the first poem I wrote for the book, entitled "The Prophet's Lament at Spring Break." It was some time later that I realized I didn't want to be done with this character, that he had something to say, that he wanted to walk the American landscape. So I set out to follow him.

Gyasi: Do you sometimes find the art of writing poetry difficult?

Fanning: Writing poetry is utterly challenging. "Difficult" is true, but not the right word, because it feels too negative. It is a deeply challenging endeavor, but a fantastically worthwhile one, even though it results in complete failure much of the time. The process of making poetry, and art, in general, involves creating problems and trying to solve them, in service of some truth.

Gyasi: What drew you to poetry?

Fanning: The pleasure of putting words beside each other, one by one, and stepping back to see what sounds and pictures they've made.

Gyasi: How long have you been writing?

Fanning: Since I was very young, probably since I could hold a pencil, though I started out writing stories mostly. I didn't write poems until high school, then I never strayed from the art.

Gyasi: Which of your own poems do you personally admire?

Fanning: I tend to admire the poems I'm working on now, because they need the most love and attention, and many of them won't make it into the world! I look at some of the work in my first collection, *The Seed Thieves*, and I'm not sure how I wrote them anymore, so I sort of marvel at them now from a distance, as an observer. But I'm very excited by the many new directions I'm headed. I don't want to be the same poet over and over again. I'm constantly trying to evolve, and each book, as well as my current manuscripts, are quite different.

Gyasi: Your chapbook *Old Bright Wheel* won the Ledge Press Poetry Award. Was it your debut book? Were you surprised to have won the award?

Fanning: Yes, *Old Bright Wheel* was my first book, a chapbook. I was ridiculously excited to have won the Ledge Press Poetry Award. My goal was always to have a book someday with my name on it. It was my first experience of that, so it was wonderful.

Gyasi: You're a professor at Central Michigan University. Is there any striking element that connects teaching to writing?

Fanning: Teaching and writing are similar in that they both involve the whole spirit—one needs to be tireless, creative, and deeply giving in order to be both teacher and writer.

Gyasi: Have you ever written out of anger?

Fanning: Oh, sure. I've written "out of" many emotions—but part of the challenge is to channel those emotions, to transmute them into something that can be felt by a listener or reader. In other words, much like transferring electricity, the writer must be the conductor—NOT the electricity. It follows, then, that to sit down and try to write in anger, or grief, or joy, or lust, will not make for a good poem. I will usually meditate before writing, to get to a space where I can be a better conductor for the material of emotion and thought into language.

Gyasi: Are you inspired by nature when you write?

Fanning: Absolutely, but I don't often directly write about nature. Walking in the woods, sitting by the river, these activities for me are great nourishment for the spirit—that I draw from when I write.

Gyasi: Do you have any writers you look up to?

Fanning: I am inspired by many writers—the contemporary scene is very vibrant.

I particularly enjoy following the work of my writer friends from Detroit: Peter Markus, Jamaal May, Terry Blackhawk, Matthew Olzmann, Vievee Francis, francine j. harris, among others. I sort of see my friends from Detroit as my writing family.

Gyasi: You are the author of two full-length poetry collections and one chapbook. Could you distinguish between a full-length book and chapbook?

Fanning: As a music lover, I often distinguish between them as comparing a chapbook to an E.P. (24-32 pages), and a full-length collection as an L.P. (48-64 pages). The former is a slice of pie. The latter, a whole pie.

Gyasi: Do you see yourself publishing more poetry books in the future?

Fanning: I see myself publishing poetry books, yes. However, I'm not sure yet if publishers see the same thing! I have completed one new manuscript, entitled *Our Sudden Museum*, and am at work on two others, one entitled *Severance* and the other *Man Carrying a Corpse*. I'm actively pursuing publication. Fingers crossed.

Gyasi: What's most important to you as a writer?

Fanning: The writing is the true playtime, the splashing around in the river and mud of words. But what's most important to me is bringing that art to others—whether in the form of giving a poetry reading, hosting a poetry reading series as I do, or teaching. I like talking about the art, sharing books with people, telling people about the poems I love, sharing my enthusiasm for the art, because I believe it is a deeply necessary, crucial human thing.

Gyasi: Who reads your books?

Fanning: Very sexy, very charming, very fashionable, highly intelligent people.

Gyasi: Is it true that writers are often boring to be with?

Fanning: Most people are very boring to be with, including me, most of the time. I'm usually a very exciting person about once a week, but unfortunately I'm often alone at that moment. Being a writer doesn't make one any more or less boring. I know stock brokers who are painfully boring. Doctors, musicians, insurance adjusters, attorneys, mountain climbers, teachers, janitors—in the immortal words of Morrissey, "the world is full of crashing bores." Writers don't, unfortunately, have a corner on the boring market.

Gyasi: Can a writer survive only by writing?

Fanning: Well, Mahatma Gandhi went three weeks without eating. So most writers would be able to live for about a month or so. However, they'd be probably hallucinating and having trouble typing after a couple of weeks. Therefore, it's good to try to eat, drink, and exercise and have some occasional social relations in between writing. In order to eat, drink, and have shelter, however, one needs money. Writing can be a way to attain money. But it's not the easiest or quickest way to attain money. Crime is much quicker, but tends to be risky. Therefore, if one chooses to write to make money in order to survive—one should plan to write books a whole bunch of people will buy. Unfortunately, poetry is definitely not the form of writing to undertake in order to attain such a readership. Thankfully, poetry is very much at odds with money. Therefore one ought to have several contingency plans of primary income if one chooses to be a poet.

Gyasi: Do you have any extra activities you engage in besides writing and teaching?

Fanning: Hanging out with my wife and kids is the ultimate pleasure. I find, when we're not busy or goofing around, I spend a lot of time just quietly looking at my wife, my son, and my daughter and admiring them. My own family, my mother, my siblings—the people we love are what matters most. The older I get, I realize that more and more. That's what matters, and maybe all that matters in the end—the people we love, the ones who will be holding our hand along the way and at the end.

Peter Specker was born in Callicoon, New York. He lived in Shandelee in the New York Catskill Mountains; Astoria, Queens, New York; Hell's Kitchen, Manhattan, New York; Hollywood in Los Angeles, California; Clearwater, Florida; and is currently alive in Ithaca, New York. He attended Cornell University 1965-1969. He has been published in over 85 literary magazines (under the mononym nom de plume Twixt), including *MARGIE, The Indiana Review, Amelia, California State Quarterly, RE:AL, Pegasus, First Class, Potpourri, Art Times, The Iconoclast, Epicenter, Subtropics, Quest, Confrontation, Writers' Journal, Rattle, Prairie Schooner*, and so many others.

Gyasi: Let's begin from where you live, Ithaca, New York. Could you tell us anything about Ithaca?

Specker: Ithaca is a town of 30,000, next to Cornell University, which has a population of 30,000—it's a college town. Deep gorges and waterfalls predominate the geology; it is at the southern tip of the largest of the Finger Lakes in upstate NY. The University gives it an international ambiance with foreign students, Buddhist priests, ethnic restaurants, and so forth. There are many gardens, an influence of Cornell's land-grant agricultural school, and lots of musicians, an influence of Ithaca College which had started as a conservatory. Downtown in the spring is a fairyland of tree blossoms along the streets.

Gyasi: You've had your poetry published in a number of magazines and literary sites including *Pegasus, First Class, Subtropics, Epicenter, RE:AL, MARGIE*, and a host of others. My question is, have you ever been rejected for your work?

Specker: I have a banker's box of rejects, which is spilling out the top—consider each reject is a small single slip. "I'm a rejects artist, which I use poems to collect."

Gyasi: When did you start writing?

Specker: As a senior in high school, I wrote two stories, and when I attended Cornell in 1965, I was part of an at-the-time experimental course in English, which had us writing journals and accounts of things that actually had happened. This was before such programs as MFA and writing courses existed, to my knowledge. As a result of this course, I transferred from a pre-veterinary program to English

132

Literature. The successful responses to my writing encouraged me, but I was already determined to write, the urge was coming to get me.

Gyasi: Can you define your voice as a writer?

Specker: I would want to communicate as free beings floating above the clouds would. But my voice, it's what it is. I have no definition for it but it.

Gyasi: Do you do lots of revisions?

Specker: I write longhand on half sheets, keeping count of syllables, pentameter-conscious. Sometimes I have word play and images that came to me written down and work to work them into a poem. Other times I start with nothing. After a couple of hours I'll look at what I've written and revise as I see is needed. A few days later I'll type them into the computer and print the few of the many that seem worth others' attention. These are put away in a folder and some time, months later, I'll go through them and discard the failures. This is a moving river, always writing, always culling as time progresses in this endeavor. If when I first write I am not satisfied, I'll write another attempt, not work over what's there. The revision is another poem, I think of it like music, like jazz: keep playing, you can't go back to what's been played. Everyone has their own flow.

Gyasi: Who are your literary influences?

Specker: Wallace Stevens, Gerard Manley Hopkins, A.R. Ammons, most importantly; Jorge Luis Borges, Guillaume Apollinaire, Rainer Maria Rilke, William Butler Yeats, I would love to be influenced by and, to some degree of emulation, have been. I am sure there are so many more.

Gyasi: Have you ever thought about why you write?

Specker: It is my way to be great. The blank pages take nothing more than me and my mind to make something beautiful and powerful. I don't have the body to be an athlete nor the temperament to sail into entrepreneurship.

Gyasi: Are you a fan of short poems?

Specker: Yes. Basho, Issa, Buscon, Ammons. The shortest means to the greatest end. Classical Chinese.

Gyasi: Do you show your work to others before it is published?

Specker: I did when my mother was alive; she was acting as my agent. I have showed my work to Taylor Stoehr and Neil Hertz, two of my professors from the Cornell experimental English class; to this day Neil is the primary angel of my support. But generally, I wear two hats: the creator, free, anything goes; and the editor/reviser, looking for what to discard, keeping only those that cannot be "disappeared" in good conscience.

Gyasi: Do you remember the line "in twilight, atoms and eve," from your poem "Flock Flight"? Could you comment on it?

Specker: I do. Like Joyce, puns and word play are my forte and my weakness. I just can't resist those discoveries in the language; they aren't my creation, they are my excavation. I intend the most compressed interplay of meanings and evocations and musical sounds, much as the Chinese poets of Li Po's and Tu Fu's day did so perfectly. Of course, in English, there's no way to also add the visual art of the calligraphy of characters Chinese affords.

Gyasi: Do you have a reader in mind when you write?

Specker: Someone who loves great work, me.

Gyasi: Do you enjoy the company of other writers?

Specker: I am out of the loop, off the beaten path, away from the highway, reclusive and solitary (add additional cliches), in that my only touch with the community of writers in the flesh is Neil Hertz. But really, reading Whitman or anyone, I am in and enjoy their company. This is also true of reviews of biographies of writers I may read. It makes me feel less nutty when I see others also pursue this activity and are accepted for doing so.

Gyasi: Do you do poetry readings?

Specker: No.

Gyasi: Could you tell us something about your poem "Apology"?

Specker: You know, I have probably 10,000 (not a typo) poems I've held onto, in boxes. I would have to see the poem to recall it.

Gyasi: Could you tell us what makes a good poem?

Specker: The essence of original creation in language. Art is nothing without freedom and awareness.

Gyasi: What are you currently working on?

Specker: I write poems three of four days a week now, that is a slow-down from earlier years. Working on seeing what might be my development by doing what I can.

Gyasi: What theme(s) do you often write on?

Specker: Space, time, spirit, water, clouds, trees, life.

Gyasi: At what time of the day do you work best?

Specker: Any time I have that wavelength inside that needs words, any time I have some time. I can and have written anywhere at any time of day.

Gyasi: What do you do to relax?

Specker: Tai Chi, which is as energizing as it is relaxing. I also am a long-term Scientologist and would term it more an advancement of freedom than relaxation.

Gyasi: Do you have any regrets as a writer?

Specker: No. I didn't write for over twenty years after I left Cornell; there are certain conditions which must be present for art to be valid, which weren't. When I began again, in 1994, so much kept pouring out it was exhausting and slightly painful. It was as it should have been, since it was what was.

Todd Davis is the author of four full-length collections of poetry—*In the Kingdom of the Ditch*, *The Least of These*, *Some Heaven*, and *Ripe*—as well as of a limited edition chapbook, *Household of Water, Moon, and Snow: The Thoreau Poems*. He edited the nonfiction collection *Fast Break to Line Break: Poets on the Art of Basketball* and co-edited the anthology *Making Poems*. His writing has been featured on the radio by Garrison Keillor on *The Writer's Almanac* and by Ted Kooser in his syndicated newspaper column *American Life in Poetry*. His poems have won the Gwendolyn Brooks Poetry Prize, the Chautauqua Editors Prize, the ForeWord Magazine Book of the Year Bronze

Award, and have been nominated several times for the Pushcart Prize. His poems appear in such noted journals and magazines as *American Poetry Review, Iowa Review, Ecotone, Poet Lore, North American Review, Indiana Review, Gettysburg Review, Shenandoah, Image, Orion, West Branch, River Styx, Notre Dame Review, Poetry Daily, Quarterly West, Green Mountains Review, Sou'wester, Verse Daily,* and *Poetry East.* He teaches environmental studies, creative writing, and American literature at Pennsylvania State University's Altoona College.

Gyasi: Your father worked as a veterinarian and your mother taught at an elementary school. My question is, what drew you to poetry?

Davis: My father had a deep love for poetry and often recited poems as we worked at the animal hospital. Hearing the cadence of these poems, as well as the fluidity of sound, pleased me. I also was drawn to the way poetry used figurative language to address many things I found most mysterious, even troubling, like death or love. But I would have never imagined myself writing a poem when I was younger. It wasn't until late in college and in graduate school that I discovered poems like "The Bear" by Galway Kinnell and "The Excrement Poem" by Maxine Kumin. These poems and these writers helped me to see that poems are made out of all kinds of experience and knowledge. Suddenly the knowledge I had as the son of a veterinarian seemed viable and appropriate for a poem.

Gyasi: What do you remember most about your family's farm in the Berkshires in Ashfield, Massachusetts, where your mother and father retired?

Davis: This farm holds an important place in my imagination, as well as in my lived physical life. It was a farm that had been built in the 1760s; my family purchased it in the late 1960s. The acreage sat just below the crest of a mountain on a one-lane dirt road, and old stonewalls traced their way through the woods, were once fields had been cultivated. We had a meadow for haying, about 20 acres of meadow, but the rest was being taken back by the forest. We had a healthy black bear population, bobcats, coyote, fisher, deer, wild turkey, beaver, etc. This wildness, the everyday motions of the natural, non-human world, left a deep imprint. I'm very fortunate that where I live today in Central Pennsylvania is quite similar to this landscape. Such places are important to my art, but even more important to my physical and emotional health.

Gyasi: What is so special about bears, something we don't know?

Davis: The bears that populate my poems and that I encounter fairly regularly in my lived experience are black bears (*Ursus americanus*). I suppose we are drawn to certain animals—some people seem to like dogs more than cats, for example. I have a deep love and admiration for many different animals, but because of where I've lived and the time I've spent watching them, reading about them, studying them, black bears are a particular favorite. They have wonderful personalities and are not an aggressive species, unless you encounter a dam-bear with her cubs and interfere or display some other aggressive behavior of your own toward them. There is something about the rhythms of a bear's life, too, that I find sensible, a symbiotic relationship with the landscape that sustains them and the seasons that dictate their activity.

Gyasi: Do you write from personal experiences?

Davis: I often remind my writing students that poetry is far closer to fiction than to non-fiction. By this I mean that the writer must satisfy the poem first, not what truly might have happened. We can recount exactly what happened, have all the facts correct, and still write a horrible poem. Having said this, yes, many, if not most, of my poems are based upon personal experiences, my own or those of people I've known. But these personal experiences only provide a foundation for the poem. I may borrow from several different experiences to write one poem; I may change the time or setting for a poem to make it work; I may change the gender of the speaker in the poem; and so on.

Gyasi: Could you comment on this line as presented in the poem "Sleep": "Sleep is a drug; dreams its succor"?

Davis: Here I had in mind a great deal of research about the importance of sleep for our physical and mental health. The body literally needs sleep to heal itself, and, as I mentioned in a previous answer, I admire animals for understanding instinctually that rest is part of a good life. In our busyness in the 21st century, I'm afraid far too many of us forget to listen to nature's rhythms. We are controlled by machines, enslaved by the very technologies we've created. So sleep is that sweet healing drug, and dreams offer succor, assistance, making that sleep reparative spiritually or emotionally.

Gyasi: Could you tell us about the state of poetry in America?

Davis: I think in many ways poetry is in the midst of a renaissance in America. What I'm enjoying about this particular moment in time in relationship to poetry is the dynamic and prolific diversity in the art form. Certainly, as in all times and places, there is work of the highest and lowest order, but often we cannot parse these distinctions when standing so close to that time and place. Yet the kinds of people who are writing poems at present, their radically different backgrounds and approaches to poetry, cannot be denied. I'm thankful for this upwelling and the opportunities it provides for celebration and lamentation, for praise and rebellion.

Gyasi: Tell us about how, in September 2002, you got to publish your first book of poems, *Ripe*.

Davis: As you know, many first books of poetry today are published under the auspices of a first-book prize. There are very few presses that publish books of poetry that are open to general submissions. I'd been a finalist in several contests for a couple of years, but I continued to seek out presses that might look at my manuscript without a contest fee or the good fortune that winning a contest demands. Jim Daniels and Jeff Gundy are two poets whose work I admire. They both had published books with Bottom Dog Press. Bottom Dog had an open submission policy, so I sent my manuscript to them. Larry Smith, who directs the press, connected with my poems and offered me a contract to publish that book. Larry continues to be a wonderful supporter of what I'm trying to do with my poems. I will forever be in his debt for publishing my first book of poems, for taking a chance on an unproven writer. In today's publishing world, these are our patrons. Larry Smith has made it possible for me to continue to write poems and send them into the world of readers.

Gyasi: Did you keep a record of how long it took you to publish *Ripe*?

Davis: I haven't been the best at keeping such records. I do think it was at least two years in trying to find a publisher for that book.

Gyasi: Perhaps the sound of the title of your second book, *Some Heaven,* unnecessarily begs the question, which heaven? So I ask, which heaven are you talking about? Or is it a metaphorical title?

Davis: The title of my second book is taken from a title of a poem in that book. In the poem "Some Heaven," I'm relating a story of my boys finding a dying rabbit and later my youngest praying that the rabbit is in heaven. I suppose I'd argue as a writer and as someone who reads in many sacred traditions, and even enjoys reading theology at times, that at this point in time any idea we have about heaven or some afterlife is metaphorical. These are gestures toward ultimate mysteries. That's one of the reasons I have more faith in poems than in theological tracts. Here's the poem:

Some Heaven

The rabbit's head is caught
between the slats of the fence,
and in its struggle it has turned
so the hind legs nearly touch
the nose—neck broken, lungs failing.
My boys ask me to do something
but see no mercy in my plan.
At five and eight, they are so far
away from their own deaths
that they cannot imagine the blessing
a shovel might hold, the lesson
suffering offers those who have
not suffered.

At bedtime, my youngest prays
the rabbit is in a heaven
where there are no fences, where
there is more than enough to eat.
He begins to cry and we rock
until sleep's embrace takes him
from me. I know his prayer is right.
What more should heaven be?
A place wild with carrot and dill,
sunflower and phlox, fields
that stretch on for miles, every coyote
full, every hawk passing over, a warm
October day that need never end.

Originally published in *Some Heaven* (Michigan State University Press, 2007).

Gyasi: It took you roughly five years to publish *Some Heaven* after the publication of your first book. Why did it take you that long?

Davis: The book was finished much sooner, but I was in conversation with Michigan State University Press about publishing it. When they offered a contract, there was a delay in the publication schedule. Since the publication of *Some Heaven* I've been on roughly a three-year pattern between each book of poems. I've just sent my most recent poetry manuscript, *Winterkill*, to Michigan State University Press. I hope they like the direction this book has taken and will publish it in 2016. The publishing process always seems a bit tenuous, something I try not to think about as I work at making the poems. Anxiety over publication doesn't help when you are trying to write!

Gyasi: As a literary critic yourself, how do you receive bad reviews of your books?

Davis: Getting a book of poems reviewed in America is a difficult thing to do. I've been fortunate over the years to have my books reviewed. Thankfully, the reviews have been favorable, and the critiques that were offered seemed fair to me. A writer cannot do all things, satisfying all readers. I'm trying to get better at making poems and hope that with each book there is improvement in the way I'm practicing the art. But a writer cannot be controlled by reviews—good or bad. Similar to the matter of publication, thinking about possible reviews, dwelling on those reviews that appear in print, does not help you write the next poem.

Gyasi: I learned from somewhere that when you're not writing, you play basketball. I am not sure if there is any link between writing and playing basketball.

Davis: I still spend time in the gym shooting, but I retired from the game in terms of competitive playing two years ago. In a few months I'll be 50, and because of some basketball injuries, my knees and ankles don't take the stress of full competition anymore. I grew up in Indiana where basketball is a very important part of the culture. My wife and I played college basketball, and my oldest son now plays college basketball. My youngest son is being recruited to play college basketball, but is still in high school. As you can see, we're a basketball family. That's why I dreamed up the book *Fast Break to Line Break: Poets on the Art of Basketball* (Michigan State University Press, 2012). The link for me between the game of basketball and writing poems is in its boundless possibilities, its call for creativity, its ability to bump against rules and boundaries and to transcend them.

Gyasi: What literature shaped your imagination as a child?

Davis: The Bible was an early influence in church. The King James Version carried such weight and authority in my ear; I liked playing with its language, hearing how such words sounded outside of the biblical context. At home I was an avid reader of comic books—both Marvel and DC; I especially liked *The Brave and the Bold* series in which Batman teamed up with many different superheroes. I also loved the short stories of Ray Bradbury and read science fiction and fantasy. If you'd told me I was going to grow up to be a writer, I would've thought I'd write comic books or be a novelist.

Gyasi: Were you troublesome as a child or were you a calm, quiet boy?

Davis: That's a good question for my mother! I'll give you my answer, although it may be tainted with self-interest. I did not get in trouble much as a child. I was usually off on my own in 60 acres of pine forest behind our house, if I wasn't doing chores or working at the animal hospital. I loved to read, which my mother says made raising me easy. I would close the door to my bedroom and read for hours at night. I also had a book with me whenever we went to the store or on a trip.

Gyasi: Coming to your poem "Prayer Requests at a Mennonite Church," my question is, are you religious as a poet? Could you tell us which church you go to?

Davis: My entire life shapes the writing of my poems. I would not call myself a religious poet, anymore than I would call myself a family poet or a nature poet. But I am a person of religious faith—even though I struggle with that faith and the doubt that must accompany it. So, yes, that dimension of my life does shape the kinds of poems I write. For the past 11 years I have been a member of University Mennonite Church in State College, Pennsylvania, although I was raised in a fairly liberal Presbyterian Church.

Gyasi: Is it appropriate to say that you wrote "Prayer Requests at a Mennonite Church" in the style of a prose poem?

Davis: Yes, "Prayer Requests at a Mennonite Church" is a prose poem. It was written in response to many prayer requests I'd heard at various Mennonite Churches over the course of my life. Mennonite Churches vary to great degrees in terms of their theological beliefs, so not all of these prayers represent my own theological perspective. Having said that, I wanted to honor the people who'd offered up these prayers, hopefully without my judgment tainting the poem. Using the prose poem allowed me to not worry about the artifice and to try to recreate a more authentic voice for the speaker.

Gyasi: Could we spend some time talking about your book *In the Kingdom of the Ditch*? When did you first conceive the idea for the book?

Davis: My books tend to come about organically, growing out of my daily concerns as a father, a husband, a son, as someone who cares deeply about the earth and all those who depend upon the earth for sustenance. I'm very much a daily writer, sitting down to my desk for a few hours each morning. As I generate poems throughout the year, they begin to talk to each other, to attach themselves to each other—creating particular themes, returning to particular images or ideas. After *The Least of These*, which Michigan State University Press published in 2010, I found myself being drawn to meditate upon how life grows out of death, how the natural cycle for things is one of birth and death and birth and death, how for one thing to live another thing must die. During my writing of this book, my own father died of pancreatic cancer. It was a difficult and painful death, yet my father continued to find elements of joy each day in the final months of his life. He insisted that while he would have liked to have been granted a few more years to live, that his 81 years had been full of blessings. That experience—being with my father in those final months of his life—had a profound effect on this book and, of

139

course, upon my own life.

> Gyasi: You solely dedicated the book in the memory of your father, your mother, your wife, and two sons. Does your family have any impact on your writing?

Davis: Because, as I mentioned earlier, my writing grows organically out of my lived experience, my family is intimately connected to my poetry. I am grateful that they allow me to write about them without protest. They are the first people to hear or read drafts of my poems. Without the love I have for them and that they in return give to me, my writing poems would mean nothing.

> Gyasi: Could you comment on this statement: *In the Kingdom of the Ditch* is your best work so far"?

Davis: Several poets, whose work I admire, have said that this is my best book to date. I'm grateful for such kind words and hope they're accurate. I certainly wish to continue to grow as a writer. As an old athlete, I see my writing in similar ways to training for athletic competition. I want to stay fit, to continue to grow stronger, to learn new skills, to learn more about the world and all its creatures, to think deeply about what interests me, about what plagues me, about what thrills me or offers joy, and to bring this way of living into my writing each day. As I mentioned earlier, I have a new manuscript completed called *Winterkill*. Those poets whom I trust with my work, who help me to revise and polish my manuscripts before I send them to my publisher, have suggested that this new manuscript is another step forward. For me, writing, like living, is a process, a way of being in the world, attending to its sacredness. This process, I hope and pray, will not end until my death.

Yaba Badoe is a Ghanaian-British documentary film-maker, journalist, and fiction writer. A graduate of King's College, Cambridge, she worked as a civil servant in Ghana before becoming a general trainee with the BBC. She has taught in Spain and Jamaica and is, at present, Visiting Scholar at the Institute of African Studies at the University of Ghana, where she is completing a documentary film—*The Witches of Gambaga*. Her short stories have been published in *Critical Quarterly* and in *African Love Stories*, an anthology edited by Ama Ata Aidoo.

> Gyasi: Let me start with your documentary film, *The Witches of Gambaga*. In fact, I had goosebumps all over my body after watching it. What inspired the film?

Badoe: I stumbled on the Witches camp at Gambaga in 1995 when I was working as a stringer for the BBC World Service in Ghana. I was shocked that, not far from where I was born in Tamale, there were refuges for women believed to be witches. What was even more horrifying was the fact that women were condemned for witchcraft through a ritual by which a chicken is slaughtered—and depending on whether the chicken dies with its wings facing the sky or the ground—a woman is forced to live in exile from her family. After spending a sleepless night at Gambaga, I wanted to make a film about the women there, because I realized that if I'd been born nearby, it was more than likely that I would be targeted as a "witch" as well.

Gyasi: Permit me to dig into the film proper. What is your judgment about the killing of a chicken and how it dies to determining whether a person is a witch or not?

Badoe: I think it's horrifying that in the 21st century in Ghana, in a country lauded for its human rights record, a woman's future can be determined by the way a chicken dies.

Gyasi: It must have been very difficult seeking the consent of the major players involved at the camp designated for witches. How did you end up with the permission to film?

Badoe: Research for the film and the filming itself wouldn't have been possible without the incredible help and support of Gladys Lariba—the care-worker at the witches camp who works very closely with the women living there—and her supervisor—Simon Ngota. Moreover, no filming or research could have taken place without permission from the chief of Gambaga, the Gambarrana, Yahaya Muni. He gave me access to research and then film the women in his custody. Gladys helped with translations, provided me with background information on women whose testimonies I recorded, and enabled me to develop close relations with them. What struck me was that many inmates at the "witches" camp were prepared to share their stories with me, were prepared to answer my endless questions and then take part in the film. Everyone who participated was extremely patient, cooperative, and accommodating.

Gyasi: In the film, I noticed that most of the accused witches are in their middle ages or are aged. In your research and in filming, did you ever stumble on teenagers or young adults accused as witches?

Badoe: No, most of the women at the camp in Gambaga tend to be middle-aged widows or elderly women. The youngest inmate at the camp while I was there was Salmata, who was around 35 years old. Witchcraft is believed to be passed from mother to daughter, so very young women are stigmatized when their mothers are accused of witchcraft. Nonetheless, unlike in the south of Ghana, accusations of witchcraft directed at children is not something I came across in the Northern Region.

Gyasi: What do you hope to achieve with this film? What has been the reception since its release?

Badoe: People who've seen the film have been moved by it and are keen to use it as a campaigning tool to change attitudes towards women believed to be witches throughout Africa. These attitudes, which scapegoat and demonize vulnerable women and children and ostracize them as "witches," need to be questioned and debated. If The Witches of Gambaga can play a part in promoting change by helping to stop violence towards women alleged to be witches, it will be a great step forward.

Overall the film has been received very well. It won Best Documentary Award at the Black International Film Festival in Birmingham in 2010 and has just won 2nd prize for Best Documentary at Fespaco 2011 in Ouagadougou. Fespaco is a biennial film festival held in Burkina Faso and is the biggest and best of film festivals in Africa.

> Gyasi: A lot of research and time must have been spent filming *The Witches of Gambaga*. How long did it take you to come up with the film? Did you encounter any challenges while filming?

Badoe: The documentary took five years to make. In retrospect, shooting the film was the easiest part of the process. I had a great cameraman, Darren Hercher; the chief of Gambaga, Yahaya Muni, was cooperative and gave me permission to film rituals that had never been filmed before; and the women at the camp were endlessly patient in telling me their stories. They soon got the hang of filming as well.

What proved to be extremely challenging was finding the funding to complete the documentary, a task which wouldn't have been possible without the help of my co-producer, Amina Mama, and well-wishers such as Yao Graham of Third World Network in Ghana, Dr Takyiwaa Manuh of the Institute of African Studies at the University of Ghana, Dr Rose Mensah Kutin of Abantu for Development, Kwasi Gyan-Appenteng of the EU's Cultural Initiative Support Programme in Ghana, and Naana Otoo-Oyortey, the Executive Director of Forward in London.

> Gyasi: Let me move on to your novel, *True Murder*. Upon first view at the title, one is likely to conclude that it is a crime or mystery novel. Can it be classified as a crime or mystery novel?

Badoe: The question people usually ask is whether *True Murder* is a crime novel or a "coming of age" story. I think *True Murder* could be described as both a crime novel and a coming of age story. I'm a huge fan of American "detective" writers—from Raymond Chandler and Ross Macdonald to Denis Lehane. Discovering the flexibility of the detective genre, its huge emotional range and resonance, helped in the creation of *True Murder*. Most important of all, it made the writing of the novel, despite the darkness of the subject matter, enjoyable. The idea was to use this most malleable of forms to equip an unlikely protagonist. Ajuba Benson, the narrator of *True Murder*, is an awkward outsider intent on unraveling a mystery, which is as much about herself as her best friend. It was my intention to give Ajuba space to inhabit the story completely, so that her positioning would disrupt the usual accretions projected on to black characters, which at times can reduce them to vehicles representing issues of social injustice. Instead, "the gaze" depicted throughout the tale is Ajuba's. As a result, her best friend's family appears "exotic," even as she yearns to become a fully-fledged family member. Hopefully, by undercutting the usual perceptions of race and framing Ajuba's story as an investigation, universal themes of love and betrayal, as well as the age-old struggle to attain happiness within a family context, are probed, irrespective of nationality, culture, and gender.

If I were forced to slot *True Murder* into a particular genre, my preference would be to describe it as a psychological thriller in the Gothic mystery tradition. A nervous heroine determined to resolve a mystery as it unfolds in the English countryside is the stock in trade of gothic melodrama. However, once the heroine is an African, another layer is added, which I hope enriches the genre, making it very much of today.

Gyasi: You solely dedicated the book to your mother. What informed this dedication? Are there scenes in the story that can be linked to your mother? And to what extent is the novel autobiographical?

Badoe: I dedicated the book to my mother because her love and enduring faith in me sustain me to this day. My mother passed away ten years ago and yet her confidence in me gave me the stamina to persist in becoming a writer. It's that same persistence that enabled me to complete *The Witches of Gambaga*, with the help of friends and colleagues.

True Murder is autobiographical in as much as I was sent to boarding school in Britain at a young age. The idea for the novel came to me when I was 14 or 15. Around that time, I found out that a girl who had been in the same class as me at prep school had been murdered. All of us who knew Clare and her family were traumatized by the event. Indeed, what happened to her haunted me to such an extent, that I decided, all those years ago, that if I were ever to write a novel, it would be about that: an event that turned the everyday rules of life completely upside down. I knew that a child was going to get murdered in the story—but how that was going to happen and who the characters involved would be took much longer to work out. Altogether, from the three months it took to write the first draft of the story, to the length of time it required to write subsequent drafts, I'd say *True Murder* took around two years of continuous hard work over an 18-year period to write! Well, you know what they say: "If at first you don't succeed ..."

Gyasi: ...try again! Isn't it? Would you then suggest this as a workable tool for budding writers who have made the first attempt and failed? Is the two years of continuous hard work over an eighteen-year period of writing not too long a time to give up—say—in the case of budding writers?

Badoe: Every writer has to make up their own mind as to how long they persevere in trying to get published. In my case, when the opportunity presented itself, I decided to keep on working on *True Murder* until, with the help of excellent editors, I made it as good as it could be. I'm very committed to the craft of writing and prepared to put in the time and effort to be as good as I can be. Some writers are very lucky and get published quickly. Getting a novel into the public domain took me a long time. When *True Murder* was eventually bought by Jonathan Cape, they did the novel proud. So in the end, the long struggle was worth it.

Gyasi: One reviewer, *Kinna of Kinna Reads,* has described your style of writing as "Completely seductive." Can you describe your style and your voice as a writer?

Badoe: I leave it to readers, reviewers, and critics to describe my style and voice. The main source of satisfaction for me is that people are gripped by the book and enjoy it.

Gyasi: I noticed a great deal of superstitions running through the novel—the fear of witchcraft, the avoidance of mirrors, and many others. Had you started your research into the making of your film before writing the novel? Or, what informed the superstitions we see Ajuba pick from her mother back in Ghana?

Badoe: I started writing *True Murder* long before I began making *The Witches of Gambaga*. I think anyone who's spent time in Ghana is aware of how religious and superstitious many Ghanaians of all ages are. Ajuba is typical in this regard.

Gyasi: Film making and writing fiction: Which of the two are you likely to be caught doing most? Do you have any preference over the other?

Badoe: I enjoy both disciplines.

Gyasi: Can you share with us how you landed your publishing contract? Was it difficult finding a publisher for your novel?

Badoe: Yes, it was a long, arduous journey, but I got there in the end!

Gyasi: The theme of divorce is also prevalent in your novel as we see Ajuba's parents' marriage breakup and the resulting effect on Ajuba being dumped off at a boarding school. In your view, do you see divorce as a disturbing force on the life of a child—say—Ajuba, in this case?

Badoe: If the story of *True Murder* is about anything, it's about an intense friendship between two adolescent girls—both outsiders, both with a load of baggage that they're humping around. Polly and Ajuba's friendship is what holds the story together and gives it its power. Their passionate friendship accommodates ambivalence and attachment in equal measure. It may be a "girl thing" but it seemed to me that the only way to convey the full emotional horror of a child's murder was to ensure that that child was loved intensely by another child—Ajuba in this case. Once I identified that this type of intense friendship between two adolescent girls was the overriding theme in the novel, writing the story was easy.

Gyasi: Should readers then overlook the sub-themes that are encountered in the story?

Badoe: Every reader takes something unique from a story. As a writer I want my readers to enjoy reading the story. What they get from it is up to them.

Gyasi: You have worked with the BBC. What kind of work did you do there? Briefly tell us about your experience with the BBC.

Badoe: I joined the BBC as a General Trainee in 1981 and was trained in radio and TV production. I was given an excellent training in broadcast journalism and really enjoyed my time working for BBC radio and television. I particularly enjoyed working with the World Service.

Gyasi: Have any writers inspired you? Any books you've loved over the years?

Badoe: Apart from the writers of pulp fiction that I mentioned earlier, I'm a great fan of Toni Morrison. I think *Beloved* is out of this world. It was voted the best novel of the last century by the *New York Times* and I agree. I love Bessie Head's and Ama Ata Aidoo's short stories. I grew up reading and loving Daphne du Maurier. *Rebecca* is a particular favorite. I enjoyed Isabel Allende's *House of*

Spirits. I adore 19th-century women novelists—the Brontes, Mrs Gaskell, Mrs Oliphant, and Ellen Wood's *East Lynne.* Contemporary Nigerian writing is excellent: Chinua Achebe, Helon Habila, and Chimananda Ngozi Adichie all hit the spot as far as I'm concerned, as does Ian McEwan's early work.

Gyasi: You wrote an interesting piece titled "What Makes a Woman a Witch?" I want to put you on the spot here. In your view, what makes a woman a witch?

Badoe: I refer you to the article: http://www.feministafrica.org/uploads/File/Issue%205/FA5_feature_article_2.pdf

Gyasi: Who should read your book? If there are any words or phrases to tell anyone to pick your book, what would it be? You may add your last words.

Badoe: The book is for anyone who enjoys psychological thrillers and likes a good, fast read with twists and turns and surprises.

Tobi Alfier is a five-time Pushcart nominee and a Best of the Net nominee. Her most current chapbooks are *The Coincidence of Castles* from Glass Lyre Press, and *Romance and Rust* from Blue Horse Press. Her collaborative full-length collection with Jeffrey Alfier, *The Color of Forgiveness*, is available from Mojave River Press. She is the co-editor of San Pedro River Review (www.sprreview.com).

Gyasi: How did you become a writer?

Alfier: I have no idea how I became a writer. I know I've been writing for over 35 years, although I did not start reading my work or publishing until 2005. I was very shy.

Gyasi: Do you remember your first piece of writing?

Alfier: It was about an article in the newspaper about a missing girl that they found. I actually still have it. It was typed on my blue Brother portable electric typewriter and it was terrible.

Gyasi: What was your first ever published work and where was it published?

Alfier: My poem "5:00pm Flight" was published in May of 2005 by *Poetic Diversity.* My poems "Deaf Escape" and "Red Plaid" were also published in May of 2005 by *Red River Review.*

Gyasi: You were born in California but lived in New York and Texas. Could you tell us anything about growing up?

Alfier: I had asthma and a lot of allergies when I was a kid, so I remember we couldn't have a dog for a long time. When we finally got one, we named him Sam Finkelstein the Third Rifkin. He was a Heinz 57 (mixed breed). I remember learning to ride a two-wheeler in Dallas. My mom would push me off and my friend Betsy's mom would catch me at the end of the street. A lion peed on my friend Betsy at the zoo. My dentist lived next door to us, and his x-rays tasted like cinnamon. I remember my dad putting my Barbie dollhouse together and I remember throwing up on his boss. That's about it. Oh, and going to The Surrey for Chicken Fried Steak and then Wil Wrights for ice cream.

When we lived in New York, I remember my dad worked in the Empire State Building and the elevator went up so quickly, you could feel it in your stomach. I remember feeding the pigeons in Prospect Park, and listening to Mr. Wizard on the radio.

Gyasi: How did you come to write *Lit Up?*

Alfier: When I started making chapbooks, I would order 100 copies, and then sell them or give them away until I ran out. I wrote *Lit Up* because I was almost done with my copies of *Carpeting the Stones*. I would go through all my poems, cross out the ones I'd already used, then pick some that I liked to go together for the next one. It's only been recently that I find myself with more than one at a time (*Lapses & Absences, The Coincidence of Castles, Romance and Rust*, and the full-length collaboration, *The Color of Forgiveness*).

Gyasi: Do you ever struggle seeking publishers for your works?

Alfier: Always. That's part of the writing life, is it not?

Gyasi: What do you regard as your best piece of work ever?

Alfier: I don't know. Would that be the poem accepted by the most high-profile journal, or my favorite poem? I hope I haven't yet written my best piece of work ever, because I'm still trying to write that one perfect profound line of poetry.

Gyasi: Who are your literary forebears?

Alfier: Anais Nin

Gyasi: Which book(s) have had great impact on your life as a writer?

Alfier: I absolutely must say *The Triggering Town* by Richard Hugo. I went through phases as I was finding my voice—I went through my Erica Jong phase, my Diane Wakoski phase, currently I say that Beckian Fritz Goldberg is a huge impact because she reminds me to "write brave." I think all work has an impact on me. Julie Orringer's *How to Breathe Underwater*, Pete Fromm's *If Not For This*, anything by Ellen Gilchrist. I loved *Crescent* by Diana Abu-Jaber—every single page is magic. I love to read. I don't read only poetry, and I think it all has an impact on my writing.

Gyasi: What is the best time to write?

Alfier: I used to write every morning from 4:30am to 6:15am. Not on purpose, I just woke up and I wrote. Now I write any time I can tell the words are ready to come out.

Gyasi: Do you care about critics when you write?

Alfier: I don't think I consider critics while I'm writing, but I certainly do care what I'm thought of. At the end of the day, if I can touch one person, I am grateful. But my worst fear is hearing someone say, "I bought this book because I liked her last one, but this one sucked!" I do want to grow as a writer, but please God let me be consistently satisfying to read.

Gyasi: What is the most boring part of writing?

Alfier: I don't think any part of writing is boring. Even the marketing machinations aren't boring. I just love to write. Everything about it.

146

Gyasi: What is the most interesting aspect of writing?

Alfier: Being able to say things in a way that other people might not think of.

Gyasi: How would you describe your voice as a writer?

Alfier: I think I have a narrative voice, and a lot of my poems seem to be love poems, no matter what they're written about. I often write about redemption and I think there's always a bit of love in that.

Gyasi: What are your main subject areas as a writer?

Alfier: It was said that I write about "food, loss, and failing bodies." That got changed to add "sex, music, and doors." Sometimes there's an overall *theme—The Coincidence of Castles,* for example, is all poems of Ireland.

Gyasi: Do you know when you've come to the end of a poem?

Alfier: Most of the time. I do sometimes have to delete the last couple lines to make a stronger poem, as we probably all do.

Gyasi: What legacy do you want to leave behind as a writer?

Alfier: I want my son to be proud of me. I want to be generous toward people who read my work, or send me work. I think it's a bit arrogant to even think I'll leave a legacy, look at the writers out there whose work is unbelievably brilliant. I am humbled by them. They are the ones who will leave a legacy.

Gyasi: What are you currently reading?

Alfier: *What is Left the Daughter* by Howard Norman, John Burnside, *A Literate Passion, Letters of Anais Nin & Henry Miller 1932–1953*, my husband Jeffrey Alfier—I look forward to reading his new poems every day.

Gyasi: Do you mind signing off the interview with anything you want to say?

Alfier: I've told this story before, so my apologies to anyone who might have heard it. One time I was doing a reading and I read a poem entitled "Life's Mysteries." After the reading a woman came up to me and said "I am sick." I said "I am too." She said "I never talk about it." I said "I don't either." To have touched one person in that way, to connect with one person and make them feel not alone for one tiny second makes me so grateful for this weird, wonderful ability to write. Every time I finish a poem I think it could be my last. I might never have any words again. But I connected. And I'm so thankful.

Margo Berdeshevsky's most recent poetry collection is *Between Soul and Stone* (Sheep Meadow Press.) Her *But a Passage in Wilderness was* also published by Sheep Meadow Press. *Beautiful Soon Enough* (University of Alabama Press), her book of stories illustrated with her own photo-montages, received FC2's Innovative Fiction Award; other honors include the Robert H. Winner Award from the Poetry Society of America, the Chelsea Poetry Award, and the *& Now Innovative Fiction Award Anthology*. Her works have appeared in journals including *Kenyon Review, Agni, Pleiades, New Letters, Poetry International, The Collagist, Gulf Coast, Prairie Schooner, Tupelo Quarterly*, and *Cutthroat*. Forthcoming, a multi-genre novel, *Vagrant*. At the gate, a new poetry manuscript titled *Blason Pour le Corps*. Born in New York City Berdeshevsky is currently writing in Paris. Her Letters from Paris can be seen here: https://pionline.wordpress.com/2015/02/05/letter-from-paris-in-february-2015/

And for more information, please see http://margoberdeshevsky.blogspot.com/

Gyasi: You're often regarded as a writer, photographer, and voyager. Is that a true reflection of what you do for a living?

Berdeshevsky: Reflection is a good word to begin on—I do see myself as all of those, yes. And I know that others may see me that way also. But first, I need to see myself as a human, trying her best to make it through each day in the world, with a little grace. As for what I do for a living … when I was a teen and was hell-bent on having a career as an actress, my scientific and business-minded father said I could never make a living as such, and suggested I view my life the way a violinist does … that is, to know that one of the strings of her bow will surely break. It was his challenge to me (which I absolutely did not appreciate at the time.) A challenge to have many strings to my bow to keep alive and afloat. Ultimately, I have cultivated my avenues of what I can do for a living. That helps in a world that is rarely supportive enough of any of us who live in the arts.

Gyasi: In what way do you see yourself as a voyager?

Berdeshevsky: A voyager to me is one who steps out and crosses bridges and cultures and belief systems. And I have done that quite a lot. Also, I have lived for shorter or longer periods of time in numerous places, by choice. And that path began when I was very young.

And so notions of patriotism and nationalism and where one lives or does not live and such were never what was most worthy to me. Rather, the idea of learning the world as much as possible has always been important to me.

Gyasi: Do you engage in the art of poetry too?

Berdeshevsky: Yes. I think of poetry as one of the arts I love most, and engage in it deeply. When I taught poetry in grade schools, I would often say that "poetry is the language of the soul." And by that, I did not mean a religious thing, but something far beyond any one faith or cult. I meant that I see poetry as a language of its own. And yes, it requires my engagement and respect.

I recently began to add this phrase to the bottom of my e mails, a phrase that I found in an interview with the editor, Michael Wiegers. I love what it says in so many ways … *"I like W. S. Merwin's contention that the first poem was the first time a mother screamed at the death of a child. We all need something that says something just beyond what words can say."* — Michael Wiegers

Gyasi: I'm wondering if one requires a special skill to become a photographer?

Berdeshevsky: Yes. Photography is about the ability to see the light and the dark and shapes and the shadows, and to have a deep sense of composition. It is not about "selfies." And it is not about snapshots of the family cat. It requires an ability to see a particular part of a scene or a face or an object, perhaps, and to concentrate on it, or to eliminate or crop away what does not serve the image being

148

finally selected and offered. At least that is so for the artistic photography that I am most drawn to do. It requires using a rule of thumb that was once given to me, and which I practice: "Take a hundred pictures with your eye, and one with your finger. It saves film and time." Photography is an art of selection from the vast array of images that constitute the world around the photographer. Selection, and the cultivation of a particular esthetic, and a desire to communicate something personal and beautiful, or not beautiful, but essential to the act of being alive. Documentary photography, which includes the more socially conscious acts of image making, and which I also do—requires an instantaneous ability to grasp the moment and to find a way of expressing it so that the viewer will feel that they could have been present at the given moment.

Gyasi: You were born in New York City. Were you raised there too?

Berdeshevsky: I was raised both in NYC and in parts of western Europe as well, because my family traveled, and we spent quite a good deal of time in France. NYC was my training ground for theatre and the intellect. Europe was my training ground for a drive toward the visual arts and history. And somewhere in between, I was always hungry for what I may call *spirit*, wherever that is raised.

Gyasi: Could you give us a brief background of who your parents are?

Berdeshevsky: Both of my parents are no longer living. My father was a Russian immigrant who was politically far to the right of either me or my mother. My mother was an old socialist, NYC born, emotionally uncertain.

Gyasi: Are you still currently in Paris? Why Paris?

Berdeshevsky: I'm mostly a world citizen, in heart and mind and activity. This morning I woke in Paris, yes. That's where I'm sitting as I type. But I could be somewhere else in the not too distant future. Why Paris? I spent time here as a child, I learned the language and love the language, I love many things about the culture and the sense of history and challenge to accepted ideas, and the esthetics of this ancient city of light. I am critical of its politics sometimes, as I am deeply critical of the politics of the USA. But as I said earlier, nationalism is not a thing I practice anywhere. I believe it leads to wars.

Gyasi: Why did you become a writer?

Berdeshevsky: Because I needed to find words for what was knocking at my heart. Because language is one of the tools I sharpened. Because it has been one of my gifts. Because it is my way of trying to comprehend a difficult and often frightening and sometimes gorgeous and fragile world.

Gyasi: What are your main research areas as a writer?

Berdeshevsky: The human thing we call woman and man and child. The human things we are often afraid to look at.

Gyasi: How did you come to write *Between Soul & Stone*?

Berdeshevsky: When asked once, at a reading I gave after the book had come out, *where was this place "between" soul & stone* ... I tried then, and I still do, to articulate that my quests to comprehend being human, being a woman in my time, being aware of the fragilities of life ... all lead me to search in the material and the nonmaterial zones. And there—is a place that I can describe as *Between Soul & Stone*. I found my way to that place again and again, in order to write the poems in the book.

Gyasi: Tell us something about your book of illustrated stories, *Beautiful Soon Enough*.

Berdeshevsky: I think my publisher FC2 said it even better than I can at this point: "It's a collection of hypnotic stories that capture the lives—worldly, sexual, obsessive—of twenty-three arresting women. … These are snapshots and collages: stories of women on the outside, looking in; of women content to end their affairs; of young women learning the power of seduction; and of older women reminiscing about past loves. They are women who cannot live without love's embrace, and women who have found it and feel that it is never enough. They are women of a 'certain age,' as the French might say, and women with naked hearts, of any age." And I so much appreciate these words that were offered about the book by the wonderful author Robert Olen Butler:

"Margo Berdeshevsky's *Beautiful Soon Enough* is a thrillingly cutting-edge work of photos and short short stories flowing together into an extended erotic dream that limns the inner lives of women deeply yearning for connection and authenticity. This is a splendid book by a fine poet turning into an equally fine fiction writer."

Gyasi: Your books have won some important prizes. For instance, *Beautiful Soon Enough* received the American Book Review/Ronald Sukenick Award for Innovative Fiction. Do prizes matter to you as a writer?

Berdeshevsky: I love this quote by Tennessee Williams:

Here is the importance of bearing witness. We do not grow alone, talents do not prosper in a hothouse of ambition and neglect and hungry anger; love does not arrive by horseback or prayer or good intentions. We need the eyes, the arms, and the witness of others to grow, to know that we have existed, that we have mattered, that we have made our mark. And each of us has a distinct mark that colors our surroundings, that flavors the recipe of "experience" in which we find ourselves; but we remain blind, without identity, until someone witnesses us.

&

… "No," he uttered, seemingly defeated, "I'm afraid that we can't continue to run from each other; I'm afraid that only in the company of these people, all of our witnesses, many of whom frighten us, can we learn who we are and what we've done."—Tennessee Williams

I will say that prizes *do* (sometimes) help to allow a book more notice in a crowded pond. And as time goes on these days, with all the writing programs and etc., the pond has become quite crowded. I'm appreciative of those awards that have come my way as a way of saying that a particular work of mine has been particularly meaningful to someone who is in a position to call attention to it, individually or via a prize. And in the case of the FC2 Innovative Fiction Award for *Beautiful Soon Enough*, it brought me into contact with a wild tribe of amazing other unusual writers with whom I was so happy to play. But the world of prizes and the "fame game" and the material world of literature and the ambitions of so many younger writers to "succeed"—whatever the hell that may mean—is worrisome. Writing is not a sport to win at. It is an art to be loved and practiced to the best of one's ability. And if the gods are gracious after that to shed a little fairy dust on it ... that's lovely! But as in so many areas of our lives, we would do well to love what we do for itself more than for the goal post. I know, how idealistic! And good luck to all of us, if we can do what we love to do as writers in our own time. There are those who may never be recognized in their time. But they have won—by doing it, all the same.

Gyasi: Can you take us through the process of writing *But a Passage in Wilderness*?

Berdeshevsky: That was my first published poetry book, and I had spent many years polishing and making it. And not finding a publisher for it. I was living far away from any big-time cities or gatherings of other poets, at the time, writing in a bubble, so to speak. But I was very aware of the world and what was happening in it and I had much that I needed and hoped to say about it, about the wilderness of our times, and making it through such metaphorical wilderness. And then, 10 pages of poems received the Robert H Winner Award for poets over the age of 40, thanks to the grand Marie Ponsot's recognition. One day she told the publisher of Sheep Meadow Press that he should treat me well. That helped! And the book gelled.

Gyasi: Why would you want your readers to read your forthcoming novel, *Vagrant*?

Berdeshevsky: It is obsessive, dis-illusory, womanly, edgy, modernist, some will say, experimental, some will some say. A *memoir poétique*, some will say. All these are apt. It is a multi-genre stand out of the box book. And I'm not shy to say that I like that. And that I hope and believe that yes, my readers will too.

Gyasi: How long did it take you to write *Vagrant*?

Berdeshevsky: Ten years. Actually, more. But who's counting??

Gyasi: Do you often show your works-in-progress to friends for approval?

Berdeshevsky: A few very close ones. Sometimes. Sometimes, too quickly, and then I have to write again and say, oh no, not *that version, this one*! I'm not a workshop person, I'm more a lone wolf as a writer. But I do have a very few very trusted fellow writers whose opinions I have treasured, and can trust. And if they tell me that something really does not work yet, I will go back to my cave and struggle with it more, and then more, and then more—until I can breathe easy with it, myself.

Gyasi: What is your greatest challenge as a writer?

Berdeshevsky: The solitudes. And the hopes for making something that might live up to the talent I think I have been given, and the time on earth that I am given to try.

Gyasi: What is your favorite book of all time?

Berdeshevsky: One—is not fair! So how about these?: W.S. Merwin's *The Vixen*. Alice Notley's *The Descent of Alette*. Theodore Sturgeon's *More Than Human*. And any of Shakespeare's oeuvre. *All of it.*

Gyasi: Of all the places you've traveled to, which of them do you love most?

Berdeshevsky: Any place I find peace.

Gyasi: You have the opportunity to sign off.

Berdeshevsky: These are a few quotes from other writers that I deeply love:

TRANS—Rita Dove, 1952

I work a lot and live far less than I could,
but the moon is beautiful and there are
blue stars ... I live the chaste song of my heart.
—Garcia Lorca to Emilia Llanos Medinor, November 25, 1920

The moon is in doubt
over whether to be
a man or a woman.

There've been rumors,
all manner of allegations,
bold claims and public lies:

He's belligerent. She's in a funk.
When he fades, the world teeters.
When she burgeons, crime blossoms.

O how the operatic impulse wavers!
Dip deep, my darling, into the blank pool.

& this:

All the poems of our lives are not yet made.—Muriel Ruckeyser

Tom Chandler is poet laureate of Rhode Island Emeritus. He has been named Phi Beta Kappa Poet at Brown University and has been a featured poet at the Library of Congress and the Robert Frost Homestead. His poems have been read by Garrison Keillor on National Public Radio on several occasions. He has written commissioned poems for the state of Rhode Island, the Rhode Island Council for the Humanities, and Waterfire, and has twice been named inaugural poet for Providence mayoral inaugurations. He is Professor of Creative Writing at Bryant University, and the founder and editor of the *Bryant Literary Review*. His latest book of new and selected poems is *Guitars of the Stars*.

Gyasi: Did you want to be a writer at an early age?

Chandler: Yes. But I got side-tracked for a couple of decades. In my 20's I played guitar and sang in bands.

Gyasi: Whom did you read as a child?

Chandler: The usual kid readings—The Hardy Boys when I had the measles. I remember *The Highwayman* by Alfred Noyes made a big impression on me. But it wasn't till I read *Huckleberry Finn* in about the 5th grade that my reading life began.

Gyasi: Do you often have a working title in mind before you write?

Chandler: Yes. I'm a big believer in the power of the title. Find the right one, and your poem will magically form beneath it.

Gyasi: Do titles come easily for you?

Chandler: Sure, but only the exactly right one leads me to a poem.

Gyasi: How did you get the idea to write "Selling Door to Door"?

Chandler: It's sales theory. A salesman is selling himself in the poem. The product he's selling is irrelevant. I think most sales people would say this is true, or at least true-ish.

Gyasi: You're the founder and editor of the *Bryant Literary Review*. How did you start it?

Chandler: When I first began teaching at Bryant University, I was offered the opportunity and the funding. This spring we will publish our 16th annual issue. That's a long run for a literary journal, and I'm indebted to Bryant for all the years of support.

Gyasi: Has the aim for which you started the *Bryant Literary Review* been achieved?

Chandler: Our only aim is to provide a respectable venue for quality creative writing from around the world. Our only editorial standard is reasonable accessibility.

Gyasi: Do you mind sharing how *Toy Firing Squad* came into being?

Chandler: I try to publish consistently in lit journals. When I have enough credits to warrant a book-length manuscript, I shop it around. *Sad Jazz* was published in 2003 by Table Rock Books. *Toy Firing Squad* came out in 2008 by Wind Publications. My most recent book of new and collected poems is *Guitars of the Stars*, also by Wind Publications.

Gyasi: You have an interesting title for your book *The Sound the Moon Makes as It Watches*. What is the book about?

Chandler: That was my first book, published just out of grad school. Much of the collection came from my thesis at Brown.

Gyasi: Do you enjoy poetry readings?

Chandler: I truly do. It scratches my itch to intro my poems and read them to an audience. Must be genetic. I come from a family of hams.

Gyasi: Do you belong to any group of writers?

Chandler: I'm doing a series of readings with my two successors as poet laureate of Rhode Island, Lisa Starr and Rick Benjamin. We call ourselves "The 3 Amigos," and read at art museums, libraries, book stores. It's great fun because we enjoy each other's poems and company.

Gyasi: Which writers have influenced you most?

Chandler: All of them. Sorry to be curt, but it's true.

Gyasi: Have you ever thought about the reason why you write?

Chandler: Yes, but I can't find an answer. No one in my family before or since has been drawn to poetry.

Gyasi: Do you care about subject matter when you write?

Chandler: Absolutely, thoroughly, and utterly! I do not care for those who hide behind empty wordplay.

Gyasi: What do you ascertain as the best time to write?

Chandler: On a good writing day, I will begin a draft about mid-morning, then work for awhile on music or something visual, but come back to the poem throughout the day.

Gyasi: Are you a fan of short poems?

Chandler: Yes, long poems sag in the middle. At some point I end up asking why the author chose the format of a poem rather than prose.

Gyasi: Do you come from a family of writers?

Chandler: No, if anything, we're musical. My dad was a singer in the Big Band era, and my brother is an accomplished pianist.

Gyasi: What are your best moments as a poet?

Chandler: When I have finished a poem I think is good, and am bathed in the blank whiteness of the page.

Gyasi: I am wondering about the challenge you've ever faced as a writer?

Chandler: The challenge never changes: If it could be about anything, what shall it be about?

Gyasi: Money?

Chandler: There is no money in poetry, but then again, there is no poetry in money.

Francesca Bell's poetry appears in many journals, including *B O D Y Literature*, *New Ohio Review*, *North American Review*, *PANK*, *Poetry Northwest*, *Prairie Schooner*, *River Styx*, and *Zone 3*. Her translations from Arabic, with Noor Al Abed, appear in *Laghoo* and are forthcoming in *Berkeley Poetry Review*. She has been nominated eight times for the Pushcart Prize and won the 2014 Neil Postman Award for Metaphor from *Rattle*.

Gyasi: One of the most striking stories I read from your biography is that you did not complete middle school, high school, or college and that you hold no degrees. My question is, were you not interested in going to school?

Bell: I was very interested in going to school, but my schooling was knocked off of the usual track very early. I was accepted by the University of Washington when I was thirteen, but my family could not afford to send me. So, instead of continuing for the next two years of middle school, I was moved up to high school. I stayed in high school for a couple of years and was lucky enough to spend six months in Germany as part of an exchange program run by my school's German teacher. I started college at fifteen and attended off and on, as I could afford to, but I did not complete a degree.

Gyasi: Do you have any regrets about not having gone to school to earn a degree?

Bell: Well, I certainly have many holes in my education, not only because I did not earn any degrees but because I skipped so many grades. I missed basic subjects like American history, chemistry, and geography, and I am not nearly as well-read as I would be had I completed even middle school and high school. It can be difficult for me to feel a part of any peer group since I tend to have different interests than those who are as uneducated as I am, and to not fit in with those who are as educated as I ought to have become. In America, poetry lives almost all of its life in the academic world, and I am most decidedly not a part of the academic world. This can obviously be, in terms of the assistance that mentors and peers can lend and the legitimacy a degree confers, a tremendous disadvantage. All of that being said, I can't honestly say that I feel much regret. There are definitely advantages to living and learning outside of the norm, to being able to develop one's own ideas and ways of thinking, and to pursuing one's writing life outside of academia. There is great freedom in having not been and in not being a part of the system.

Gyasi: You were raised in Washington and Idaho. Do you remember anything about your childhood?

Bell: I have very vivid memories of my childhood, beginning at the age of two. Some favorite memories are of my mother's cooking and garden; of car rides through the big, dramatic landscapes of Idaho and Montana; of night-skiing with my father; and of Saturdays when our family of five would visit the library and then spend the rest of the day in silence, each one of us immersed in our books.

Gyasi: What eventually took you to California?

Bell: I moved to California twenty-three years ago in order to marry my husband. I had told a girlfriend a few months before meeting him that I would never, ever move for a man. God is still laughing over that.

Gyasi: Do you remember when you started holding a pen?

Bell: I remember very distinctly when I started holding a pen because learning to write was a terrible struggle for me. Kindergarten was traumatic because I had to learn to write the letters, and I would make mistake after mistake and then erase them until the paper was shredded. In second grade came the absolute horror of trying to learn to write in cursive. I am left-handed, and learning to write in cursive from a right-handed teacher was nearly impossible for me. I still don't hold a pen properly, and, if I must write something by hand, I plan ahead in order to use the fewest words possible.

Gyasi: Did you know as a child that you would become a poet?

Bell: I hoped so. I fell in love with and memorized (with my sister's help) a poem for the first time at the age of five, wrote my first poem at six, and submitted my first poem when I was eleven. That said, my journey toward becoming a poet has been slow and full of enormous gaps. There have been many years when I was too busy with other responsibilities to pursue my writing.

Gyasi: Is there any difference between a poet and writer?

Bell: I am not sure you are asking the right question. I think that poets are one genus in the family called "writers." Poets use different tools and have a different focus than, say, journalists or novelists, but I think all three can be called *writers*. Poets and other types of writers are all makers in the world of words.

Gyasi: Your poem "I Long to Hold the Poetry Editor's Penis in My Hand" reminds me of my own personal rejections from editors. Did you write this as a result of a personal experience?

Bell: This poem is the result of years of reading rejection slips and feeling the snark that sometimes seems to ooze from them. The lines of rejection in the poem are lifted, more or less, from rejections I have received over the years.

Gyasi: How often do you receive rejections from publishers or editors?

Bell: Constantly.

Gyasi: Can you tell us about the genesis of your poem "For My 1st Ex-Lover to Die"?

Bell: Last year, I heard for the first time that an ex-lover had died, and it was a strange feeling, a feeling I wanted to explore in a poem. It was not exactly sadness. In fact, I would say it was the absence of actual sadness that struck me. It was like taking a fall, assuming you must have been injured, but finding nothing amiss when you get back onto your feet. It occurred to me, while writing this poem, that only after years had passed was I able to see the situation with anything approaching clarity, about myself or about my lover. It reminds me now of a line from a poem that Noor Nader Al Abed and I recently translated from Arabic. The poem is called "The Orbit of a Possibility," by Bisan Abu Khaled, and the line is this: "Eventually we will know what happened between us." I've come to think that may be the best we can hope for in any relationship: to eventually understand what it was.

Gyasi: What is the best time to write?

Bell: For me, the best time to write is between 10:30 in the morning and 2:50 in the afternoon on weekdays. Because my children are in school, I have been out for my daily run, and the house is empty and quiet.

Gyasi: Do you know who reads your poems?

Bell: I admit that I feel very pleasantly surprised to learn that anyone reads them at all. One of the most exciting developments in my life as a writer has been watching my website's statistics this past year. I have been amazed and humbled to see my website being read by people from more than 75 countries. Another blessing from living in the internet age is that I can see when people post a poem I've written on their blog. That can still make me cry.

Gyasi: How do you get ideas to write?

Bell: I tend to get a lot of my ideas when I am running. Sometimes, if I am lucky, I can write a whole poem in my head over the course of four miles. I also get a lot of ideas from free-writing, from just letting myself write down anything that comes to mind. When I go back and look in my free-writing notebook later, I will often find material to make a new poem with. The most magical way to make a poem, though, is to awaken very early and find that I've been writing one in my head as I sleep. This does not happen often, but I have gotten some whole poems this way.

Gyasi: Do you have any personal favorite among all the poems you've written?

Bell: Generally, I admit to a special affection for the newest thing I am working on, the poem that hasn't had a chance to disappoint me yet. Of work I have lived with for a long time, two poems come to mind as favorites: "The Yearning to Be Supple" and "Too Many Men, Each One Leaving."

Gyasi: What excites you about writing poetry?

Bell: The making of connections, the shaping of metaphors in order to more clearly see the shape of the world, the stunning emotional intimacy of it.

Gyasi: What sort of preparation went into the manuscript for your first book, *Bright Stain*?

Bell: The manuscript for my first book contains poems written over many years. There are poems I wrote in my early 20's and poems I wrote in my 40's, and there are nine years completely unrepresented by poems because I was too busy to write any. Three years ago, I sent seventy pages of poems to April Ossmann. She is herself a beautiful poet and is also a professional editor and manuscript consultant. I asked her if she thought there might be a book in those seventy pages, and, to my amazement, she said *Yes*. She gave me line editing advice about all of the poems, and she also shaped a selection of the poems into a manuscript. She has been a tremendous help and support to me.

Gyasi: You won the 2014 Neil Postman Award for Metaphor from *Rattle*. Which of your poetry won this award?

Bell: My poem "Where We Are Most Tender" won this award.

Gyasi: Is there any single writer you look up to as a role model?

Bell: As a role model, I look up to Stephen King. Most of his books are too scary for me to read (I have a very vivid imagination and a long memory), and I don't write much fiction myself, but there is so much to admire and emulate about his life and his life as a writer. King faced adversity at so many points in his personal life, from fatherlessness to family financial problems, drug and alcohol addiction, and the suffering of severe bodily injury. As a writer, he faced the usual onslaught of rejection, though he faced it early since he started to submit at fourteen. He kept writing and submitting even when he was a struggling, young father of two, even when his work was rejected and rejected and rejected. After his first novel was published, he was advised to stop writing horror in order to avoid being pigeon-holed, but he didn't. His genre and his books are often looked down on by academic writers and critics, but he keeps writing what he loves to write in the voice that he has. He does not give up. He does not try to be anything he isn't. He just keeps writing.

Gyasi: If you were to point to just one book that has affected your writing, what would it be?

Bell: *On Writing* by Stephen King.

Gyasi: What do you hope to achieve with your writing?

Bell: On a personal, private level, I hope to achieve greater understanding through writing poetry. Understanding of my individual life and understanding of humanity's collective self and the lives we lead as a group. On a public level, I hope that my poems can give voice to what others might be unable to speak about. I hope that my poems can be accessible to and find their way to readers who do not necessarily have advanced degrees and teach at universities, to readers who maybe do not even write poetry. I hope that my poems can provide moments of intimate humanity, moments when people who happen to read them will feel themselves seen in all of their staggering beauty and devastating flaw.

Debra Kang Dean is the author of *News of Home* and *Precipitates*, both from BOA Editions; two prize-winning chapbooks, *Back to Back* and *Fugitive Blues*; and *Morning's Spell*, a chapbook of renku written with Russ Kesler. Her poems have appeared in many journals, including *Rattle* and the thirty-fifth anniversary issue of *Bamboo Ridge*, and have been featured on *Poetry Daily*, *Verse Daily*, and *The Writer's Almanac*. Her essays have most recently appeared in the expanded edition of *The Colors of Nature: Culture, Identity, and the Natural World* and in *Until Everything Is Continuous Again: American Poets on the Recent Work of W. S. Merwin*. A member of the faculty of Spalding University's low-residency MFA in Writing Program since 2003, she is a regular contributor to the program's blog.

Gyasi: Before I begin, I want to send my warmest greetings to Bashô and Cricket.

Dean: Thank you, Geosi, if I may address you by your given name. Both of my feline companions have now gone over.

Gyasi: How did you come to write *Back to Back*?

Dean: I'm not someone who writes to projects; I remain, essentially, a lyric poet who writes one poem at a time, although that idea has moved beyond the short poem and into longer sequences. So I don't so much write books as discover among the poems I have written recurrent ideas and obsessions. As you may have noticed, many of the poems in this chapbook are in *News of Home*, my first full-length collection. I put that chapbook together just before a contest deadline because I wanted a stand-alone tribute to the women in my family of non-readers. I'd reached a point where I thought I'd taken *News of Home* as far as I could, and if, by chance, my full-length collection were accepted somewhere, I realized that I wouldn't be able to go backwards and publish the chapbook.

Gyasi: *Back to Back* won the Harperprints Poetry Chapbook Competition. How did you feel at the time, as it was your first poetry collection?

Dean: A very odd thing happened. I was notified that the late Ruth Stone had selected *Back to Back* for that contest, and within a couple of weeks, if I am remembering these events correctly, I received The Call from BOA about *News of Home*. I walked around in a daze for some time after that.

Gyasi: Is there any special reason why you wrote *News of Home*?

Dean: I think of this book as reflecting my apprenticeship in poetry—and perhaps that may be evident in its formal range—but by learning how to bring content to form, it was also where I came to recognize what my core subjects are. Robert Frost wrote, "A poem begins as a lump in the throat, a homesickness or love sickness." For me that longing was spiritual, not literal. I grew up in Hawaii only vaguely aware of how it was being transformed from a place of sugar and then pineapple plantations to strategic military outpost to a tourist destination; when I began writing, it was out of a kind of homesickness even as I was aware that the world I longed for wasn't there. I was discovering, however, that I could evoke and momentarily inhabit that world through writing. I sometimes think of the poems in that book as my "Fern Hill" and my answer to "Fern Hill."

Gyasi: How long did it take you to write *News of Home*?

Dean: I wrote many of the poems while I was in the MFA program at the University of Montana. It took seven more years for me to write the poems I needed to complete the big poem that is the book.

Gyasi: What inspired your book *Precipitates*?

Dean: I wanted to extend my range as a writer and at the time I was thinking about the ways that I faced both East because of my upbringing and West because of my formal education. *Precipitates* is comprised of three sequences. My writing of the poems in the second section called "Heart Sutras" began with my reading and reflecting on the Buddhist text called the "Heart Sutra"; over a period of about five years, I wrote more of these poems than are included in the book. The sequence called "Traces," which comprises the fourth section, was written in the space of ten days during the summer of 2000, I think, and came out of my reading and reflecting on "Ecclesiastes"; when I finished it, I realized I might have the makings of a book. I wrote "Patchwork of Selvage," which surrounds these sections, stanza by stanza in 1999 with the idea of putting into my writing practice the daily discipline I'd observed in my taiji practice and also under the influence of Bashō and renku writing.

The catalyst for "Patchwork of Selvage" was photographer Jim Brandenburg's book *Chased by the Light*. In the preface to this book of photographs, Brandenburg, whose work involved shooting rolls of film, talks about his decision to take only one photograph a day. I wanted to challenge myself to write toward greater "objectivity" to counterbalance the subjectivity of my writing. I use these terms in the way that Bashō is quoted as saying, "The trouble with most poetry is that it is either subjective or objective." I made a decision not to use the first person. I'd regarded what became "Patchwork of Selvage" as a worthwhile undertaking because I learned in the process to see better and to use the third person, but when I finished "Traces," I realized that it was perhaps something more than that.

Gyasi: Why did you decide to become a writer?

Dean: From what I've written so far, the answer to this question may be predictable. I can't really mark a moment when I made that decision. In one of his essays, Seamus Heaney quotes Patrick Kavanagh as saying, "You begin dabbling in verses, and they become your life." That seems true of my experience.

Gyasi: Do you have a favorite among all the books you've written?

Dean: Last year *Fugitive Blues*, which won Moon City Press's Blue Moon Poetry Chapbook Contest, was released. It is currently my favorite because its shape—it has what I think of as a tunnel in the middle—is one that I had wanted for the full-length manuscript from which many of the poems came. I have since revised the full-length manuscript into a more conventional structure, so this shape, which I think comes closest to reflecting the movements of my heart/mind, now exists only in *Fugitive Blues*.

Gyasi: You're a contributing editor for *Tar River Poetry*. Could you tell us something about *Tar River Poetry*?

Dean: I haven't been as actively engaged with that publication since Peter Makuck, a friend and mentor, was the editor of that journal. It was as a result of his confidence in me that I began writing reviews and subsequently co-conducted interviews with Louis Simpson, Betty Adcock, Patricia Goedicke, and Colette Inez.

Gyasi: What inspired your forthcoming poem, "Single-Lens Reflex"?

Dean: It's been awhile now since it appeared in print, but this sestina started as an assignment I gave myself to use six words from photography. I think this may have been triggered by a memory of seeing footage of a reporter who had just been shot saying to the cameraman, who kept filming, something like "Help me, for God's sake, I've been shot!" It was a disturbing reminder of what one risks in cultivating too objective an eye.

Gyasi: What is your poem "Distance" all about?

Dean: This poem is dedicated to Greg Pape, who was one of my teachers and is my colleague in the low-residency MFA in Writing Program at Spalding University. I wrote it during a period that is often referred to as life-after-the-MFA. It was triggered by a casual remark he once made about duck hunting, which changed the way I thought about that activity after I realized that what he had said could be understood as a metaphor for writing poetry—that it was an activity that required getting up and then outside in the dark and having the patience to sit out in the cold, watching and waiting with the expectation that those waterfowl might descend from the sky and into view, and the sensation of seeing them if they did. I thought of the poem as something given in gratitude for a metaphor that sustains me still.

Gyasi: Could you tell us the difference between prose and poetry?

Dean: I am an advocate for the line, and so I have a half-serious answer to the question: poems have a ragged right edge. However, what I've come to believe is the essential difference between prose and poetry is something C. K. Williams wrote many years ago: the form or shape of a poem is a part of the meaning. Carolyn Forché's prose poem "The Colonel" is a classic example, and more recent ones are some of the poems in Claudia Rankine's book *Citizen*, which won the

National Book Critics Circle Award. These poets went beyond the line because there was no other way to say what needed to be said; we see simultaneously, as we do in acts of civil disobedience, the line drawn and the crossing of that line but as significant gesture more than as action. To me, that manner of expressing a sense of urgency makes it different from poetic prose.

Gyasi: Could you tell us something about your prose "Ten Thousand Leaves"?

Dean: Peter Makuck invited me to write an essay for the twenty-fifth anniversary issue of *Tar River Poetry*, and it was the nudge I needed to explore in writing what I thought and felt about the place of politics in poetry. *Precipitates*, which deals more with the natural world than my first book did, was soon to be published, and it coincided with the appearance of the Poets against the War movement in protest of the invasion of Iraq. Against the backdrop of these public events, I was also dealing with difficult personal circumstances, and the essay was my way of trying to gather my thoughts toward a provisional answer. The title of the essay is an allusion to the "Man'yōshū," a classical Japanese anthology compiled in the eighth century. I have since written another essay that deals with Nature/nature called "In the Valley of Its Saying," which was published in the revised edition of *The Colors of Nature: Culture, Identity, and the Natural World*.

Gyasi: In your view, what is the difference between teaching and writing?

Dean: As a teacher, I want for my students what I want for myself. So I try to provide them with tools that will help them to become better readers, which I think is also a way for them to become writers equipped to craft poems that can engage the whole of their complex selves. I also like to introduce them to some received forms so that they can choose to write within and/or against the forms—and, by implication, the traditions out of which the forms come; I hope as well that in the process of scrutinizing the form they may find, across space and time, their own community of kindred spirits, spirits that can, paradoxically, fortify them in the work of finding and going their own way, rather than following the currents of fashion. I don't want my students to write like me, so it's not unusual for me to be teaching one thing and doing something else in my own work. It's a little like something my mother used to say to me when I was a teenager: "Do as I say, not as I do."

Gyasi: You were nominated for the Pushcart Prize in 1990, 1993, 1999, and 2003. What are your thoughts about nominations, awards, and prizes?

Dean: There were also subsequent nominations in 2006, 2010, and 2013. Such things are fleeting, but I have always been grateful to have my work acknowledged, particularly by people I've never met; it can help stave off the next round of doubts an introvert like me is susceptible to. Your e-mail note out of the blue and your interest in my work are a related kind of gift—thank you!

Gyasi: Who are your literary forebears?

Dean: The American poets who have been most important to me are Elizabeth Bishop, Stanley Kunitz, and Robert Hayden, and it's probably not a coincidence that these are poets whose volumes of collected work are comparatively slim, which I didn't know when I gravitated toward their work in anthologies—and in subsequently reading around the poems themselves, I would discover points of contact and connection. Seamus Heaney and Eavan Boland through their essays, in particular, have also been important in the way that Bashō, of course, has been. Each of these poets has helped me to think about the vocation of poetry, and I am often still bewildered by how someone like me came to be a poet; so I do think of them as forebears but more so as mentors that, with the exception of Heaney, I've never met in person. As my interests have shifted, Buson, who was known for both his painting and his poetry, has become increasingly important to me for the clarity and resonance of his images. Ellen Bryant Voigt and Louise Glück are contemporary writers whose body of work exemplifies the continual growth I aspire to.

Gyasi: What do you want to be called—poet or writer?

Dean: I'd rather inhabit a verb, and though it doesn't succeed, I can live with One-Who-Writes-Poems.

George Szirtes was born in Budapest in 1948 and came to England as a refugee in 1956. He was brought up in London and studied Fine Art in London and Leeds. His poems began appearing in national magazines in 1973 and his first book, *The Slant Door*, was published in 1979. It won the Faber Memorial prize the following year. After the publication of his second book, *November and May*, 1982, he was invited to become a Fellow of the Royal Society of Literature. Since then he has published several books and won various other prizes including the T. S. Eliot Prize for *Reel* in 2005. Szirtes lives near Norwich with his wife, the painter Clarissa Upchurch.

Gyasi: You're often referred to as a Hungarian-born British poet. My question is, where do you actually belong: Britain or Hungary?

Szirtes: Britain.

Gyasi: You went to England as a refugee in 1956 at the age of eight. Do you remember your childhood in Hungary?

Szirtes: Some of it, in flashes.

Gyasi: Could you tell us anything we ought to know about Hungary?

Szirtes: Small, landlocked country that used to be much bigger, with an isolated language and a great musical and literary tradition as well as some major photographers and filmmakers.

Gyasi: What was it like to be a refugee at that tender age?

Szirtes: Exciting, numbing.

Gyasi: Do you think moving to England has impacted your life in any positive way?

Szirtes: Of course. I have spent almost fifty-eight years here and was brought up in England. It gave me the English language, the English literary tradition, the word-hoard, safety, my wife, my children, my work. It gave me all a country could give.

Gyasi: I am wondering why you decided to study Fine Arts in London.

Szirtes: I lived in London. London was the first step, then Leeds, then London again. I studied Fine Art because having fallen in love with poetry in my last year at school I next fell in love with painting. I couldn't study English with my science A levels, but I could study art.

Gyasi: What circumstances led you to become a poet?

Szirtes: One moment in a school corridor when I read a bad poem and, for the first time in my life, knew what I wanted to do and to be.

Gyasi: What do you often write about?

Szirtes: I have written some fifteen books of poetry and much other poetic material over forty years, so have written about a wide range of subjects. My first couple of books had a lot of poems on art, the next few had many about history and the rediscovery of Hungary, there was a period when I wrote a lot about Britain, when I wrote about photographs and cinema, then about memory and language itself. I have always written poems about and out of love.

Gyasi: How did you come to write your first book, *The Slant Door*?

Szirtes: I didn't write the book. I wrote a lot of poems that I edited down to make a book and called the result *The Slant Door* after one of the poems. First books often happen that way.

Gyasi: Was it easy getting your first book published?

Szirtes: No. It is never easy. Nothing should be easy. I had been writing ten years when my first book appeared. When it did it was partly due to the agency of other older poets who believed in me.

Gyasi: From where do you get ideas to write?

Szirtes: Very wide range of inspirations—from small moments or events in life, from pictures, from words, from big events, from lines that occur to me.

Gyasi: Did you see great changes when you returned to your birthplace, Budapest, for the first time in 1984?

Szirtes: No. I recognized everything. That was the shock.

Gyasi: What does it take to be a translator?

Szirtes: A good source text, a gift for languages and, if translating poetry, a good sense of what makes a poem in the original language and, even more importantly, what makes a good poem in the language into which you are translating.

Gyasi: You've won a number of prizes for your work, including the Faber Memorial Prize and T. S. Eliot Prize. Which of them do you feel most proud of?

Szirtes: The T. S. Eliot Prize. But I have felt proud of them all—and surprised by all of them.

Gyasi: Could you tell us about the literary scene in Norwich, or the place where you live?

Szirtes: Very active. A good number of outstanding writers have emerged through the art school and the university, and the founding and developing of the Writers Centre has helped organize and encourage meetings, events, and festivals.

Gyasi: You ran The Starwheel Press with your wife, Clarissa Upchurch. How did you start this press and how is it doing?

Szirtes: Starwheel started in 1976 with a set of etchings I still had from art school. Two other small presses already existed in Hitchin where we then lived. One of them, Mandelville, was prepared to publish the etchings with new poems by me. To do that we had to buy an etching press. After a couple of years we bought a large letterpress machine too and set up to publish anthologies of poetry and etchings by other hands. We ran till 1985 when I started returning to Hungary and translation took over.

Gyasi: Do you think painting has anything in common with writing?

Szirtes: Yes, a great deal, since they are both expressive arts. They are not each other's equivalents: they work through different senses in different ways, but their perceptions have much in common.

Gyasi: Tell us about how you came to write "Mony Mony."

Szirtes: I was fascinated by the YouTube video of Tommy James and The Shondells performing it back in the late sixties. The video itself was very simple and frontal. That is what was exciting about it. It was like watching a doomed cage of time full of exciting music that remained exciting.

Gyasi: Are there any writers who have inspired you as a writer?

Szirtes: Many at different times. Here are a few among the moderns: Arthur Rimbaud, T. S. Eliot, Max Jacob, Martin Bell, W. H. Auden, John Crowe Ransom, Sándor Weöres, Wallace Stevens, Elizabeth Bishop, Anthony Hecht, Joseph Brodsky, Derek Mahon, Louis MacNeice, Theodore Roethke, Ágnes Nemes Nagy, Rainer Maria Rilke. Earlier: Donne, George Herbert, Alexander Pope, Swift, Byron's comic verse.

Gyasi: Do you ever regret, as a writer?

Szirtes: No. I have been enormously fortunate to have found an art that is exciting, unpredictable, mysterious, and majestic and has given me encouragement and reward enough for me to continue

Gyasi: Do you feel you've achieved all there is to achieve as a writer?

Szirtes: Certainly not!

Zenobia Frost is an Australian writer and editor whose debut poetry collection, *The Voyage*, was released in 2009. Frost (Brisbane) is the assistant editor of *Cordite Poetry Review*. Her work has been published in *Voiceworks*, *Overland*, *Southerly*, *The Lifted Brow,* and *Rave Magazine*. Frost was shortlisted in the 2013 Overland Judith Wright Poetry Prize and won second place in the 2013 John Marsden Prize for Young Australian Writers. Her debut collection, *Salt and Bone*, is forthcoming from Walleah Press.

Gyasi: Between page and stage, which one is your first love?

Frost: Page, I think. Writing poetry was how I learned to be happy with my own company. I can fiddle with one line or one piece of punctuation for hours on end. Sometimes, when I write a new poem, I'm excited to wake up the next morning just to see it with fresh eyes and make it better. When it comes to other writers' poetry, time spent reading quietly with a cup of tea is sacred.

Gyasi: The stage is constantly in motion: performing or reading poetry. How do you translate the static, tactile pages to the stage?

Frost: I aim to choose poems that have a distinct conversational voice or rhythm. It's true that some poems live in and on the page—they need time and rereading to be absorbed. For me, the best performative poems marry rhythm with semantic resonance. Musicality and meaning.

Gyasi: Do you ever regret venturing into this business of writing?

Frost: I think it was inevitable. I'm grateful that I've found my way into jobs that help me balance the writing life with getting the bills paid. I find that full-time professional editing, especially when working from home, can eat up the motivation to write creatively. I much prefer having a day job that differs drastically from writing and editing (though the occasional freelance contract helps keep me sharp).

Gyasi: Your debut poetry collection, *The Voyage*, released by SweetWater Press (Brisbane) in May of 2009, brought you much attention. Moving on, how has this attention been managed?

Frost: I wouldn't say that it brought unmanageable attention. It did, I think, catalyze some fantastic opportunities, like touring around Australia with the Arts Queensland Touring Poets program in late 2009. But I'm still a quiet voice in Australian poetry—I'm not sure, to be honest, if I'm emerging or emerged.

Gyasi: Ross Clark said of your debut chapbook: "This first collection somehow combines undertones of both *The Ancient Mariner* and *The Hunting of the Snark*, while remaining determinedly in her own voice." Have you therefore found your own voice and how would you describe it?

Frost: I think I have, especially in the last couple of years. I expect it's a very Brisbane voice; I find myself returning again and again to Queensland's architecture, weather and animals — if not to our Brissie lingo, mate. I've finished proofing the book that will be out, hopefully, within the next couple of months: *Salt and Bone* (Walleah Press). (Forgive the plug.) It's been fascinating reading it with distance: to pretend I'm an editor who's never heard of me. I think I'd describe my poetic voice as lyrical and assertive.

Gyasi: Do you consider place an important ingredient in the writing process?

Frost: For me, definitely. A poem can be a way to visit or revisit a place, via scent or sound. In writing, I find a poem can be a way into an old memory; I spent my early childhood in New Zealand and the UK; all those memories are sensory. I also think I feel an obligation to exalt Brisbane, a city that's sometimes a little embarrassed of itself. I've lived a lot of places and this one is home. I think artworks that unabashedly live in and for Brisbane are important.

Gyasi: "... cotton-gloved rabbits/a few aeons late/to taste the blade's full thrust." (From your poem, "Archaeology") The question is, where do you purchase your diction?

Frost: To answer this question, I have dragged up old drafts of "Archaeology" to look back on early iterations of those lines. I think the diction emerges, like a sculpture, via a process of whittling. My early drafts are often very verbose; later edits are slimmer and slimmer. My hope is always that the end product will be a concise, clear image.

Gyasi: May I query you on the caption on your blog—*A Storm of Tea Cups*? Are you obsessed with tea?

Frost: Heh. A bit. Yes. A visitor recently remarked, "You seem to have bought the whole tea shop"—or something to that effect. There's something to be said for the ritual of tea. Having a pot always brewing nearby seems meaningful. I've always been a black tea drinker, but recently I had to cut down on caffeine, so suddenly I have a new shelf: rooibos, mint, honeybush, lemongrass, ginger ...

Gyasi: Who would you likely pick as your literary influence?

Frost: Just the one? Eep! Early on in my writing, I might have said Oscar Wilde, because I was obsessed with *The Picture of Dorian Gray*. As an adult, my influences are many and variable, but often include lyricists. Josh Pyke and Glenn Richards (Augie March) certainly stand out to me as musicians whose lyrics have a poetic, distinctly Australian flavor. My favorite novels are poetic and surreal: Virginia Woolf's *Orlando*, Janette Winterson's *Sexing the Cherry*, Italo Calvino's *If on a Winter's Night a Traveller*. I'm no good at following one writer's whole career, but I read a lot of bits and pieces.

Gyasi: What did you have in mind at the time of writing your poem "Early Rituals"? How much of your personal life is reflected in your poetry?

Frost: When I was around 11 or 12, Mum would let me put temporary colors in my hair—usually purple-ish or reddish washes. These would last as long as the holidays—but sometimes, if I was careful, a little longer. I always liked that my mum was complicit in these subtle rebellions against dress code. This ritual—something Mum and I did together—was emblematic of her support as puberty kicked in, with all its attendant rites of passage.

More often than not, my poems might be considered confessional. I certainly write fictional poems, but I find that writing from memory comes easiest.

Gyasi: You work as a writer and editor. How do these two complement each other?

Frost: I think writing and editing are inseparable: editing is just the biggest chunk of the process known as writing. As soon as the first draft is down, the editing begins. They complement one another, as do two sides of the same coin.

Gyasi: This may sound silly, but here it is—how did you fall in love with graveyards?

Frost: When I first moved out of the family home, I lived in a sharehouse two streets away from Brisbane's biggest cemetery. In the Victorian tradition, Toowong Cemetery is a parkland first and graveyard second. I spent a lot of time there: walking, writing, meeting with the friend whom I'd wind up falling in love with. To me, graveyards signify new beginnings and nature. They have just enough inherent weirdness to please my inner teen-goth too, I admit. They're such a funny, human thing: a beautiful botanical garden dotted with little stone shrines to our ancestors. In the 1970s, a large number of tombstones were removed from Toowong Cemetery with the aim of increasing its sense of park-ness—some land was even cleared as a cricket or picnic area. You can imagine how well that went down. This clearing, pockmarked with grave-shaped indents, remains quite un-picnicked. Except by me. So there you go.

Amy Miller's poetry has appeared in *Bellingham Review*, *Cascadia Review*, *Nimrod*, *Rattle*, *Willow Springs*, and *ZYZZYVA*, and in anthologies including *The Knotted Bond* and the upcoming *Clash by Night: A London Calling Anthology*. She won the Cultural Center of Cape Cod National Poetry competition (judged by Tony Hoagland), the *Whiskey Island* Poetry Prize, and the Poetry Storehouse First Anniversary videopoem contest, and has been a finalist for the Pablo Neruda Prize and the 49th Parallel Award. Her chapbooks include *In the Hand*, *Botanica*, and *Tea Before Questions*, and her articles on writing and chapbook design appear in *The Writer's Journal* and *The Poet's Market*. A longtime book editor, she now works as the publications project manager at the Oregon Shakespeare Festival.

Website: http://writers-island.blogspot.com.

Gyasi: Tell us about the Cultural Center of Cape Cod National Poetry Competition you won.

Miller: The Cultural Center of Cape Cod is an arts center in South Yarmouth, Massachusetts, that puts on exhibitions and performances serving the arts community of Cape Cod. They hold a national poetry contest each year, judged by a well-known poet and advertised in the "big" venues like *Poets & Writers*. The year I entered, Tony Hoagland was their judge. That year it seemed like Tony's name was on everyone's lips—he was red-hot, and I was just getting familiar with his work, which I loved. I was thrilled to bits to win that contest. In a funny add-on, I got to take Tony to a play a couple of years ago when he came to read and teach a workshop in my town. I meant to thank him for being the judge in that contest, but he was such a fun, down-to-earth date that I forgot to say that to him, and we never even talked about poetry. Instead we talked about washing machines and hearing aids and real estate.

Gyasi: You've also been a finalist for the Pablo Neruda Prize. Have you read Pablo Neruda?

Miller: I have read Neruda and admire his work a lot, though I'm not an expert in it. The Pablo Neruda prize isn't necessarily for poetry that's like Neruda's (probably lucky for me); it's *Nimrod*'s annual competition. *Nimrod*, published by the University of Tulsa, is one of my favorite literary journals. I often read poems in there that I like so much that I immediately go look up the author on the internet, or friend him/her on Facebook.

Gyasi: When did you become a writer?

Miller: I started writing when I was 7 or 8 years old. I had some glass animals—little dogs and ducks and horses that were cheap and popular at the time, that I got at the local hardware store—and I used to write elaborate adventure tales about them. They braved great storms, fell in love, got sick and died ... all kinds of drama. I started writing poetry around age 12, mostly in response to reading e.e. cummings, whose playfulness I really liked.

Gyasi: Do you mind telling us about your work as an editor and publications manager with the Oregon Shakespeare Festival?

Miller: The Oregon Shakespeare Festival is a huge deal in Southern Oregon; it brings thousands of tourists to the region and is a crucial part of the local economy. I've worked in publishing most of my life, for magazines and book publishers, and now I'm the project manager for most of OSF's printed pieces: the playbill that you grab on your way into a show, the season brochures with all the ticket info, the souvenir program with glossy photo spreads of all the shows that year, and many other brochures. I edit and sometimes write the text, choose photos, work with designers and freelancers, do layout in InDesign, and make sure everything is approved by the people who have a stake in it, everyone from playwrights to box office managers. It's a big job, a hell of a lot of work, and during the busiest times it takes up most of my energy. But it's an artistic, creative environment where everybody strives to do great things—one of our shows, *All the Way*, went on to Broadway this past year and won the Tony award for Best Play. We all got to spend a little time with the Tony statue, like hockey players with the Stanley Cup.

Gyasi: What influenced your book *In the Hand*?

Miller: That book started out as one thing, then changed into something different. I was gearing up to teach a workshop on printing books through CreateSpace, Amazon's self-publishing platform, and wanted to publish a small book with CreateSpace as a case study. So I started putting together a manuscript of short poems with a "miniature" theme, small poems that sort of fit in the hand. But as I chose which poems to put in and which to leave out, a narrative began to emerge about confinement and oppression and the tight spaces that we—women, in particular—sometimes find ourselves in. I ended up abandoning the "miniature" idea and bringing in some longer poems that expanded on that new theme. Then the new theme dictated the cover, which I had a *really* good time designing.

Gyasi: What is your book *Botanica* all about?

Miller: I'm a longtime gardener (though my backyard is a mess right now), and I've written many poems about plants, flowers, trees, etc. *Botanica* collects some of them. I also do the National Poetry Writing Month (NaPoWriMo) poem-a-day challenge every year, and since it's always in April, I often end up writing poems about spring and all the crazy stuff blooming and bees and the headiness of abundance after the cold winter. Several of those NaPoWriMo poems made their way into *Botanica*.

Gyasi: What is the greatest challenge you've ever encountered as a writer?

Miller: By far, the greatest challenge I face as a writer is just to keep doing it. Writing can be a frustrating business—rejections, critiques, self-doubt, keeping track of journals and publishers, and the constant hard work of the writing itself. In my late 20s I got so fed up with it that I gradually stopped writing and sending stuff out without realizing I was giving up on it. Then, about ten years later, I came down with a serious illness that made me think hard about what I wanted to do with my time here on Earth. And I realized with horror that I'd quietly stopped writing—a thing that had once given me joy and that I felt was important, in spite of all the frustrations. It scared me, how easy it had been to just give up on it. I try to keep that in my mind all the time. It's easy to get discouraged and say, "Oh, I'll do that later" and quit without even knowing you're quitting. I've seen some very good writers do that.

Gyasi: Who are your literary forebears?

Miller: I was influenced early on by e.e. cummings, as I mentioned. His rule-breaking really appealed to me as a kid (still does). In high school in Massachusetts, I had a great English teacher who had us read a lot of Anne Sexton, who was also a Massachusetts poet. As a teenager I soaked her up like a sponge, all that imaginative language and strange word choices and brutal honesty. I also loved Dylan Thomas, for many of the same reasons ("night above the dingle starry"). Louise Glück has strongly influenced my more recent work. I like her mix of tenderness and cynicism, and her work is full of surprising leaps.

Gyasi: When and where do you often write?

Miller: I usually write poetry late at night, in bed, with a pen and notebook. I sometimes wake in the middle of the night and write then, a fruitful time for me, with the subconscious closer to the surface. On the other hand, I tend to write nonfiction and blog entries on the weekends, in the daytime, at the computer. Prose tends to be a daytime activity; poetry is mostly a nighttime one.

Gyasi: What is the best poem you've ever written?

Miller: Oh, that's like trying to say which is your favorite kid! All are flawed; some are beautiful in some types of light. Today I like this poem; tomorrow I'll hack it to bits. The fact that we can constantly edit our poems gives them a sort of perpetual imperfection. That said, right now I'm high on a prose poem I wrote about a trek in the New England countryside during hunting season that really, under the surface, is about the crapshoot nature of our decisions. That sounded like a really bad elevator pitch.

Gyasi: Do you remember your first piece of writing?

Miller: I think it was a short story called "Eight Sacred Horses" that I wrote at age seven or eight. It was, as I recall, an action-adventure-romance-sci-fi-Western.

Gyasi: What theme(s) do you often write on?

Miller: When I'm stuck for an idea, I tend to go back to a couple of topics: horses, and my youth in western New England. I suppose I'm always trying to write the perfect horse poem, the impossible task of making a poem that comes anywhere near the beauty of a horse. And my teenage years in Massachusetts were full of things that formed me as a person—first love, first loss, first exposure to a lot of literature, the historic landscape itself, "old" families and newer communities of immigrants, abandoned mills and bygone industries. It's peculiar that the place that sparks the most ideas for me is the one I don't live in anymore. Or perhaps that's not peculiar at all.

Gyasi: How did you get your first piece of work published?

Miller: The first piece of writing I had published in a real journal/magazine was a personal essay in *Fine Gardening* in the mid-1990s. I sent in the submission, then heard nothing for a year and gave up on it. When the acceptance letter finally arrived, I was so surprised that my knees literally gave out and I sank to the floor while reading the letter. After I signed the contract, it was more waiting: two more years went by until one morning when I got a phone call from an editor at the magazine. He said the editor I'd been working with had left the company sometime ago, and my essay had been lost in a filing cabinet. He apologized and said he was running it in their next issue. It came out a few months later with a beautiful layout, and the magazine nominated it for a Garden Writers Association award. I learned some lessons from that experience, but mostly the value of patience and being a good sport. It turned out fine in the end.

The first poem I had published was in *Rattle*. Stellasue Lee, the editor at the time (this was before Tim Green, "B.T.G."), called me up to accept the poem and suggest a small revision. We talked for about a half hour. To think that acceptances used to come in phone calls! Seems quaint now.

Gyasi: Do you often get rejections from publishers?

Miller: Oh gosh, yes. I've had hundreds. I think I got three last week (and one acceptance, yay). Most of the time, rejections are no big deal; they're part of the process. I wasn't always this thick-skinned (see "quit for ten years" above), and once in a while a rejection still hurts a lot. When that happens, I allow myself to feel bad for 24 hours. By the next day, I'm usually over it and can move on.

Gyasi: Do you have any ritual you do before you sit down to write?

Miller: I actually don't like writing rituals or superstitions. I hate routine, and writing works best for me when it feels new and fresh; rituals run counter to that impulse. The only thing I'm fussy about is pens. I write poems with cheap ballpoints swiped from hotels. When I find a hotel pen that has good poems in it, I use it until it's out of ink, and then I have to audition a few new hotel pens (I pick them up wherever I go) until one coughs up a good poem. Then it's the anointed pen for as long as it lasts.

Gyasi: Do you write love poems?

Miller: Sure. Love is one of those bottomless, infinitely complex topics. I also think that, in a way, all poems are love poems. I mean, why would we want to leave our writing behind in the world if we didn't love and believe on some level?

Gyasi: What is the best response you've ever received from a fan of your work?

Miller: I got an e-mail a few years ago from a professor in England who wanted to use one of my poems in a class she was teaching on "The Poetry of Home." A lot of her students were immigrants and young people away from home for the first ime. The concept of "home" has always been a thorny one for me because my family moved a lot, so that was kind of serendipitous.

Gyasi: What is the relevance of poetry?

Miller: Such a hard question. There's so much talk now—maybe always—about whether poetry can have an affect on the world, whether it can be used as an instrument of change with all our social turmoil going on. To that I say, absolutely, it can. Just as songs work their way into our heads to give us a way to articulate something we've been thinking, so do poems, with their inherent musicality, stick in our memory. But I get awfully self-conscious thinking about whether what I write is relevant. That feels like the enemy of creativity; it imposes a sort of authoritarianism onto an act that should, at its heart, be anarchistic and heedless. And who is to say what is important or relevant? I think our treatment of animals is one of the most important issues facing human civilization. It's on my mind all the time, so I write about it. And if somebody gets my lines in their head, never mind if I'm only preaching to the choir, then maybe they pass it along and it becomes relevant to somebody else. Every step is important.

Gyasi: Do you do poetry readings?

Miller: Yes, I love doing readings. I love making eye contact with people in the audience and reading *to* them; I enjoy seeing their reactions and feeding off that energy. I'm extremely shy, even sociophobic at times. But doing readings and open mikes for all these years has made me a "situational extrovert"—put me on a stage, and I turn into a big ham.

Gyasi: What is the most boring part of writing?

Miller: I love this question! I would have to say "making myself do it." Or maybe feeling bad about not doing it, that negative space between the writing, when I'm thinking, "Good lord, I don't want to write because it's so bloody hard." I mean, I love writing, but a part of me always has to be dragged to it kicking and screaming. Logging in rejections is also pretty boring and demoralizing. I have yet to come up with a way to make that fun. Make a drinking game out of it.

Gyasi: How do you begin a poem?

Miller: They begin in all sorts of ways. Sometimes the title or a line presents itself in something I overhear or some unusual phrase that comes to mind. Sometimes it's a response to an event layered with a complex mix of emotions, something that I feel two or three or four ways about at the same time. Sometimes it begins with a surprise, something I wasn't expecting to see or feel, or a sentence in my head when I wake up that comes from a dream I can't remember. Then it's a matter of finding the phrasing and voice, and sometimes that's just trial and error; I'll often go through several "beginnings" until I hit on a syntax, tone, and visual style that feels fertile and interesting.

Gyasi: How do you end a poem?

Miller: I find this one of the hardest parts of writing poetry. I'm a big fan of ending a poem with an image rather than a statement or abstraction, something I picked up from Dorianne Laux and Joe Millar when I took a workshop with them a few years ago. Occasionally I stray from that, but it's a great go-to method for finding an ending that's strongly evocative yet doesn't try to sum up the poem or tell the reader what to think. Of course endings are still a challenge with every poem; I change them all the time. I always hope I'll find the ending is already in there buried in a bunch of junk I can trim away.

Gyasi: Do you want readers to like what you do?

Miller: I certainly want some readers to like it a lot. But, that said, it's difficult to predict what readers or editors will respond to. I can't tell you how many times I've sent a batch of poems to a journal with three or four poems that I think are perfect for them and one that I'm not sure about, only to have them pick the "not sure" one. Happens all the time! So my gauge for "people will like this" is always out of whack. I try not to think about it too much; I try to write poems that excite me, and let the rest take its course.

Gyasi: My favorite title of all your books is *Tea Before Questions*. Could you tell us how the book came into being?

Miller: I'm very glad you like the title. I can't take credit for it; it's from a great book called *The Last Speakers: The Quest to Save the World's Most Endangered Languages* by linguist K. David Harrison, in a story about how he traveled to Tuva to stay with a family and study their language. The full quote goes like this: "I carried a letter of introduction ... They could never have dreamed an American linguist would be dropped at their doorstep. Yet they reacted with aplomb, offering me, in true Tuvan style, tea before questions." That kind of practical acceptance and kindness is, in my mind, an ideal way to live life.

Joy Gaines-Friedler is the author of two full-length collections of poetry, *Like Vapor* (Mayapple Press, 2008), which was among the press's top seller, and *Dutiful Heart* (Broadkill River Review Press, 2013), where one critic wrote that the book lets the reader "Understand sorrow and love—not as two antagonizing partners—but as complementary and necessary things encouraging human interaction. It is then that we can begin to find cures and contentment, joyful apertures." Her work is published in over 50 literary journals and anthologies, including the *Poets in Michigan in Poetry Anthology* and *The Bloomsbury Anthology of Contemporary Jewish American Poetry*. The recipient of numerous scholarships and awards, including *The Litchfield Review* National Poetry Series Award for a series of poems based on the journal of her friend Jim who died from AIDS, Gaines-Friedler's work has also been recognized and nominated for prizes including a Pushcart. Her work can be found in, among others, *The Pebble Lake Review*, *The New York Quarterly*, *Rattle*, *The Paterson Literary Review*, *The San Pedro River Review*, *The Writer's Digest*, *Poetica*, and others.

Gaines-Friedler teaches Advanced Poetry and Creative Writing for non-profits in the Detroit area where she teaches and facilitates workshops with, among others, Detroit Public Schools, mental health care provider services, universities, private schools, women's conferences, and historical societies. Gaines-Friedler teaches with the philosophy that writing is transformative, and that every writer is a part of the history of all writers. A troubled young man once told her, after working with her for six weeks, that what he learned from the workshop is that "I'm not as unhappy as I thought I was." At twenty-one Gaines-Friedler traveled cross-country with a band called The Midnight Special. For twenty years, before publishing poetry and essays, before university studies and teaching, Gaines-Friedler made her living as a photographer in the Detroit area photographing, among others, dignitaries such as Mayor Coleman A. Young, Roger Smith (the once CEO of General Motors), and a number of well-known news anchors. For Gaines-Friedler, photography and poetry, all art, is an act of respect and historical documentation.

Gyasi: Growing up in Oak Park Michigan, do you have any fun memories about the place?

Gaines-Friedler: Oak Park Michigan was one of those newly minted 1950s suburbs (of Detroit) with little brick houses, freshly planted oak trees, sidewalks, a ton of kids where about the most dangerous thing we ever did was play with cap guns and vaporize insects with a magnifying glass. What I particularly remember is playing Pin-The-Tail-On-The-Donkey at birthday parties in our basement made of knotty pine walls, and because my mother never learned to drive, being taken by taxi to Hebrew School. I was the youngest of three kids, and because I had a childhood illness that kept me hospitalized a lot, from age 5 through 13, and because we moved from there when I was eleven, my memories of Oak Park are small; they take place in small spaces, and for small periods of time. I didn't feel particularly connected to others in the neighborhood the way my brother and sister did.

Gyasi: How did you become a writer?

Gaines-Friedler: I have always been a creative person. I needed it. I liked Paint-By-Numbers and Sparkle Paints. I liked helping my father put things together, a new shoe rack, or the metal swing that I still own today. As a teenager I would sit on my bedroom floor and recreate in pencils the album covers of Led Zeppelin. Creating and recreating was something I had to do. I kept diaries off and on. "Dear Di" I would start each passage and then pour out my adolescent angst about a boy named Larry whom I lived and breathed for.

I went to college, essentially for the first time, when I was 40 years old. My first class I was asked to read the journals of Sylvia Plath and Anais Nin. I was captivated as much by the craft and quality of the writing as I was the content. Then I saw the video *Where The Soul Lives* narrated by Bill Moyers. There, Robert Bly reads his love poem "Ferns" while strumming a mandolin, and Lucille Clifton makes the argument that poetry can be fun—that a poet can have fun with language. Then, she reads poems about her body parts. I was smitten. But what really nailed poetry for me was reading Pablo Neruda, Wendell Berry, Anne Sexton, and Sharon Olds. I had no idea people were out there expressing what mattered to them with such craft. They were artistic essays on life come alive. They were music that reached madly into my soul, they were like photographs, simple images, simple language but deeply metaphoric. I got it. I get it. I crave it. I read poetry every day. Every single day and have for years. I learned the craft of poetry from reading it. I also learned from attending workshops. Lots of them with lots of amazing writers and teachers of writing.

Gyasi: Could you share the story of your travels with The Midnight Special band?

Gaines-Friedler: At twenty-one, having just quit a job as a medical assistant at a busy Detroit walk-in clinic (I hurt an old man while drawing his blood and quit on the spot), I was invited to join the travels of an agented band called The Midnight Special. They were a top 40s bar band originally from California. My best friend Linda and I went to hear them every night at a hotel bar called Dewy's. We got to know the band members, really nice guys, and the female singer, Becky, whom I am still very close with. I went on the road with them for five months. We went to South Padre Island, Texas; Colorado Springs, Colorado; and Redlands, California. The band broke up in California. I stayed on in L.A. and went to photography school for two years at The Artography Academy in North Hollywood.

Gyasi: What do you aim to achieve with your writing?

Gaines-Friedler: My aim is always communication. Communication is what creates connection. I crave connection. To me a poem is a conversation, a conversation that continues as we, the poet and reader, think more and more about what's being said and from what personal history the poem is experienced. A poem is like the 2:00 am phone call to say more, the all night discussion about God, the confession, the joke, the tears and laughter of connection. My poems obviously won't communicate with everyone. But to those who are open to hearing what is written on that page, I hope they find a bit of themselves there, find something in my voice that is their voice, their experience, and I hope they feel a little less alone.

Gyasi: Is it true that you're a professional photographer?

Gaines-Friedler: Yes, I made my living as a photographer. I always liked working. I've had a lot of jobs, and I worked in my father's small manufacturing plant. I loved working in the plant with the noise of the machines. I went to photography school in California when I was 21, after the band broke-up and I did not want to go back to Michigan. But, it turns out, I was lonely in L.A. My best friends, Linda and Jim, wanted me to come home, so I returned to Michigan where I lived in Jim's basement in Inkster for a time. Linda came over almost every weekend. It was there that I began my own business as a freelance photographer, a career I had for 20 years. I had a showing of my nature photography at The Botanical Gardens in Ann Arbor, but I made my living photographing people and products. I photographed families, models, fake food, houses, horses, and occasionally a wedding. I photographed a lot of dignitaries including the Mayor of Detroit, Coleman Young.

Gyasi: Why did you decide to enroll in Oakland Community College?

Gaines-Friedler: In 1985 my life changed completely. My best friend Jim was diagnosed with AIDS. In 1988 I divorced my husband of nine years. In 1990 Jim died. Two years later I had had breakfast with Linda, the closest person I've ever had in my life, with whom I laughed more than with anyone else. She could barely talk. She was trying to tell me something that was, it seemed, terribly humiliating for her. Finally, she told me that she was leaving her husband. She had at the time a three-year-old son. She couldn't tell me why she was leaving Michael, but promised she would. I was confused and concerned but I trusted her. I hugged her goodbye and told her that I loved her. I phoned her that night. She didn't answer, so I left a message. The next morning I received a phone call from Linda's friend Joan. Linda and her husband Michael were both dead, she told me. Michael had shot and killed Linda. Then killed himself.

In the course of three years I'd lost the most important people in my life; I'd lost the people I could turn to with "remember when's." It was as though my adult history were erased. It took a couple of years for me to have legs again. But when I did I saw that I had a new life. I remarried. I took photography jobs all over Michigan. And then one day, more than anything, I wanted to study. I enrolled in community college (and would continue through to the university and to graduate school.) I was 40 years old.

> Gyasi: Could you tell us something about the creative writing seminars and workshops you run?

Gaines-Friedler: I teach privately and for non-profits. I teach poetry and memoir to adults of all writing experiences, from beginners to well established writers. I also teach for community health networks which service young adults "at risk," parents of murdered children, and battered and abused women. I learned about the "underdog" from being one, and from knowing them in their iron lungs and full body casts. I learned from the cancer patients and burn victims in the hospital children's wards. I learned, and was exposed to great writing from gracious and devoted writers and teachers of writing. And, most importantly, from my own reading and writing, I learned that writing is a transformative art, that the page is a place for self-discovery.

I am lucky to be able to combine my few talents, such as they are, in order to offer something to a community that I know needs to be heard, acknowledged, and recognized—sometimes heard by themselves more than by anyone else. To write three things you saw today is to honor what you pay attention to. To describe an abstract feeling in a concrete way is to give that feeling an image, to then see it more clearly, to own that feeling in a different way. I work with young adults who have issues of gender identification, bullying, suicide, homelessness, drug abuse, sexual abuse, and more. I work with young mothers and teenagers who have gotten themselves adjudicated to group homes. I work with people who are grateful for two hours of art that may have nothing (and everything) to do with their losses. By writing a love poem, an ode to something seemingly mundane, the sky for instance, by listening to poems, by making objects in the room "talk," they are in a different part of their brains and something magical happens there. Something, I've been told more than once, is so much better than therapy (apologies to the psychologists).

> Gyasi: How difficult is it to teach people how to write?

Gaines-Friedler: It is not difficult to inspire one to write. I simply ask students to describe what they see around them. I start each workshop by reading aloud something amazing, then talk about how the poet/writer used craft. We are all gods I tell them. We are the great manipulators. We can make people feel and think and see. Craft can be taught. It is, however, more challenging to get people to take risks, to be brave enough to mine their own psychology—to release themselves from guilt—to acknowledge that they actually have something to show us or to say. The simple can be meaningful. The personal, universal. If they read enough, they usually get it. This is art. I wouldn't tell Van Gogh to use less purple or stop painting sunflowers.

Gyasi: How did you come to write "Capitalism, South Carolina"?

Gaines-Friedler: People who know me know that I am politically sensitive, meaning, I am keenly aware of who has power over whom. I am a person who is perhaps hypersensitive to the excesses of power. And, as a poet and photographer, I am a keen observer. My husband and I had taken a road trip from Myrtle Beach, North Carolina, to Savannah, Georgia, to Charleston, South Carolina. Along the way I saw the crazy number of hilariously themed miniature golf courses in North Carolina. We saw the endless number of cargo ships in and out of the ports in Savannah. We saw the old black men selling handwoven baskets along the road in South Carolina. We stopped and toured what was once a cotton and brick plantation where some of the slave houses are still kept, now as a tourist attraction. I can't remember what it cost to take the tour of that plantation, but I was horrified by everything about it. Everything is economics. We fought a civil war over the slave economy. Thus the connection in my poem to the fake worlds of the miniature golf courses created by Styrofoam mountains, and Fort Sumter (which seems to float "like Styrofoam") out in the Charleston harbor, where the first shots of the civil war, that war over economic freedom to own human beings as slaves, were fired.

Gyasi: How do you start a poem?

Gaines-Friedler: Poems seem to come to me in two ways: often from an image, something I've imagined or actually seen (the hand of a large, tattooed man gently holding the hand of a child for example, or, my mother at the sink weeping when my father was dying. Or a firefly.) I'm deeply moved by images. Or, a poem will start with a line—a line that comes to me when I'm doing something else—like making a cup of coffee. Recently I heard a cardinal singing during a rain storm—the line came to me "Even in the rain/the birds sing/the birds fly." It felt wonderfully metaphorical and wound up being the last line of a recent poem.

Gyasi: How do you end a poem?

Gaines-Friedler: My poems tend to end on an image. I like a poem to open up at the end. I don't make summary statements at the end of my poems—I let the images create or deepen meaning. That being said, I will sometimes end on a statement—but a statement that opens up thought.

Gyasi: Are there times you feel like not writing?

Gaines-Friedler: I never feel like not writing. There are times when I can't write for various psychological reasons and I accept that. I try to be patient with myself. I try not to compete with myself or others. If that period of not writing poems goes too long I might start to feel frustrated, but returning to my journals to circle good lines or sentences, or journaling anew, or reading another's poem actively, meaning circling and taking marginal notes, almost always gets me writing again. The process of writing is the process of discovery.

Gyasi: Could you introduce us to your book *Like Vapor*?

Gaines-Friedler: The title poem of the book *Like Vapor* introduces the mother in this book of characters. She is a person who appears and disappears both figuratively and literally in the life of the speaker. My mother suffered depression in an era before Prozac. She was suicidal at times and her joy, her "self," would come and go without a moment's notice. She, like so much of life, is someone who metaphorically cannot be grasped, known, or held onto; she, like everyone, is like "the clouds misty edges/ she will disappear again"—The metaphor of trying to draw her with colored pencil, "white pencil on white paper/ gray on gray," I think, speaks to the book's entire volume: What we think we know is nothing compared to what we don't know. As I learned from the murder of my friend Linda. I had no idea what was going on in my best friend's life. I spoke to or saw her almost every day for twenty years. It turns out, I didn't know what was going on in her life. This is a book about accepting this, even celebrating it. Even Eve is misunderstood in my poem "Eve," for she was "blamed for something she knew nothing about." All Eve craved was Adam's "untamed touch." There is a miscarriage, there are poems created from the AIDS journal of my friend Jim (that he "willed" to me.) There are poems about domestic violence, divorce, about the loss of my father from cancer and how I grew closer to him during that time. There are even Distracted Angels. But, along with loss in this collection there is splendor, humor, redemption, and above all, love. The poem "Grief" explains this: "I call on sorrow/ to remind me that life is/ not external or hollow/ but rather full of content/ in moments that only sorrow can awaken in me.

Gyasi: Do you know who reads your works?

Gaines-Friedler: It is such a wonderful surprise for any writer, I think, to hear from a reader. I hear from readers occasionally who tell me they loved such and such a poem and thank me for writing it. Can you imagine that? That someone, a stranger, would find you and thank you for your art, which is your heart, your soul, yourself.

Gyasi: What is the most boring part of writing?

Gaines-Friedler: The most boring part of writing is submitting. It's something I'm not very good at. I read a lot of literary magazines and journals. Every year I rotate subscriptions. I want to support the efforts of these editors. But going through submission guidelines online—and making "packets" for submission? Ugh. By the way, I have a wall in my office I call my *Wall of Rejections*. It reminds me that someone besides me and my husband are reading these poems. It helps me see my history and to honor those poems that might not have found their homes immediately, but eventually did. It reminds me why I do this ... to communicate something meaningful and to honor what it means to be human—including rejection.

Gyasi: How different is your book *Dutiful Heart* from *Like Vapor*?

Gaines-Friedler: My second book, *Dutiful Heart,* continues this weaving of loss with transcendence, knowledge, and awakening. We are different human beings every day. This book becomes more introspective, more spiritual I think. It is a book about my mother's eight year disappearance from dementia. I was her care provider. The last poem in the book, "Harbors," was nominated for a Pushcart. That poem, and "Poem for Place," express how everything is what it is. It's a book of acceptance. A lot of the poems in *Dutiful Heart* are lyrical narratives, but the narratives are not necessarily my factual truth. They do, however, speak to a spiritual truth. Again, truth is filtered through humor and observation, "the elderly line up in their wheelchairs along the wall like soldiers with no enemies," for example (from "Assisted Living: Caring for the Irreducible"). Love transcends loss. It's a book about love. Aren't all books?

Gyasi: Is your poem "Another Field" your shortest poem ever?

Gaines-Friedler: "Another Field" is indeed my shortest published poem. I love that little powerhouse.

Gyasi: Do you often perform your poems?

Gaines-Friedler: I do quite a lot of readings. I believe, strongly, that poems belong to the world. So too, one certainly experiences a poem more richly, I think, from hearing it. I like to make a reading a kind of full experience. I like to come up with a theme for a reading then plug my poems into that theme. Without being didactic, I want my readings to be an awe inspiring way to learn something about ourselves. Kinda like a play or a musical concert.

Gyasi: What are your literary future aspirations?

Gaines-Friedler: I aspire to write poems. Writing a poem pleases me in a way that nothing else does (it is close to how I feel when I play piano). Writing makes me feel full and satisfied. It feels more real to me than anything else. I also love to teach. I love bringing this amazing art to the hands, hearts, and fingers of others. When I write a poem I imagine my audience as a someone who loves me and wants to hear what I have to say. I also want to be that audience for others. I'm always thrilled when poems get picked up for publication. I aspire to that, and to the creation of my next books, but the deepest satisfaction comes from creating the work itself.

Gyasi: Do you care about subject matter when you write?

Gaines-Friedler: I've learned to let my poems have their own say as to subject. I wish I could be even more brave than I am. I admire poets, especially women, who own brash, brave voices. I've been told my voice is quiet. Strong, but quiet. I try to fight the impetus to write "about" something. I start with an interesting line or image and I let myself write. I let myself pile image upon image, thought upon thought, then I set the poem aside and come back to it later. It's at that point that it is starting to tell me its subject. I may help it along, or I may take what the poet Jack Ridl calls "a blue highway"—an off-ramp into another direction. I like tension in a poem. I like dichotomy, for life is always two things happening simultaneously. Sometimes dichotomy is paradoxical, seemingly unexplainable, yet totally true. Love contains pain. Pain comes from love. Dark is filled with light, there is beauty in the ugly, as Shakespeare says, one can be "sick with joy." I write what is going on in my world and how I choose to observe it. That is why it is always a good idea to go off to Florida or a Truck Pull Contest or somewhere else; it's good to get away from looking out of the same old window.

Gyasi: Is it possible to say that your poem "Assisted Living" is a prose poem"?

Gaines-Friedler: If you mean "Assisted Living: Caring for the Irreducible" (in *Dutiful Heart*), no. I would not consider that a prose poem. I think it is a lyrical poem in that the images and language create an unstated "knowing." It may have a narrative quality to it—but that narrative it is not lineal. It is a lyrical poem in related sections (13 of them.) I also have an essay titled "Assisted Living." It's a personal narrative essay written in second person (whew!) that has a poetic lyrical quality to it. It is close to being a prose poem. "Assisted Living" is considered a memoir and is published online. It is not in any print journal or book.

Gyasi: Which of your poems do you regard as your best?

Gaines-Friedler: I don't know. It may be the next poem. It may be the first poem I ever wrote. Because, as I said earlier, I am a different person every day. It's a difficult question to answer, as at any given time it changes. I had a person once send me an email reprimanding me for a poem of mine she feels is "unfair." She wanted to know why I personally (not my speaker?) would behave with such anger. Another person contacted me about that same poem thanking me for writing it, asking if he could teach it to his class. Another poet/teacher told me that the poem wasn't angry enough. So go figure. I guess the point is, one must like their work and be satisfied with it. I love my poems. I find something useful and meaningful to me in them all. Even the ones I hate.

Emmanuel Sigauke teaches English at Cosumnes River College in Sacramento, California. The Zimbabwean wordsmith, educated at University of Zimbabwe and California State University, is the founding editor of *Munyori Literary Journal*. He has published poetry and fiction in numerous magazines such as *The Pedestal*, *NR Review*, *The Rattlesnake Review*, *African Writing Online,* and *StoryTime*, to note a few. Sigauke is the sole editor of the *African Roar* 2013 anthology of short stories, a selection of thirteen stories sourced from a bigger pool of fifty from writers all across Africa. His collection of short stories, *Mukoma's Marriage and other Stories*, was published in 2014. He is currently working on a novel.

Gyasi: Perhaps we could begin from home. How often do you return to Zimbabwe?

Sigauke: Every two years, although I now want to go there more often. Interesting things are happening on the ground. I am working on launching an annual summer writer's workshop; quite a big deal to me. And somewhere in the chaos of life there, one salvages something good; just like all returns to the sources should be.

Gyasi: What is your assessment, from the writer's point of view, of the current political situation in Zimbabwe?

Sigauke: It's what it is. Now I just watch from a distance. I seem to worry more about the direction of American politics, about the disturbed racial waters of America, than concern myself with the drama of Zimbabwean politics at the moment.

Gyasi: When did you actually leave Zimbabwe? Why did you decide to go to America?

Sigauke: I left in 1996, following a fiancée, chasing love.

Gyasi: Would you have been a "serious" writer today if you had not left Zimbabwe?

Sigauke: Leaving Zimbabwe took away some of the seriousness at first. America had its own demands for dealing with the new realities of how to make a living. With the time I spent in menial and part-time jobs, and attending school full-time, and raising a family, etc, I stopped writing seriously for a number of years, but then around 2004, when I started college teaching, I resumed writing, and by 2007 I was publishing again in magazines and journals, and was finally, through social media and other means, reconnecting with literary friends like Memory Chirere, Ignatius Mabasa, and others, who had by then already published serious books. America almost killed my writing ...

Gyasi: Growing up in Mazvihwa, were you aware of the apartheid system in the neighboring South Africa? How similar, in your view, was the apartheid system to the then white minority rule of Rhodesia?

Sigauke: Mazvihwa is closer to Pretoria than to Harare, so yes, we were very much aware of the dreadful presence of apartheid South Africa. Nearly all my elder brothers went to work in South Africa in the 70s, so they brought back stories, scars, and sweets. At Zimbabwe's independence, I remember some apartheid threats to the new Mugabe government playing on our radios. There were times when in Mazvihwa we could easily tune in to South African radio than we could to Zimbabwean, so I remember South Africa saying things like, "We will destroy your little Harare in a second," or something to that effect. It wasn't a good thing for apartheid South Africa to have an independent northern neighbor apparently. As to similarities, the minority government in Rhodesia used the same segregationist methods as those used in South Africa, but it seems the latter also destroyed more traditional values than in Rhodesia. In Rhodesia we had our intact villages, the Mazvihwas, the Mberengwas, with a strong sense of home and tradition. Our southern neighbors urbanized even their villages (because I'm told a village in South Africa is not the same idea of village we have in Zimbabwe). The dynamics are obviously deeper than this.

Gyasi: Could you tell us about your childhood memories of Mazvihwa?

Sigauke: Too many to pinpoint. I do a better job of recalling memories in my writing. One thing though is, although I have grown to fully accept Mazvihwa as home, it never quite accepted me when I was growing up there; I had a foreign last name; they said I came from Chipinge or Chimanimani, or Mozambique. The truth is I am the son of a Mozambican father and a Zimbabwean mother from Masvingo. So Mazvihwa was right; I wasn't quite from that area. In fact, one enduring memory I have is of a dizzying bus ride from somewhere, when I was two; the bus ride from Masvingo rural, where I was born; then it was decided I should grow up in Mazvihwa. Happy memories point to the time after I started writing, when the Mavihwa people of my age realized that I was writing stories about our Mazvihwaness. Then when I went to secondary school and I would get number 1 all the time, at our little Mazvihwa secondary school, I got to be accepted more.

Gyasi: Do you think that the political situation in Zimbabwe is so bad that one just can't survive there?

Sigauke: People are surviving in Zimbabwe. It's something I don't understand, but it is happening. In fact, there is so much laughter there, and so much U.S. money being spent like nobody's business, so much survival it makes you feel inadequate in some essential way. The infrastructure is crappy, the roads are dying, there is growing corruption even by ordinary people. Things don't move if you don't bribe your way; only it's not called bribery: they want to think of it as tips, "money for coca-cola," "money to help your sister, or your brother." One dollar here; two dollars there. Rarely do they seem to ask for a lot; the little dollar here, five dollars there, and before you know it the one hundred dollar bill you broke this morning is gone. By the end of two weeks you can't quite account for three thousand dollars. Everything you want seems to be there, but then you also lose your cash fast. It's mostly cash we use there (not credit or debit cards or cheques). Zimbabweans don't seem to hesitate to spend the USD as it comes: in fact, one Shona statement I heard in the village was: "Takadherera dhora," and I am not going to translate this. Of course, much of the quick spending reflects the reality that most people don't make enough to save; it comes, it goes.

Back to your question: Politics seems to be something happening in the background while people figure out ways to earn the dollar. The roads are dying (I already said this), but the cars are getting bigger, more Toyota Hiluxes, the Pajeros, the Range Rovers. The smaller ones thrive, and the drivers have become experts in zigzagging their way. I tried to drive straight and I popped a tire in a pothole during a rainy day in Harare. And that taught me fast to zig-zag.

The water gets cut frequently; some people have drilled boreholes on their properties; electricity goes often, generators get turned on; etc. ... Of course, not everyone can afford these alternative means, and forcing a whole country to be used to inconvenience seems mean, is actually citizen abuse; but surprisingly, it seems a good number of the people understand the situation, are used to it, and sometimes even defend the government, mention Western sanctions, etc. In some ways life in the city has become similar to the village. In Borrowdale you see women carrying water buckets in the same fashion the ones in Mazvihwa do it. What happens is that when the weekly water cut happens, there is at least one home with a borehole water supply that neighbors can access, so you see them line up, some pushing wheelbarrows, others carrying buckets, stocking up for the remainder of the week. You look at this and something within you breaks, but of course, you have to be helpful, go help fetch the water!

Sometimes trying to discuss with the locals on the state of things leads nowhere, as some people seem not to want to participate in a discussion critical of the status quo, sometimes not out of fear, but out of topical exhaustion, a realization that you can talk all you want, but that's not what brings food on the table. So then before the debate ripens, there is some distraction, perhaps it's the beer you are drinking (how cheap it seems, that beer, at one dollar a pint, even at club rate!), or a car with a pot of mazondo meat arrives and everyone rushes to it to buy the beef foot for a dollar each, and next, the man who grills gizzards starts his fire and we are all gathered around him in anticipation, because he used to be a real chef for a well-known hotel.

> Gyasi: Emmanuel, the truth is that, you ought to explain to our understanding, the meaning of "Takadherera dhora."

Sigauke: We spend the U.S. dollar without hesitation; it's what we do easily, like it's nothing. In other words, we don't have much respect for the dollar. Poor translation, this, but one direct statement I heard in the town of Gweru, was: We brought our own dollar to nothing (hyper-inflation); next, it's going to be this U.S. dollar. Of course, it was said with humor.

> Gyasi: Do you have any hopes of returning to Zimbabwe to resettle?

Sigauke: My friends have convinced me to resettle ("You don't have to come back to stay, per se; but buy property, property has value; it's a big investment."). It's a country of people who are believing they can survive anything, and they can do anything for themselves. So you begin to dream of owning property in a place like Borrowdale Brooke, only to realize you can't afford those million-plus dollar homes. There is a way Zimbabwe and its Zimbabweans (those who never left, or those who left and resettled) makes you feel inadequate, makes you feel poor, as if you drive the wrong car (which is often true), or you live in the wrong neighborhood in your America (which is also true, because these people have stretches upon stretches of land on their property, etc). But you also see serious poverty here and there, yet never a lack of smiles and laughter. If you offer to give them the remaining dollars in your wallet, they will not say no, but after a while you will realize you didn't have to do so necessarily. In fact, you are the one finally broke; I don't know if you can be broke from being already broke. Each time I go back to Zimbabwe, I don't have enough time to understand the new Zimbabwe; but it's a great experience; I always come back more educated.

> Gyasi: So for Zimbabwe and its numerous worsening issues, do you really think you'll succeed in establishing the annual summer writer's workshop you're planning?

Sigauke: I think so, as much of its success depends on my determination and the support of my sponsors, who already do other projects in Mazvihwa. They employee indigenous innovation using what resources the land provides for its own progress. My workshop follows a rural model in which I bring the professional writers to the rural areas and they spend a week with local

(Mazvihwa) budding writers, facilitating intensive writing workshops.

Gyasi: Could you clarify this for me: Are you a poet or writer?

Sigauke: I am both. I am other things too: essayist, memoirist, playwright.

Gyasi: What was your main role when you helped found the Zimbabwe Budding Writers Association? I am much more particular about the word "budding."

Sigauke: I joined the organization early, but the founding was done by Albert Nyathi and a group of young writers who attended the one meeting I didn't attend, because I was in Mazvihwa on holiday. I remember the word "budding" referred to the stage at which our writing was, more than it referred to our ages. We ranged from primary school students to university professors to grandmothers or grandfathers who had felt the calling. We were vibrant; we were loud and proud. At one point we received serious funding from a Nordic country, and we opened branches, what we called chapters, all over the country. I was the secretary-general for a number of years, and I went to help launch all these chapters. We were a serious bunch. A lot of the prominent contemporary writers in Zimbabwe used to be members of BWAZ.

Gyasi: You studied English and Linguistics at the University of Zimbabwe and went on to study English at California State University. What is it about English you wanted to study to the highest level?

Sigauke: The one time I wrote the best essay at Gwavachemai Secondary School in Mazvihwa led to every teacher steering me towards English. No one seemed to care that after a while my Mathematics was beginning to suffer; it was enough that I was good in English. I loved the attention. That, compounded with the fact that I had also become the "writer in residence" for my school, and the English police, and the debate chairperson, etc. And I enjoyed reading; I enjoyed the English too. By the time I reached California, it was too late to change my habit, and I am glad that now, as an English professor, I am serving English well, just as it is serving me.

Gyasi: What was the main medium of language you spoke at home in Zimbabwe?

Sigauke: We used Karanga, but once the English bug caught on, some of us started throwing in some phrases of English in our Shona, even as we herded cattle. English is a very good cattle-herding language.

Gyasi: Does the place where you live matter to you when writing?

Sigauke: It does. I am able to distance myself from the setting of my stories. I like this ability to write about Zimbabwe from a distance. I can be imaginative.

Gyasi: Could you name just one writer who has been so influential to you as a writer?

Sigauke: D. H. Lawrence.

Gyasi: You are the founding editor of *Munyori Poetry Journal*. Why did you decide to set up this journal? How is it doing?

Sigauke: It started as a result of my interest in web design. I had just finished a course in HTML and I wanted to practice what I had learned. I had many choices, and I took the literary route, since I was already a writer. Then once I made a call for submissions, I knew I had reached a point of no return. Now I am looking forward to turning this into a small press that will publish books. I have received enough material to start anthologies.

Gyasi: How do you know when a piece of work is right for your journal?

Sigauke: I select works that feel right the first moment I read them. If the work needs more work, I often work with the writer to improve it.

Gyasi: What is your greatest achievement as a poet/writer?

Sigauke: The publications I have made, one a poetry volume and another a short story collection. But the time I did a poetry blog and blogged 400 "poems" felt good. Of course, later I would discover that most of those pieces were crappy. Still, I saved them, and once in a while, when I want to feel the pain of their failure, I revisit them, and occasionally, I am able to turn one into polished work.

Gyasi: When do you anticipate retiring from writing?

Sigauke: I don't yet feel like I have even started; so retirement isn't a thought I have entertained.

Gyasi: Does your poetry book *Forever Let Me Go* have anything to do with your sojourn in America?

Sigauke: Excellent question. The book was originally entitled *The Eyes that See Me Go*; then my editor recommended that I use *Forever Let Me Go*. I had a poem with that title; which came as a response to Kazuo Ishiguro's title *Never Let Me Go*. But to answer your question: Yes, there was a time when my stay in the U.S. had begun to cause me to think that this was a forever, that I would never set foot in Zimbabwe again, so then it was a request to the eyes that saw me go, that should I be gone forever, please, let me go, forever. But when you read that poem, you may never guess; the poem itself is about someone soaring, following their dreams, succeeding in life. I like to read it to high school students, to help them follow their dreams in life. But yes, I remember that time when America made me feel like I would never return to Zimbabwe ever. Notice that the feeling had nothing to do with Zimbabwe; it had everything to do with America ... and how it made me feel. I have since recovered from that state of stasis.

Gyasi: Could you tell us how your poem "Hurry, A Zimbabwean in Concert!" came into being?

Sigauke: I wrote it after attending a Tuku concert. It was great day, the true point at which I was reconnecting with the Zimbabwean community in California.

Gyasi: I am not sure why I should be asking you this, but do you have any secret flaw as a writer?

Sigauke: Yes, working on projects for too long; feeling bad for a while about it, but then getting used to the prolonged effort until I justify it as the essence of that work's artistic process. There is a novel I have been working on since 1999. And still, it's not going anywhere. I'm glad it's not a secret anymore.

Gyasi: Which specific genre of books is often found on your bookshelf?

Sigauke: Literary fiction, poetry, and drama. I have lots of short story collections too; the literary kind. Blame it on my training. Once in a while I sneak in a science fiction work, which I end up not reading for one reason or another.

Gyasi: Do you think talent matters in the making of a great writer?

Sigauke: It does. But hard work counts a lot too.

Gyasi: Tell us about your book *Mukoma's Marriage and Other Stories*...

Sigauke: I think I spent more work on it than I should have. It went on forever; the work. It's a collection of connected stories. My editor suggested once that I should turn it into a novel, but I wanted it to be a short story collection, for the pieces to stand alone, to allow me to be inconsistent if I had to, without the pressure for a seamless whole. To some, the book will seem autobiographical, but really, it's not. I just happen to have had many brothers out of whom the brother figure in the book was shaped (just a few borrowed features and characteristics). It features maigurus too (sisters-in-law), and a great moment early this year was when I took a copy of the book to Mazvihwa and one of my sisters-in-law started browsing it; she spent a few hours with it, and I had a sigh of relief when she commented: "Amazing how you are able to make all this up."

Gyasi: Is there any question you think escaped me?

Sigauke: Not really. You worked me hard already. Thank you for these questions though.

D. R. James is the author of the poetry collection *Since Everything Is All I've Got* (March Street, 2011) and four chapbooks, the most recent being *Why War* (Finishing Line, 2014). Poems have appeared in various anthologies and journals, and an article on Adrienne Rich and Audre Lorde is forthcoming in *The Writer's Chronicle.* He lives in Holland, Michigan, where he's been teaching writing, literature, and peace-making at Hope College, now going on thirty years.

Gyasi: Did you know as a child that you would one day become a writer?

James: No, not at all. I won my school's 5th-grade Memorial Day writing contest and then didn't appear publicly as a writer again until in my college's lit magazine. Even then I didn't think of myself as a writer. Around 30, after my first round of grad school, I thought I would like to be a nonfiction writer, but didn't make any substantial moves toward it. Not until around 50 could I say I was actually a writer writing.

Gyasi: Is it true that without talent one can never succeed as a writer?

James: I don't really know. I suppose it depends on what you mean by success. I've experienced many books, even so-called successful ones, whose writing, in my opinion, showed no particular talent. I've also worked with students who showed no writing talent but went on to write fine work. Perhaps the greats (what does that mean?) have inborn talent that they then have to develop. Maybe just as important is enjoying writing and what it produces.

Gyasi: How did you come to write *A Little Instability without Birds*?

James: The more accurate question would be how did I come to put that chapbook together, since I didn't write its poems with putting them together in mind. I started journaling during a rough patch in my mid-40s, which turned into writing poem-like things, which then turned into a few published poems, which I then combined with a few unpublished poems when I thought I had enough combinable pieces for a chapbook. They ended up having a woe-is-me-turned-brighter outlook theme, and several were about birds, so they hung together pretty well. Finishing Line Press thought so, too, and voila, *A Little Instability without Birds*, which thrilled me to death.

Gyasi: Do you mind telling us about the inspiration behind your book *Lost Enough*?

James: The title comes from lines in a William Stafford poem: "If you're lost enough, then the experience of now is your guide to what comes next." I had continued writing poems like those in the first chapbook—in fact, all the poems were mixed together in their production—but things were looking up, especially after I considered my seemingly lost life in those terms. Like *Instability*, the chapbook *Lost Enough* has a low-to-brighter-outlook arc, and once again Finishing Line liked what they saw.

Gyasi: What sort of preparation goes into the writing of a book of poems?

James: I think the theme here, for me anyway, is none. I write the poems and then find a combination when I think I have enough to combine. One of my mentors, Marvin Bell, reminds me just to write poems; my obsessions will come out automatically. And they do, so there's always a combinability.

Gyasi: Do you show your manuscripts to friends before you send them out to publishers?

James: Yes, though probably not as much as would be helpful. I tend to be a loner, so seeking feedback sometimes *feels* more like intrusion than help, but every time I do, I get wonderful input. I did go to a Colrain manuscript-consultation weekend, which helped me reconceive and put together my full-length collection, *Since Everything Is All I've Got*, though I then redid it again, thanks to Jack Ridl's help, before March Street Press accepted it.

Gyasi: How do you often begin a poem?

James: In all kinds of ways, but often with just a phrase or line or maybe a title or a line that then becomes the title. Sometimes I have an "idea," but if I'm too set on that a poem rarely emerges, because I then will manipulate things to bring the idea out. Sometimes I know I'm somehow going to recount a personal event, but I usually don't know what will come of it. I love surprising myself.

Gyasi: What is the best time to write?

James: For me, beginning something goes best in the morning, but I love to revise and tinker, and I can do that at almost any time.

Gyasi: How do you combine teaching and writing?

James: With difficulty. I don't teach poetry writing but composition, mainly, plus a fall intro peace studies class and sometimes lit. I also work in an academic support center, so I'm either with students in class or one-on-one or preparing to be or reading papers, and for a low psychic-energy person like me, that all takes it out of me. That's why writing in the morning is best, before the day has a chance to have its way. But reserving mornings doesn't always happen.

Gyasi: Do you write on a computer or in a notebook?

James: I start things in a notebook and then switch to the computer when I think I have something. I revise and do that tinkering on the computer.

Gyasi: Tell us something about *Psychological Clock*?

James: Like for the other books, the title comes from one of its poems and is a play on biological clock. I didn't start writing seriously until my late 40s, and by the time that poem and then chapbook came along I saw myself entering the second half of my life (I'm optimistic about living to 100). The second half was looking to be way better than the first because I was finally paying attention to my psychological clock. A fun thing about this book is that I emailed it to Pudding House around noon one day, and by late afternoon it had been accepted. I could hardly believe and once again was thrilled.

Gyasi: Did you write *Since Everything Is All I've Got* from a personal experience?

James: Nearly everything I write germinates out of some personal experience, whether I end up rendering it explicitly as that or not, and so the poems in *Since Everything* are by and large no different. But this book, too, wasn't written as a book but came together in a way similar to all the others. Its poems are mainly responding to various personal experiences.

Gyasi: Which writer(s) inspires you?

James: Initially Billy Collins's *The Art of Drowning* helped me see what some actual contemporary poems could be and that I could write poems, but also: Jack Ridl, Marvin Bell, Mary Oliver, David Wagoner, Ruth Stone, W. C. Williams, Joe Millar, Denise Levertov, William Stafford, David Hernandez, Adrienne Rich, Hayden Carruth, Stephen Dunn, Kwame Dawes, Bob Hicok, David (L.) James, and many, many others. I read poems all the time and have shelves and shelves of poetry books.

Gyasi: Do you feel that there are more books you ought to write?

James: I want to write more poems, and I reckon they'll come to together as books sooner or later. I have no "projects."

Gyasi: Is there any conflict between the names David James and D.R. James?

James: Well, the D. R. comes out of a conflict of sorts. When I finally got around to publishing poems, another poet, in my state even, was already publishing as David James, a fine poet in his own right whom I highly recommend. So I had to come up with some other moniker. D. R. hasn't been ideal as it turns out, since if you search-engine it all kinds of Dr. James's crop up, of which there are many. The other David James and I have also experienced some interesting cases of mixed-up identity, especially because we live in the same state and have books published by the same publishers, but mostly it's fun, and we've become pretty good friends. I could have gone with David R. James, but that just seems like what I sign to get life insurance and car loans.

Gyasi: What inspired you to go to the University of Iowa?

James: In the late 70s and early 80s, in addition to the Writer's Workshop, which I did not attend, Iowa was hosting a crew of famous composition experts, and so we grad students got to take classes from them in addition to those of the regular faculty, some of whom were famous in their own right. Since I wanted to become a comp expert, it was a logical and do-able choice. It turned out great and propelled me into what I have been doing since. A side note: at the time, Marvin Bell was already a poetry household name and teaching in the workshop, so I heard all about him from my office mate, who'd done poetry and was now doing comp. I never met him there, but low and behold, 33 years later, Marvin was my fourth of four mentors in the Pacific University MFA program, from which I graduated in 2013. He's also coming to my college next week to read and rub shoulders with our creative writing students.

Gyasi: Besides English, do you write in any other language?

James: Nope, but I hear translating is a great way to hone one's art and skills, and I would do that from French if I ever did.

Gyasi: What is the relevance of poetry in the modern world?

James: Good question, and one that haunts most poets daily. The lucky ones can ignore the question and just do their art. The less lucky, like me, see that there are a million poets and relatively few poetry readers, given the available volume, and torture themselves with how little poetry seems to be valued outside of the circle of poets. I know I have to keep reminding myself that I write first for me, because I enjoy it and it helps me process my life, and second for readers, since chances are I won't have many or any anyway. I think if more non-poets knew what the vast array of contemporary poetry has to offer, contrary to their poetry experiences in school, more would read it and discover its insights and joys.

Gyasi: Is it difficult to teach people how to write?

James: Yes, especially those who come in hating it, thanks to school. I see my main job as a college composition teacher to be helping students leave my classes not hating writing, or not so much. And since most of my classes are required, it's a tough sell. If I taught poetry writing, maybe—probably—I'd have a different answer.

Gyasi: What do you generally regard as the most important thing to you as a writer?

James: Time, psychic energy, and a playful, don't-worry-about-writing-poems frame of mind.

Ace Boggess was locked up for five years in the West Virginia prison system. During that time, he wrote the poems collected here and published most of them. Prior to his incarceration, he earned his B.A. from Marshall University and his J.D. from West Virginia University. He has been awarded a fellowship from the West Virginia Commission on the Arts, and his poems have appeared in such journals as *Harvard Review*, *Notre Dame Review*, *Southern Humanities Review,* and *The Florida Review*. His first collection, *The Beautiful Girl Whose Wish Was Not Fulfilled*, appeared in 2003. He currently resides in Charleston, West Virginia.

Gyasi: I find it difficult to ask this, but what took you to prison and how long did you spend there?

Boggess: I was a drug addict for many years—Oxycontin and the like. Over time, that took away most of my sanity, and I ended up robbing pharmacies for drugs. I spent five years in the penitentiary.

Gyasi: Your most recent book, *The Prisoners*, published by Brick Road Poetry Press, has most of the poems written while in prison. Were you allowed the liberty to write in prison?

Boggess: Yes, all of the poems in the book were written while in prison, and probably 2/3 of them were published while I was locked up, in magazines such as *Atlanta Review, River Styx, Rattle, J Journal*, and so on. The first poem in the book was written on the day I arrived at the penitentiary, and my acceptance letter for the book arrived on the day of my release. I lived with that book for five years, constantly obsessing over what belonged in there and what didn't.

Gyasi: Do you regret having been incarcerated?

Boggess: It's a mixed bag. I hate that I lost everything I ever owned, lost track of friends, not to mention five years of my life. At the same time, I wrote that book while I was there and, in doing so, proved something to myself. It was the one thing no one could take away from me, and I achieved success in a way that I couldn't have imagined. Plus, it often takes losing everything in order to figure out you didn't need any of it to be happy.

Gyasi: What's the most profound joy—if any—you got from prison?

Boggess: I found it in odd places: a library book, a conversation, working as the legal rep and trying my best to help other inmates with their problems. Of course, my first year there, the Pittsburgh Steelers won the Super Bowl, and watching that was probably the happiest time in my five years. There's a poem about it in the book.

Gyasi: Was it difficult finding a publisher for *The Prisoners*?

Boggess: Finding a publisher is always difficult, and more so from prison. Most publishers and probably 3/4 of journals have moved to electronic submissions, and in prison there's no internet access. Still, I was writing and publishing before I got myself arrested, so I knew what books and magazines to order to help me find places to submit. In this case, though, Brick Road Poetry Press was the first place I sent the complete manuscript. I really didn't know how the editors would respond. Luckily, they loved it. I'm still shocked when I see how folks react to this book. It's not something I expected.

Gyasi: How different is your first book, *The Beautiful Girl Whose Wish*

Was Not Fulfilled, from *The Prisoners*?

Boggess: The first book was more traditional, with what I often call philosophies of nothing and the moon. There are love poems and depictions of scenes with friends, writing experiments, notes on Camus and Hemingway. It's all over the place. Of course, I was a drug addict when I put that book together, and I think that can be seen in the sadness and loneliness that haunt its pages.

Gyasi: From the title, can I query you on who constitutes/constitute the prisoner(s)? I am most interested in the last letter, "s."

Boggess: "The Prisoners" is the long poem that wraps up the book. It's a note of sorts on the suffering of those around me. In five years, I probably encountered two thousand people, and many of them had the same troubles: wives and girlfriends leaving or fooling around, the growth of either a religious pleading or its opposite in wild desperation, money troubles, child support for children the inmates never saw. What I observed in these shared troubles was a grayness in eyes and spirits. That became a theme of the poem, and to a greater extent, the whole book.

Gyasi: Do you remember some of the friends you met while in prison? Have any of them become writers?

Boggess: I'm still in touch with a handful of folks. None have become writers as far as I know. Maybe they should try. They would have their own perspective on that world. It might prove fascinating.

Gyasi: How did you get into writing?

Boggess: The same way I got into drugs. I've dealt with severe social anxiety all my life, although I didn't recognize it as such early on when I started writing and taking pills to help myself deal with my fear. This is all looking back, of course. That was the end of the 80s and the early 90s. I didn't understand what was happening to me and what I was doing to cope. But, both the writing and the pills were a big part of my life after that for a long time. The weird thing to me, though, is that I always considered myself a novelist. It still amazes me that my novels haven't sold, but my poems have taken off. Que sera sera.

Gyasi: Was the place where you wrote from prison very much conducive or environmentally friendly?

Boggess: In West Virginia, prison is mostly just a warehouse filled with loud, obnoxious people. There's plenty of time for writing, but you have to be able to tune out the noise. Some days that worked, and some days it didn't. What's important is that there were plenty of things I hadn't seen there. The newness of, say, a shakedown or smoking a cigarette that someone had smuggled in in his butt was fascinating to me. My training was in journalism, and like a reporter I wanted to give those scenes to other people. I tried to capture everything I saw. Again, it didn't always work, but a lot of the time, it did.

Gyasi: Who inspires you to write?

Boggess: The poets I love to read are Bob Hicok, Billy Collins, Natasha Saje, Kevin Young. I read constantly. I saw a study recently that suggested reading poetry triggers things like introspection and nostalgia. I find that to be true. So, I read whatever literary journals I can get my hands on. At the same time, the book I always go back to is David Lehman's *The Evening Sun*. I read that a decade ago when I was reviewing books for *The Adirondack Review*, and it blew me away. I even ordered a copy of it while I was locked up. I also have an attachment to *Velocities* by Stephen Dobyns, because it was the only poetry book in the prison library when I first got there, so I read it many times.

Gyasi: Could you define what a love poem is? How much liking do you have for love poems?

Boggess: To me, it's a search for connection. When I write what I consider a love poem, it's often the description of a scene in which I and someone else share something beautiful: a walk along the riverbank, a sunset, a movie, a moment of intense passion. I always enjoy love poems if they're well done without being sappy. I read Neruda early on, and I go back to his books. They just have a certain feeling to them without wasting time talking about that feeling. It's hard to explain. I guess for me a love poem is like any other poem except that I have a co-author who provides me with something other than the words.

Gyasi: Do you have a specific purpose as to why you write?

Boggess: The main thing I try to do is take a photograph or make a home movie and then share that with others. I'm writing about my life and my stories and the things I see, but I always hope I'm doing it in such a way that the reader will connect with it and wonder if I've been watching him or her through a window. If the reader finds a connection to her own life, I consider that a win.

Gyasi: Do you have a particular target audience when you write?

Boggess: I don't have a particular target audience. Ideally, everyone would read my work. Knowing that won't happen, I just cast my line and hope I get a few bites.

Gyasi: The gap between your first and second books is quite huge. Why is that so?

Boggess: Yes, a decade passed. Half of that I spent in prison. Book-ending that time are—on one side—a couple years of the worst phase of my drug addiction, descent into despair and madness, time in rehab, etc., and—on the other—the two years since my release while I've been focusing on the new book and trying to sell several others. I have two manuscripts left over from before I got locked up, and I'm trying to find homes for them, plus a handful of novels that are still making the rounds. But, I had no access to any of my older manuscripts while I was inside. So, my focus was entirely on *The Prisoners*, which I built from scratch and hovered over as if it were my sick child. Anyway, I hope it won't take nearly as long for the next one to find a home.

Gyasi: Tell us a bit about the literary scene in Charleston, West Virginia, where you currently reside.

Boggess: Honestly, I don't know that much about the Charleston literary scene. I grew up in Charleston, but I hadn't lived here for a couple decades before my release from prison. So, I'm still exploring. However, West Virginia as a whole has a marvelous literary tradition, with recent poetry books by wonderful authors such as John McKernan, Kirk Judd, Ron Houchin, and A. E. Stringer, and novels out recently from amazing authors John Van Kirk, Andrea Fekete, and Marie Manilla. There's much to be praised here. I'd like to see it become more visible everywhere else.

Gyasi: Could you describe the typical American prison system? Do you think American prisons have any flaws?

Boggess: Ah, now there's a rub. The West Virginia prison system is, from what I understand, not typical of the American system. As I said, it's mostly just a warehousing system for people the state wants to be rid of for a while. There's a lot of dead time. I'm sure the intensity and craziness you hear about in most prisons happens here, too, but I didn't see much toward the extremes. It's just passing time. There are many flaws, but they're American flaws and, as such, mostly stem from apathy. I'll leave it that.

Gyasi: If you were asked to give advice to a group of drug addicts, what would you say?

Boggess: The best advice I can offer is this: ask for help. You can't beat the habit alone, but your junk-hungry brain will tell you that you can. You'll try everything you can think of, but it's always back to the dope in the end. Don't get me wrong. I'm not anti-dope. The drugs helped me survive something I couldn't understand inside me that might have destroyed me. They opened doors in my writing, also. But, taking drugs and being an addict are worlds apart. Once the addiction gets you, ask for help, or you will destroy yourself.

Gyasi: I would not let you go without telling me the inspiration for the poem "Mango Smoothie." Of course, that's how I encountered you!

Boggess: It's pretty straightforward. I set out to write a love poem for a new love, and she happened to be sick at the time. It started me thinking about what we do for love, even when we know it won't work. I found my moment of beauty and connection in what was otherwise an ugly, disturbing scene.

www.ingramcontent.com/pod-product-compliance
Lightning Source LLC
Chambersburg PA
CBHW022007080426
42733CB00007B/514